Suburbia in Transition

Suburbia in Transition

Edited with an Introduction by
Louis H. Masotti
and Jeffrey K. Hadden

A NEW YORK TIMES BOOK

New Viewpoints
A Division of Franklin Watts, Inc.
New York   1974

Library of Congress Cataloging in Publication Data
Masotti, Louis H   comp.
    Suburbia in transition.
    "A New York times book."
    Bibliography: p.
    1. Suburbs—United States—Addresses, essays,
lectures. I. Hadden, Jeffrey K., joint comp.
II. Title.
HT351.M32   301.36′2′0973   73-5907
ISBN 0-531-06494-8 (pbk.)

Acknowledgments

WE WANT to thank publicly the students who have helped locate, assemble, and edit *The New York Times* materials which appear in this book—Deborah Ellis Dennis, Susan Lee, Martin Finkel, and Mary Anne Richardson. This book is dedicated to them and their fellow students, who will inherit and inhabit the suburbia now in the process of becoming.

L. H. M.
J. K. H.

Contents

2. The Suburban Surge

RACE, CLASS, AND NUMBERS

COMMERCE AND INDUSTRY

3. The Exclusion of "Undesirables"

THE ISSUES

THE FEDERAL GOVERNMENT'S ROLE

ALTERNATIVES TO EXCLUSION

4. Problems That Won't Go Away

5. The Politics of Suburbia

6. Suburbia Revisited

THE OUTER CITY: AN OVERVIEW

SUBURBAN LAND DEVELOPMENT

Suburbia in Transition

Introduction

"THE FUTURE belongs not to the city but to the suburb," sociologist Charles Zueblin concluded in 1905. Twenty years later, in the first detailed study ever made of the suburbs, Harlan Paul Douglass reaffirmed this perception.[1] To him, the suburbs represented an urban area in its early stages of development. And now the speculations and projections of these two sociologists and a few others seem to be reality.

Suburbia, invariably defined as the politically separate but economically dependent communities located within commuting range of the central city, is in transition. The area outside the historic city has long lost its distinction as the encampment of the affluent, although recent developments have not entirely purged the conventional wisdom image of suburbia as the bedroom for the organization men who live in "split-level traps" with a "crack in the picture window" and crabgrass in the lawn. This image—some call it the "suburban myth"—is based on what the critics of the fifties perceived as homogeneity, standardization, conformity, and isolation. The myth is simply not supported by the diversity and dynamics of suburbia today, and indeed it may never have been a very accurate view.

The suburbs, rejecting efforts to metropolitanize government, remain politically distinct entities, each jealously guarding the

1. Harlan Paul Douglass, *The Suburban Trend* (New York: Century, 1925).

power to control its community's "character." Largely because the freeway system keeps the time-distance ratio at an acceptable level, most suburbs are still within commuting distance of the central city, even though they sprawl in ever-widening circles around the city. However, commuting patterns are also changing, with fewer suburbanites holding jobs in the cities, more urbanites working in the suburbs, and a considerable amount of intersuburban commutation. This reflects what may be the single most important change in the suburban-city relationship—the increasing economic independence of the suburban ring. While the suburban economic "tail" does not yet wag the urban "dog," the decentralization not only of industry but also of commerce, retailing, and, most recently, popular culture and entertainment is dramatic.

The *result* of these centrifugal forces within the metropolitan areas is a phenomenon which *The New York Times* now refers to as "the outer city." [2] The *process* by which urban functions, activities, and life styles "deconcentrate" might be labeled "the suburbanization of the city" or, perhaps more accurately, the "urbanization of the suburbs." [3]

But whatever label we put on it, the facts clearly indicate a significant change in the dynamics of metropolitan America. And it has occurred while most of us were still caught up in the mythical suburbia produced by the fifties or concerned about the real urban crises of the sixties. But the seventies give every indication of being a decade dominated by the problems and potential of suburbia and suburbanization.

Harlan Douglass may have been right in 1925, when he observed that "the suburb is a footnote to urban civilization," but today that relationship appears to be changing. The directions and intensity of that change will have serious implications for the future of both suburbia and the central city.

The suburbanization of the city has various dimensions—the *migration of more and different kinds of people,* who leave the city

2. See Part 6 of this volume.
3. For a book which explores this theme, see Louis H. Masotti and Jeffrey K. Hadden, editors, *The Urbanization of the Suburbs* (Beverly Hills, California: Sage Publications, 1973).

attracted by what the "outer city" can offer or repelled by what the central city does offer; the *physical relocation* of industries, businesses, shops, and activities from city to suburb; and the *exportation of urban life styles,* such as ethnic communities, apartments, specialty stores, singles bars, good restaurants, and professional sports.

But more people, more firms, and new life styles also create a diversity that challenges existing practices and values. Confrontations between those who promote change and those who desire to protect the status quo are inevitable. The new urban battleground is suburbia, and the war has already begun.

Early in the sixties, the suburban share of the metropolitan area population exceeded 50 per cent for the first time, and by 1970 it had reached almost 57 per cent. Furthermore, during 1970, America became a suburban nation: more people now live *around* central cities (37.6 per cent) than *in* them (31.4 per cent) or in rural areas (31 per cent). Between 1960 and 1970, the suburban population grew (by migration and natural increase) from 59.5 million to over 76 million (a 28.2 per cent increase), while the central cities increased less than 6 per cent, or by about 3.1 million persons. (See Table 1.)

In twentieth-century perspective, the more recent growth of the suburbs relative to the cities is even more dramatic (see Table 2). The suburban share of the national population grew only 8.8 per cent from 1900 to 1940. Since then, and in effect since the end of World War II, the suburban proportion of the total United States population has almost doubled. On the other hand, the central cities' proportion of the population has remained remarkably stable at about 32 per cent from 1930 until the recent census indicated a slight decrease.

These numerical shifts in population, significant as they are, tell only part of the suburbanization story. If the question is *who* is suburbanizing—that is, the personal characteristics of the new suburbanites rather than *how many*—the trend takes on added meaning. At this time, limited empirical evidence is available to support the strong impression that a broader spectrum of class, age, and race is represented in the suburbs.

TABLE 1
U.S. POPULATION DISTRIBUTION
BY METROPOLITAN-NONMETROPOLITAN RESIDENCE: 1970 AND 1960
[Numbers in thousands]

Race and Residence	Population 1970	Population 1960	Change Number	Change Per cent	Per cent distribution 1970	Per cent distribution 1960
Total	203,165,699	179,323,175	23,842,524	13.3	100.0	100.0
Metropolitan residence	140,155,868	120,158,786	19,997,082	16.6	69.0	67.0
Inside central cities	63,824,480	60,630,027	3,194,453	5.3	31.4	33.8
Outside central cities	76,331,388	59,528,759	16,802,629	28.2	37.6	33.2
Nonmetropolitan residence	63,009,831	59,164,389	3,845,442	6.5	31.0	33.0
White	177,612,309	158,831,732	18,780,577	11.8	100.0	100.0
Metropolitan residence	121,256,426	106,373,098	14,883,328	14.0	68.3	67.0
Inside central cities	49,450,484	50,057,231	−606,747	−1.2	27.8	31.5
Outside central cities	71,805,942	56,315,867	15,490,075	27.5	40.4	35.4
Nonmetropolitan residence	56,355,883	52,458,634	3,897,249	7.4	31.7	33.0
Negro and other races	25,553,390	20,491,443	5,061,947	24.7	100.0	100.0
Metropolitan residence	18,899,442	13,785,688	5,113,754	37.1	74.0	67.3
Inside central cities	14,373,996	10,572,796	3,801,200	36.0	56.3	51.6
Outside central cities	4,525,446	3,212,892	1,312,554	40.9	17.7	15.7
Nonmetropolitan residence	6,653,948	6,705,755	−51,807	−0.8	26.0	32.7
Negro	22,672,570	18,871,831	3,800,739	20.1	100.0	100.0
Metropolitan residence	16,826,430	12,760,092	4,066,338	31.9	74.2	67.6
Inside central cities	13,147,738	9,913,801	3,233,937	32.6	58.0	52.5
Outside central cities	3,678,692	2,846,291	832,401	29.2	16.2	15.1
Nonmetropolitan residence	5,846,140	6,111,739	−265,599	−4.3	25.8	32.4

Source: U.S. Bureau of the Census, Census of Population and Housing: 1970. *General Demographic Trends for Metropolitan Areas, 1960 to 1970,* Final Report PHC(2)-1 United States. Washington, D.C.: U.S. Government Printing Office, 1971.

TABLE 2
METROPOLITAN DISTRIBUTION OF THE U.S. POPULATION,
1900–1970
[Percentages]

Year	Central cities	Suburbs
1900	21.0	10.7
1910	25.0	12.7
1920	28.9	14.8
1930	31.8	18.0
1940	31.6	19.5
1950	32.3	23.8
1960	32.6	30.7
1970	31.4	37.6

Source: U.S. Bureau of the Census.

Some authorities have argued that only the high cost of suburban housing in general, and the shortage of new, moderate, and low-income housing in particular, is keeping the lower-middle class, and what is left of the middle class, in the central cities. In the New York area, for example, it has been estimated that a family needs a minimum annual income of about $17,000 to buy into the suburban housing market. The National Council Against Discrimination in Housing estimates that this excludes at least 80 per cent of New York's families. Even so, there is some evidence which indicates that the class composition of suburbia now includes an increasing number of blue-collar, working-class residents who are following their jobs or escaping the city and its problems.

The age characteristics of suburbanites also appear to be changing. One strand of the suburban myth has linked suburbia with families, and particularly with child-centered family units. Indeed, the postwar concentration on single-family dwelling units and the relatively small stock of housing units, especially apartments for singles, childless couples, and the elderly, plus the occupational and entertainment sterility of suburbia, made this pattern inevitable. But recently, the suburbanization of commerce and retailing and the apartment boom have increased the number of singles, couples, and retirees who call suburbia home. Furthermore, the wider range of suburban housing alternatives, including the so-called environmental or amenities apartment complexes, have made it unnecessary for "empty-nesters" (parents whose children are away at college or married) to return to the city.

The racial composition of suburbia is also changing, although the absolute numbers are less impressive than the relative shifts. For example, the number of nonwhites in the suburban rings has increased 1.3 million (40.9 per cent) since 1960, while the white increase has been 15.5 million (27.5 per cent). Because of the large number of whites who left the cities during the decade (about 2.5 million), the ratio of suburban blacks to whites changed imperceptibly (from 4.2 to 4.5 per cent) despite a more rapid black suburbanization rate.

These data tell us little about the degree to which suburban blacks are racially integrated. Impressionistically, it appears that many are. But there are also ghettos in suburbia, some of which are urban spillovers. And of course there are the black suburbs—for example, East Cleveland, Ohio, and Compton, California—and there will be more. Class ghettos in suburbia have always been more or less accepted, although they are now being challenged seriously. But are we to re-create the urban racial ghettos in suburbia?

Even urban housing styles are being imported by suburbia. For the first time since World War II, the number of multi-unit dwelling-starts is greater than that of private, one-family houses. There was a 37 per cent increase in the number of metropolitan area multi-unit dwellings in the sixties; the increase for the central cities was only 17 per cent, while the number of suburban units almost doubled. In absolute numbers of units constructed in the suburbs there were almost as many apartments (2.5 million) as private homes (2.6 million).

Some officials explain this phenomenon on simply economic grounds—suburban land is less expensive and cost is a basic factor in investment decisions. But land cost alone is insufficient to explain the trend. The demand for apartments in the suburbs suggests the acceptance of the suburban apartment life style by those who need smaller living units outside the city: the elderly concerned about living in the city with all its problems, and young adults with increasing employment, recreational, and entertainment opportunities in the suburbs. Many of the newer apartment complexes offer a full range of amenities at an acceptable price closer to the most rapidly developing job market. The suburban apartment boom appears to some observers as a logical concomitant of the decentralization of other urban functions.

The suburbanization of industry, corporate headquarters, major and minor retailers, and even professional athletic teams represents a significant symbolic change in the city-suburban relationship, as well as a significant shift in the distribution of such economic goods as property and sales-tax dollars and accessible jobs. This is a trend of major proportions, with little indication of abating. The hard facts will be available after the next census of business in 1973, but the signs are unmistakable. The U.S. Department of Labor reports that between 1960 and 1967, more than 50 per cent of all new industrial buildings and 52 per cent of new trade facilities were constructed in the suburbs. Each of the nation's twenty-four metropolitan areas with populations of 1 million or more experienced an absolute decrease in the number of manufacturing, trade, and service-industries jobs. During the last full decade for which data exist (1954–1963), central cities lost more than 500,000 jobs while the suburban areas of those twenty-four metropolitan areas gained over 1.5 million jobs. And the Regional Plan Association has estimated that two million of the 2.4 million new jobs developed by 1985 in the metropolitan New York area will be outside the city.

The trend toward industrial suburbanization is not new, nor are the reasons for it: cheaper land, new technology and transportation, revised production, and facility needs. It has been alleged that some business executives have moved their corporate headquarters to the suburbs as a matter of convenience, since it is no longer a necessity to locate businesses in the central city. Convenience may be a factor, but it is also true that there is now a substantial pool of skilled office workers in the suburbs. And retail stores have been attracted to the suburbs because that is where the customers are; the success of the ever-larger, ever-increasing number of shopping centers appears to endorse the economic wisdom of this retail migration.

The industrial, commercial, and retail migration has serious consequences for the city thus deserted. The decline of jobs in the central city and the inaccessibility to growing suburban economic opportunities have exacerbated racial and class isolation. The cities are becoming "reservations" of poor blacks and other minorities, while suburbia reaps the economic benefits.

The suburban wall is not easily toppled or scaled by the urban poor who seek to follow the job market by living in the suburbs. Each suburb, as a separate political jurisdiction, has traditionally attempted to maintain or enhance its "character" by establishing a variety of restrictive policies and practices—large-lot ("snob") zoning, minimum house-size requirements, and arbitrary building codes—which can be employed to exclude those defined as undesirable. To date, these exclusionary practices have been highly effective. But they are currently being challenged as discriminatory by civil rights groups like the Suburban Action Institute, the National Committee Against Discrimination in Housing, labor unions, some agencies of the federal government (for example, H.U.D. in Warren, Michigan, the Department of Justice in Blackjack, Missouri, and the Equal Opportunity Commission), and sometimes corporations themselves. Unfortunately, President Richard Nixon has taken a position which in effect endorses economic discrimination as long as it is not also racial.

If exclusionary practices are changed, it will come only through political pressure brought to bear on individual communities by civil rights and labor groups (such as the "fair-share" housing plan in the Dayton-Miami Valley area), economic pressure exerted by corporations (Quaker Oats made Danville, Illinois, pass a fair-housing ordinance before it would move its plant in), or a judicial breakthrough which overrides local zoning authority (as in Madison Township, New Jersey).

Up until quite recently, suburbia has been thought of as an escape from the problems of the city. In suburbia one could avoid the urban condition—congestion, apartment life, crime, the drug culture, bad schools, poverty, integration, and so on. But as suburbia urbanizes, more of its residents come to realize that the "new city," the "outer city," is much like the city they thought they left behind. The problems are becoming much the same, although there may still be significant differences in intensity.

Suburban taxes have always been high (except for industrial or commercial enclaves), but as the range of services and service costs increases, the increased residential property rates have taken the bloom off suburbia for many of its residents.

The 1970 Census shocked many when it revealed that 21 per cent of the nation's poor live in suburbia, as compared with 30 per cent in the central cities. (The rest live outside metropolitan areas.)

The suburban crime rates are growing more rapidly than those of the central cities (see Table 3), but for the time being, it is still safer to walk the streets of most suburbs. Crimes of violence are still predominantly an urban phenomenon, but crimes of acquisition are rapidly increasing in the suburbs.

TABLE 3
CITY-SUBURBAN CRIME RATES
[Percentage of increase over preceding year]

	1968	1969	1970	1971
Cities [1]	18	9	6	3
Suburbs	—	11	14	11

1. With populations of 250,000 or over.

Source: *The New York Times* (September 1, 1971; December 30, 1971).

A Senate subcommittee reported recently that the environmental problems of the city, particularly air pollution, are "wafting to suburbia." The increase in suburban industry and the number of cars needed to transport suburbanites around the outer city will guarantee this.

Nor does living in the suburbs prevent exposure to drugs, apartments, skyscrapers, noise, integration, or any of the other characteristics of cities. If suburbia is in fact the "new America," "the outer city," or the "city of the seventies," it must learn to cope with the problems which attend urbanization. Perhaps the most serious challenge it will face is how to govern and administer what one pundit called a "growing, pulsating thing." It is centerless and potentially unmanageable. The suburban seventies present us with an interesting and difficult new challenge. The adequacy of our response will determine the future of the historic city and the quality of life in the new city—suburbia.

Part 1

MYTH AND COUNTERMYTH

A New Life Style

by Ralph G. Martin

YOU CAN still remember walking up to your new house, in this new Long Island development, that day it was legally yours. You didn't see the unlandscaped mud on your lawn, you saw thick green grass and flowers, all kinds of flowers. And when you opened the door —what a feeling it can be to put a key in the door and open it!— you didn't see the emptiness, you saw a cozy furniture arrangement around the fireplace. Looking out of the huge living room window, you didn't see the tractors busy leveling the land, you saw a future park, all dressed up in thick trees and birds, so many, many birds. And as you walked around the room, just touching things, it was so easy to imagine noises in the silence—your wife busy in the kitchen making another fancy dessert, the crying of a brand-new baby. . . .

The idyll of a first home in the suburbs—it is that—but this is not the familiar suburb, which comprises a little of everything from a General Grant mansard to a three-room "ranch house." This is one of those new developments with a pattern all its own. Our development sprang up—and there are dozens like it on Long Island—mostly to accommodate veterans who wanted a place away from the in-laws, far from exorbitant rents in dank Manhattan basements. The notable characteristic of these developments is that they emerge out of nothingness and in a few months a community is formed. The result is a new way of living—and a new kind of person, what might be called the Development Type.

Of course, it's not *the* country. It's not Bucks County, Pennsylvania, or Old Lyme, Connecticut, with the tinkling brook running past the doorstep. More likely to be seen here is a neighbor, quite friendly, sunning his newborn in front of his own house, one or two hundred feet away. And near by, more houses, hundreds of them, and more kids. Nor is it like one of Long Island's old semi-country townships, some of which have been thriving outside New York City since before the Revolution. Those neighboring communities have both old folks and new folks, old houses and new houses, grandmas, tall trees, overstuffed attics and Established Ways.

It does, however, have some of the charm of any country village. When you walk around at night, this place is a cork blanket. No buses, no streetcars, no jangling taxis, no baby-sitter parties blaring out of the windows.

"I'm lucky. I work out here. I don't go to the city unless I have to," said Lester Grolnick, an "old-timer" who has lived here since the community was born, several years ago. "I've developed the hick attitude, I guess. All of a sudden now, I get overwhelmed by the hustle and bustle. I'm so used to the quiet that when I go to visit my folks in Brooklyn, I can't sleep because of the street noise. Honest. And I was born in Brooklyn, lived there all my life. Can you beat it?"

Our particular development sits on a flat stretch of land, about thirty miles from New York and halfway from either the north or south shores of Long Island. When we talk of the Island, we usually mean only Nassau and Suffolk Counties, both outside the city limits, stretching out about 100 miles long, twenty miles wide. Since 1940, Nassau alone has had almost a 50 per cent population increase. In the past two years, there have been a dozen brand-new communities created out of farmland, with whole new sections added to twenty-five other communities—actually, 60,000 new homes since 1947.

My community isn't just a bedroom of New York City, even though it's only fifty minutes away. Every day it becomes more of a separate place. It has a new bank, a post office, and a telephone building. Two more schools are getting ready to open, several more churches, always more clubs. The local paper has announced a concert series. A veterans organization picked its own local beauty queen. Stassen and Lehman both thought it important enough to make a special speech here the same night before election. They're even bringing a grand opera company here.

Who wants Coney Island, when it's always ten degrees cooler here, when all you have to do is walk a few blocks to your nearest swimming pool? (There will be one huge pool for every 1,000 homes.) Who has to go to Broadway for first-run movies, if you can find them in nearby towns? If you're a joiner, you have more than two dozen clubs to choose from here, including the recipe-traders at the Home Bureau, the singers at the Major and Minors, the hard-fighting Home Owners Association, and even a Dartmouth Club.

Or maybe you like to dance? It doesn't cost a nickel at the Village Green restaurant every Saturday night. Somebody once explained the big turnouts by saying, "I guess we're all at the same dance age."

They're alike in so many other ways. Besides being in the same age group (25–35), almost every one of the 9,000 homes has at least one child (and only 100 of the 8,000 children are old enough for high school). Nobody keeps up with the Joneses because they almost all have the same income (about $4,000 average). Nobody talks about the war much, because they've all been in it. And most of the men have the same Long Island Railroad commuting problem—which many have solved by car pools. All this helps cement neighbors into friends.

The Howard Handlers have lived here only since September, but when Howard talks about his neighbors—welding boss John Phillips, city fireman Tom Carney and air-conditioning expert Dick Hollis—you'd think he was talking about his closest kin.

"Phillips' wife had a birthday last night and what a time we all had," Howard said. "Hollis brought over his kid and put him in the same bed with the Phillips' two kids and then he took out his guitar and played and played and we just sang all night long.

"I tell ya, the four of us really have it worked out. When the girls go to a garden club meeting, we boys get together and baby-sit and play pinochle. Or one night we'll all go bowling down at the Village Green. And now we're all taking some of these adult education courses down at the school one night a week. Dick and I are taking a course in 'How to Finish Your Attic' and John's learning photography."

He told how they shared everything they learned: the best stuff to clean tile floors, the cheapest insurance for their thermopane windows, that there was a small ventilator opening that should be screened to keep out field mice. When Howard brought back fresh flowers from his mother, all four homes got some. Each woman already had spliced a piece of her potted plant to give to the others. They even compared electric bills, to see if any one bill was out of line.

"See that door windbreaker," said Howard proudly. "It got loose, so Hollis made angle irons for all four of us. And when I wanted to buy a garbage can, he wouldn't let me. He made me one out of a fifty-pound grease drum. Now isn't that a beautiful garbage can?"

People who lived for years in apartment houses without ever really knowing their neighbors come here and start living Dale Carnegie. For newcomers it sometimes becomes overwhelming. You come home from work to find your neighbor (whom you hadn't yet met) had put your milk in her refrigerator so the sun wouldn't spoil it. If you don't have a car, neighbors with cars are always asking your wife, "I'm going shopping. Do you want to come along?"

Before you can ask somebody for the neighbor's lawnmower, he usually volunteers it. One woman left her faucet running and came back to a flooded kitchen, but six neighbors were already mopping it up. If your car gets stuck here, don't worry, the next car that comes along will stop to help. When polio victim Norman Modell came out of the hospital and needed some strong arms to support him while he tried to walk again, he had all the volunteers he needed.

Perhaps all this explains why Mrs. Edwin Niles said, "For the first time since I left Fordyce, Arkansas, I really feel at home."

There's a small-town friendliness at the Village Greens (there are three so far, more coming up fast). Modernly styled, the Green is the shopping center for each area—and something more. People are always stopping to talk to each other there. Nobody rushes.

This is a paradise for children. "There are so many babies here that you would think everybody would be blasé about them," said Mrs. Alice Miller. "Still, when a new one is coming, all the neighbors make a fuss over you. I had to go to the hospital soon after I moved in, and neighbors I hadn't even met yet just came in and took over. They pack your bags, drive you to the hospital if your husband's working, take care of your other baby if you have one. And they wouldn't let me buy anything for it either. That carriage isn't mine and neither is the crib, and my other neighbor said we could have those baby scales as long as we need them. Somebody here always has a baby a year older."

The slightly older ones never had it so good. If they leave their toys on the walk sometimes, or if they overrun into somebody's back yard—there is a deep, patient understanding by the neighbors, because they probably also have a child. Children have space to run in, grass to roll in, wading pools, and playgrounds. Mothers don't worry too much about cars, because there's almost no transient traffic. People who drive here live here. They don't have to be told to watch out for children—they have their own. And the short, curved streets slow down the strangers.

When you talk to the pediatricians (there are six here now, more due any minute), they tell you how much better physically children are here, compared to city kids. But that's a thing you see for yourself. If that was the only reason for moving out here, it would be reason enough for most families.

The best is none too good for the children. When Mrs. Betty Gurwitz moved in and saw there wasn't any nursery school, she wrote a letter to the editor to find out who else was interested. Twenty women answered, so Betty called a meeting. It was a stormy, snowy night, but fifty people showed up.

"My kitchen was just covered with rubbers and galoshes," said dark-haired Betty. "I never belonged to any organization before in my life and here I had helped start one. I got the feeling of people wanting to do things together." They finally found an old schoolhouse seven miles away. The husbands built chairs, toys, swings, blocks, easels, cubbies (for the children's clothes). For expenses, these women published a town directory themselves and sold advertising space in it.

In the regular public schools (there will be three open soon, with sites for five more set aside) there are more than thirty new admissions a day. Slightly more than two years ago there were only thirty-seven pupils in this whole district. Now there are 1,180 pupils in grades one to eight, a thousand more expected by September 1950.

The children themselves don't seem to regard schools as torture chambers. Maybe it's because the young teachers guide instead of push, or maybe it's because the half-million-dollar modern buildings have huge windows that let the sun in. And parents are always comparing notes, how their little Marjorie is so much more advanced than her city cousin in the same grade. It may even be true.

Parent-Teacher Association members, all 640 of them, are eager beavers. When only one school was open, working a double shift, they helped solve the transportation problem with buses. They were the ones that got after the police to set up enough safety zones. And when they saw cars driving too fast, even on the Turnpike, which divides the town, they copied down license numbers and reported them. They persuaded Mitchel Field to donate seven pianos to the school. Last spring they got together with the local American Association of University Women and went from house to house collecting nickels and dimes until they had the $600 to finance a summer playground for the children.

While the PTA concentrates on an individual school, the AAUW canvasses the broader picture. They get acquainted with top school board officials, learn about local tax structure and county government, invite an expert to tell them how to start a town library.

This "our town" spirit takes on a sharper focus when people talk about their homes. The houses take on the personalities of their owners. Different kinds of garages, a concrete patio, a huge wagon wheel, a rustic fence, an unusual signpost, special flower arrangements, and every home has a different paint job. Working around the house isn't a chore, it's mixed up with a deep feeling of pride.

"Now he knows how to hammer a nail," said Betty Gurwitz,

pointing to her husband. "And he knows all about the nitrogen content of the soil. You should have seen our tomatoes. We didn't buy a single tomato, and we eat a lot of them."

Her husband rubbed his chin reflectively. "We had corn, too," he added, "but it wasn't successful this year. Didn't have enough space. Next year I'll try several varieties so I can have cross-pollination. Which reminds me, I need more mulch." He laughed at himself. "Mulch—that's a hot one. I never even heard the word before I came here."

But not everybody's happy here. Slightly more than half the homes are rented and there's a small population turnover. Some people leave because they think it's too rural; they want more excitement, more Broadway. Some families grow so large that they need a bigger place than these 4½-room homes (although some homes have attics converted into two more, a room over the garage, a utility room in back of it).

One woman moved because "a house isn't a house if it doesn't have a basement," even though she admitted the radiant heating was wonderful. Another woman was moving back to New York "because I like to live where I can walk with my baby carriage and see stores instead of houses."

For others it's a financial question. Monthly payment for home owners is $58, which covers equity, interest, taxes, everything but heat and electricity. But there's always the monthly commutation ticket ($17) plus bus and subway fares, unless you've connected with a car pool. Another frequently brought up criticism is that this town isn't typical of the real world. You can tell your child about old people, but you can't show him any. The same is almost true of teenagers.

Some people move back to the city because they find these small communities too friendly. They're introverts who like invisible moats around their homes, or else they don't know how to cope with overexuberant neighbors who insist on coming in without knocking. Usually, though, people here who want moats, have them —without moving.

But people have other reasons for moving. You have to live in a house for a while before you find the kinks in it. Maybe your wife will develop a phobia about always walking on hard tile? Or maybe you get sensitive about having an overlarge living room window when your view is nothing but the overlarge living room window of your neighbor? Or maybe it's the size of the rooms, or the layout, or perhaps your wife never did like fireplaces?

After a while you may find all kinds of things you'd like to change, especially if your repair bills are high. The dream house is always a continuous dream. Houses aren't like cars—you can't trade them in every year. For most people here, this is it. For others, this first home is only the first step, a sort of education in what a house is. If their income grows as big as their expected family, then they plan to build what they really want.

The case for this sort of new semirural community isn't clear-cut. It depends on who you are. But if you want a place where you can walk safely down the street with a pet live duck; if you want a place where you can start a small symphony orchestra simply by writing a letter to the editor, as automobile salesman Lawrence Eliscu did; if you like to get up in the morning and go right out into the fresh air—not smoke or dirt, but real fresh air; if you prefer folk dances to the juke box, buttercups to Broadway; if all your life you've unconsciously been running away from the pushing, blaring, hurry of the city—then this is for you.

For the Sake
of the Children

by Anne Kelly

EVERY SUBURBAN PARENT is familiar with the phrase "for the good of the children." It explains very neatly why he's living where and as he's living in 1958. Experts began pointing out a score of years ago the importance of green grass as an adjunct to child development; parents heard, heeded and began what has become a near stampede to the suburbs.

And now, as they compute the monthly mortgage payments for their little semicountry homes, what are these parents hearing? That for the young, that outward trek may not have been such a good idea after all.

Who says so? The experts—the very same sociologists, mental hygienists, and other specialists who encouraged the massive suburban shift in the first place. The suburbs, they say, are homogenized like peanut butter—grouping families all too much alike in age, income, education, and pattern of life. The areas are likely to be child-centered, focusing on offspring all attention not necessarily directed to the commuter's timetable and the snow shovel. Pressures on children to conform, to be popular, to achieve, and generally to fit in with the group amount to a squeeze. They are

Original title: "Suburbia—Is It a Child's Utopia?" From *The New York Times Magazine,* February 2, 1958, copyright © 1958 by The New York Times Company.

so overincluded as to have no time left for daydreams or mumblety-peg.

On the other hand, experts say that suburban children may feel shut off from and rejected by society because the new communities fail to provide roots ready-made for them. Harking back to the "stable" small town of 1900, one social worker of national repute charged not long ago:

> We do not bother to evaluate the new suburban society —how it excludes the children, whether it gives them a sense of our love and concern. Fifty years ago the children grew up in a town that automatically encompassed them. Neighbors knew one another and their children and had a concern for one another. Children grew up with this sense of concern.

So, we are told, the children are simultaneously fattening on a diet of spoon-fed attention, and—wait a minute—rootless and starved for love. It all depends upon which expert we've tuned in.

And there's still more to come: suburban life, for children, is overorganized; the father has little time at home because of commuting demands; the mother becomes sole disciplinarian and 24-hour chauffeur; population turnover is great, with a resulting lack of stability; materialism is glorified, with sports cars, patios, hi-fi, and country clubs set upon an altar and cocktail parties celebrated as a sort of social low mass; despite the dedication to the child's interests, children in the suburbs do not distinguish themselves in tests devised to measure mental health.

To the complete indictment, there is only one possible response: a sober nodding of the head, in recognition of the fact that parenthood is a battle which can never be won. Everything they say is true, but—

It might be interesting to consider why many of us, seeking a lair in the middle-class wilderness, chose the suburbs as the place to have and rear our children—and what alternative we had.

That cozy small town of 1900 was, except in fantasy, out. (And was it really a children's developmental paradise, anyway? Was it not sometimes labeled provincial, snobbish and ingrown by the scholars who did research projects on it? Was it invariably "stable"?)

Therefore, we had as possible choices the city itself (the place where most suburban parents earn the money to make the mortgage payments); the isolated countryside (possible only if the father (1) changes his vocation to sheepherding or (2) lives so far from work that families are together only at vacation times); the "smaller places adjacent to a city," as Webster defines the suburbs.

Heeding the experts' earlier warning that a concrete sidewalk was not a recommended training ground for our young, and believing, too, that urban life would involve private schools, summers in the country, and other flourishes clearly beyond our budget, we made the move to the suburbs because we felt neither rich enough nor poor enough to homestead within the big city.

For the most part, a suburb attracts monogamous settlers of procreative age and inclination who are able to read and write, are accustomed to inside plumbing, and generally exhibit a marked sameness right down to a basic tendency to wear shoes. As a vantage point for studying a "cross-section" of life, then, it is definitely less favorable than an automat or night police court.

These alleged rootless, shifting, homogeneous souls are likely to have been transplanted from other sections of the country or from other lands. But a recent spot check in the Connecticut town of Darien—a suburb in every sense of the word—revealed that, while some elementary and junior-high youngsters, if given their choice of the place they would like to live, might elect Majorca; Beloit, Wisconsin; New York City; Maine, or California, the majority preferred a suburb like Darien. Of the seventy-eight children in the fourth, sixth, and ninth grades questioned, all but three said they are happy with the suburban way of life. Children may be in no position to determine whether or not they are happy, but at any rate this is a touching testimonial, if only to the status quo.

Children of these families, moved from one community to another according to their fathers' business fortunes and their mothers' social ambitions, may lack the sense of continuity their grandfathers knew from growing up in the same town where *their* grandfathers were born. But at the same time they have an awareness of their country and the world that grandpa never had.

Day dawns early in the suburbs. Most fathers make a coattail departure for the 7:57 and may not reappear until the evening meal looks as if it had been embalmed. To a large extent, then, the daytime hours are truly of matriarchal and child-centered quality. Children go to nearby public schools and can vacation, if necessary, in their own back yards. They have sleds in winter and wading pools or town beaches in summer; they have trees to climb. They can see all but the fiercer animals without going to the zoo, and they can plant zinnias in the ground instead of in pots. They associate freely and handily with their "peers" by the simple gesture of opening the back door.

They can also—as any suburban mother who has turned the ignition key forty-eight times in one week will testify—enjoy Cub Scouts, Brownies, ballet class, day camp, Sunday school, Little League, birthday parties, library reading hour, school fairs, trick or treat, haircuts, dental checkups, and cooky sales, all on their own tight suburban island. A child who declines to join in these activities will share the same sense of exile his parents feel in rebuffing neighborhood, church, civic, political, educational, arts-and-crafts, or Friday-night-bridge groups. In the suburbs, a non-conformist is conspicuous and, just as in the small town of 1900, he or she is likely to draw a certain amount of attention from the highly active, intrasuburb information services.

Because of transportation complexities, a suburb is likely to be self-contained socially, and suburban weekends find fathers drawn into the same backyard, neighborhood, and town-center activity programs that have occupied mothers and children throughout the week. However, books reach the suburbs, as do periodicals, news-papers, the comics, and TV. And, as the experts may or may not have heard, suburban children are also occasionally taken by their parents into the wide world beyond. They thus have an opportunity to observe life at grandma's, at the top of the Empire State Build-ing, in a motel, and at the museum. The breadth of their experi-ences is determined more by the metabolism and muscle tone of their parents than by group dynamics.

Granted that New Suburbia has its drawbacks, are they neces-sarily inherent in and restricted to suburban life? Or do they reflect, perhaps, the swing our total American culture has taken in recent years toward conformity, conservatism, group adjustment, and a balanced budget?

And if suburbs are, as they surely seem, child-centered, may it not simply be because in these residential communities there are so many children to center lives around? Regardless of their habitat, most parents are likely to concede that not only their lives but their life insurance, sewing baskets, and desk drawers are notably child-centered. This is one of the facts of parenthood.

As for the tendency of suburban children to want to be popular and yet indistinguishable from the rest of the group, any parent anywhere who has ever tried to force a child into corduroys when other children are wearing blue jeans may suspect that this trait is universal. There is even a nice, neat psychological phrase for it, used indiscriminately in city and village in reference to both grownup and child—"group approval."

Where suburban children may, with or without knowing it, feel the pinch is in their opportunities to see and be with their own fathers. But here again we may have a problem of relativity. There is on fathers everywhere a certain regrettable pressure to remove themselves from the family hearth at intervals and sell shirts, fill teeth, or even compile sociological studies, in order to bring home a paycheck. Time en route to and from work may be increased for the suburban father, but the problem will not be finally delineated until some research team measures the time spent by all fathers, of varied residential settings, away from home—at work, on the golf course, playing squash, or gone fishin'.

And is the quantity of parenting necessarily more important than the quality? What delicate measuring device of the social scientists can weigh the intensity of attention a father gives his child in any one minute? And isn't the question of father-child companionship one that, finally, must be worked out between two individuals rather than on the pages of research reports?

To the twin charge that, while father is too little present in the suburbs, mother is too much so, mother herself would probably be the first to agree. Mother, particularly Den Mother and Room Mother and Car Pool Mother, often has difficulty locating—not to mention measuring—her own "sense of personal freedom." There are times, too, when her self-esteem is at low ebb and the "we" feeling threatens to overwhelm her. There are even times when she envies father his two daily commuting hours—spent sitting down, with a newspaper in hand. But mothers everywhere are known to be involved in intricate problems of time and space and balance, and if the emphasis is different in suburbia the basic proposition of motherhood is not.

Parents being as they are, suburban parents included, it is doubtful that they can now—at the experts' new crash call—remove their children from the center of their lives or set about simultaneously administering affection, security, family roots, stability and togetherness in scientifically controlled doses, guaranteed neither to smother nor to reject. They can continue to worry, as they always have, about whether or not their children are happy, but to establish a definite answer to this puzzler would take a mightier analyst than any parent or any specialist.

If the pendulum now swings gradually away from emphasis on possessions, on sameness, on artificial recreation, and on earning a living at the expense of living a life, children and parents everywhere will surely benefit, in suburb and out. And the specialists who point out our cultural inadequacies will deserve—once again —our gratitude.

Meanwhile, suburban parents can take comfort from the fact that the imitation small town they live in is a good deal like other places, only more so, and that its imperfections belong, in varying degrees, to our way of life at large—rural, exurban, suburban, interurban, urban, and houseboat.

And there is an additional comfort available for suburban parents, too: In the year 2000-plus, when man has set up new and shiny residential areas on the face of the moon, a new generation of experts will peer closely and compile detailed reports. Parents will then read that their children miss the old earthly gravitational pull, that no child knows what part of the solar system to call his home, that children are overprotected beneath their plastic sky-domes and that one face looks just like the next inside a space suit. Then someone will hark back nostalgically to the suburbs of 1958.

The Suburban Apartment Boom

by Jack Rosenthal

APARTMENTS IN the suburbs, once an almost unimaginable sight through the picture window, increased at a spectacular rate in the nineteen sixties, according to the first major national housing report of the 1970 Census.

The number of all housing units increased by 18 per cent in the decade, but the number of suburban apartments increased by 96 per cent.

The growth has been so strong that now there is one suburban apartment for every two city apartments. The 1960 ratio was one to four.

The 1970 total of 5,244,000 suburban apartments includes every type of multi-unit dwelling, from garden apartments near Disneyland to Planned Unit Developments—clusters of various kinds of housing and industry—in New Jersey and high-rise condominiums outside Cleveland.

Experts here have already described such development as decisive evidence that suburban areas are being urbanized into Outer Cities. But even they expressed surprise at the magnitude of the Census Bureau findings.

Original title: "Suburb Apartments Up by 96% in Decade." From *The New York Times,* December 9, 1971, copyright © 1971 by The New York Times Company.

"And if you think the sixties were the decade of suburban apartment building," said Arthur F. Young, chief of the bureau's housing division, "just wait till the figures are in for the seventies."

U.S. HOUSING PATTERNS, 1960–1970 [1]

	1960	1970	Per cent change
Suburbs:			
Multi-unit dwelling	2,674,162	5,244,350	96.1
Single-unit dwellings	15,179,739	17,793,206	17.2
Mobile homes	334,031	673,196	101.5
Central Cities:			
Multi-unit dwellings	9,335,193	10,919,260	17.0
Single-unit dwellings	11,002,478	11.471,239	4.3
Mobile homes	95,784	175,396	83.1
U.S. Total:			
Multi-unit dwellings	13,789,663	18,859,968	36.8
Single-unit dwellings	43,758,556	46,900,548	7.2
Mobile homes	766,565	1,847,326	141.0

1. Figures are extracted from summary report of 1970 Census.

The new report also provides a mass of other data for 243 standard metropolitan statistical areas. These are cities of 50,000 population and over plus their suburbs. Other findings include the following:

• Median monthly rents are higher in 18 other cities than in New York City. The highest figure—$135—was for San Jose, Calif. In New York, where many apartments come under rent control, it was $96. The national median for the cities was $91.

• While luxury apartments in some cities clearly command the highest rents, typical rents were significantly higher in the suburbs in almost every sizable metropolitan area. The national median figure for the suburbs was $113. The highest specific suburban figures were: San Jose, $149; Washington, $148; New York, Chicago, and Orange County, Calif., $142.

• For owner-occupied housing in the cities, the highest median value was in Honolulu—$43,200. The New York median figure was $25,700. The national figure was $16,500.

• By far the highest value for the typical suburban house was recorded around Stamford and Norwalk, Conn., "$50,000 plus." In New York's near suburbs, it was $29,500. Nationally, it was $20,800.

• Nationally, the typical family was significantly smaller than in 1960, but it had larger and somewhat better lodgings. The typical suburban family, for example, had 3.5 people living in 5.1 rooms in 1960. In 1970, there were 3.3 people in 5.3 rooms.

• The proportion of all families who own their homes remained at about 63 per cent, but it increased among black families to 42 per cent from 38.

• While virtually all housing units in Northern cities and suburbs have adequate plumbing, the picture was different in many Southern suburbs. In the suburbs of Memphis, 23 per cent of all homes do not have complete bathrooms. In suburban El Paso, the figure is 21 per cent; in suburban Shreveport and Nashville, 18 per cent.

One category of housing—mobile homes—increased faster, proportionately, than suburban apartments. The 1970 Census counted 1,847,000 mobile homes, a jump of 141 per cent.

But in absolute numbers, there were more than two new suburban apartments in the decade for every new mobile home.

The urban authorities offer a series of explanations for the dramatic surge in suburban apartment building, but the most common is land cost.

"Our central cities are our histories," said Dr. Charles G. Field, a research official of the Department of Housing and Urban Development. "But investment decisions are based on present costs, not history. And suburban land is cheaper."

The Census Bureau's Mr. Young cited life style changes as another important explanation.

"People who could never afford an answering service, a pool, special security, and extensive social facilities in their own homes," he said, "can get these amenities in a plush apartment."

And the market for such apartments in the suburbs, Mr. Young said, is both big and booming. Many aging suburbanites do not want to care for big houses any more with their children grown.

"Plus their grown kids—marrying later and having kids later —need places to live," he said. He continued:

"The parents, concerned about security, don't want to go back into the cities. And the young people—having grown up in sub- urbs—don't have even sentimental ties to the cities any more."

Other housing authorities regard the suburban apartment boom as a reflection of the decentralizing of other city functions. As jobs, stores and recreation have moved outward, they say, it is inevitable for people who want smaller living units to follow.

"It used to sound farcical for someone to suggest building an elevator apartment out in the boondocks," said one H.U.D. econo- mist. "Not any more."

In the words of another authority, referring to developments far south of Washington: "It's the ultimate urban irony—apart- ments and town houses twenty-five miles from town."

Isolation in Suburbia

by Linda Greenhouse

THE QUESTION is a painful one, and the women here waited a long while before they started asking it, even of themselves.

"Chappaqua is a good address, after all," said Phyllis Sanders, who moved here three years ago with her husband and five children. "The real estate agent's pitch is that you'll be here in your pretty house, surrounded by trees, and nobody will bother you. Your husband wanted a place with a green back yard. He's gone every day from 7 A.M. till 7 P.M., and you're left with the green back yard. Does the nice house and the green yard make for happiness?"

That is the question. For a growing number of women in this appealing, almost rustic commuting suburb twenty-five miles north of New York City, the answer is no. The women range from young mothers to those whose children are grown, with the most vocal of them well into middle age. They are well-read, well-traveled, active in their church or temple, and impeccably middle-class.

They draw back almost perceptibly at the suggestion that their thoughts, if not their language, sound very much like women's liberation, saying that they don't want to be labeled. Within the last few years, these women have begun to tell themselves—and now feel ready to tell outsiders as well—that the life of the suburban housewife is often one of isolation, boredom, and loneliness.

Original title: "These Wives Found Cure to Some of the Ills of Suburban Life." From *The New York Times,* October 1, 1971, copyright © 1971 by The New York Times Company.

They know that neither they nor their town is unique—indeed, the idle, frustrated housewife is almost as much a cliché as the battle-ax mother-in-law.

But people do not think of themselves as clichés, and for each of about sixty women here—they are not organized and have no name for themselves—the realization that the stereotype applied to them was a very individual process. The process was precipitated by different events for different women. For one, it was when she stopped feeling sorry for her husband because he had to commute. "All winter the trains would be an hour or an hour and a half late, and I'd wait for him and tell him how terrible it was that he had to sit in the train all that time," she said. "He would tell me he hadn't even noticed. It's not the men who suffer over commuting. It's the women. For a man, the train is a welcome cushion of time when he can be alone, when the phone won't ring, and no one will bother him."

Mrs. Sanders says her feelings were confirmed the summer her family was host to a black fourteen-year-old from the Bronx as part of a summer school program. Critics of the program, she recalled, had said that it would be psychologically damaging to the black children because "they'll see how happy we are here and they won't be able to face living any other way." But at the end of the summer, when she asked her guest how he had enjoyed Chappaqua, he told her that he felt very sorry for her two sons, who lived too far to walk to visit their friends and who had to depend on their mother to drive them everywhere. At home, he said, he was independent and surrounded by friends. "It's so lonely here," the boy said.

The women started meeting in the Spring of 1968 as a discussion group to read and talk about the Kerner Commission report on civil disorders. The group was sponsored by the United Church Women but it included women of all religions. Last winter, several of the women who had first met during those talks organized a series of six discussions on "The Quality of Life in Suburbia." The series drew about eighty women, and the initial call for suggestions attracted a surprising increase—and, to the sponsors, a surprisingly negative set of comments. The comments, typed and mimeographed for group discussion, included such descriptions of Chappaqua as "as escape from the world," "retreat into a comfortable existence of good schools," "inner needs of educated women often unmet," "no community feeling," and "mother a taxi driver much of the time."

"We saw that everyone felt the same way, but no one had ever verbalized it before," said Claire Marcus, who met recently with several others of the original participants at Mrs. Sanders's house to discuss their collective experience.

As they talked, the women agreed that similar problems do exist in many other suburbs. But they felt the problem to be especially acute in such places as Chappaqua, where the houses are too far apart for casual neighborliness; where trains make the hour-long run only once every two hours after the morning rush, and where husbands are often in executive positions that call for frequent travel.

In addition, Chappaqua, with perhaps 10,000 residents, is not incorporated. It is a residential village, part of the town of New Castle; therefore, the government that most clearly represents its people is the Chappaqua school district. However, women who do not have children in school miss even that community link. Chappaqua has few sidewalks, no movie theaters or nighttime recreation, no newspaper of its own, and no parks or places where women can gather during the day to see other adults.

The series of meetings gave the women some concrete ideas about what Chappaqua needed: a park, facilities for child care, some way of publicizing community events, at least one woman on the New Castle Town Board, and some occasion that could focus residents' attention on Chappaqua as their community.

"We realized that our husbands have no idea what our needs are," said Loree Elliott, the wife of a minister and one of the more active members of the group. "They've run Chappaqua, but they've never really lived here. What we have to do is not yell at them, but to educate them."

When they first started talking to community leaders about what Chappaqua needed, Mrs. Sanders said, the women hesitated to present themselves as a group of women. "We didn't want to seem too threatening," she said. When people asked her whom she represented, she mumbled something about "a group of people."

To the amazement of the participants in the series, most of the needs they identified have been or may soon be met. A woman, Sally Martin, received the Democratic nomination for one of three vacancies on the Town Board. The trustees of the First Congregational Church agreed to provide space for "play care," where mothers can bring their children on an irregular basis for $2 a morning. The session started last week and has been heavily oversubscribed. A committee of women working with the local Red Cross is offering a six-week course to train and certify baby-sitters. Eighteen junior high school youngsters have enrolled so far. Another committee plans to compile and post a daily listing of town events. No park has been created, but the town fathers are talking about including one in longstanding plans for a new town hall.

And, finally, a summer of planning culminated in "New Castle Community Day." Sixty separate events and exhibits, ranging from a free pig roast to a peace vigil to an illustrated lecture on the life of Horace Greeley, Chappaqua's favorite son, drew between 3,000 and 5,000 people, even though the local Chamber of Commerce president had told Mrs. Sanders: "I don't think you can sell it. This is a place where people come to get away from other people."

The community day, which included many husband-and-wife teams on the planning committee, was the first nonathletic family event that anyone can remember here. It led to plans to set up a permanent showcase for local art, and the day itself will become an annual institution.

The women are under no illusion that this rapid series of events will solve all their problems. There will still be lonely times in the green back yard; there will still be the long vigils at the railroad station, motors idling on dark winter nights, waiting for the commuter trains to pull in. The child care program and reliable baby-sitters will give them more mobility, certainly. But what the women talk about most is their change in attitude.

"There's a spirit of hope, that something can be good about suburbia," Mrs. Elliott said, "We've discovered that we can make a difference."

Don't Knock It

by Harvey Aronson

WHEN I WAS a kid growing up in Queens, relatives from Brooklyn and the East Side used to visit on Sundays and sit in our small back yard on folding chairs and talk about how nice it was to be "out on Long Island." They were wrong, of course, but the mistake persists; there are still people who live in Manhattan, and you mention places that are really New York City, like Bellaire or Laurelton, and they say that's Long Island. Well, don't try to tell that to anyone who really lives on Long Island.

Long Island, for better and worse, begins where New York City ends. That is a matter of life as well as geography. To a good many New Yorkers who can't get away from fun city fast enough in the summertime, Long Island is strictly places like the Hamptons and Quogue. This is as stupid as saying that New York is strictly the Waldorf-Astoria or that America is "My Three Sons." The real Long Island is centered in places about which the plastic groupies of Davis Park, the biased anachronisms of old-guard Southampton, and the chic radicals of new-guard Easthampton know very little. The real Long Island is not those asinine dances and nude-in-the-pool parties you read about on *The Times'* society page. The real Long Island is communities like East Meadow and Syosset and Commack and Patchogue. The real Long Island is suburbia.

Original title: "Long Island Is Not to Be Scoffed At." From *The New York Times,* May 22, 1971, copyright © 1971, by The New York Times Company.

I am passionately aware of the real Long Island's faults—some of which, such as single-stratum neighborhoods and segregated slums, also scar the city. I am aware that many communities look alike, that integration is still token, and the majority of my neighbors probably think Spiro Agnew makes a lot of sense. I am aware of that national abomination called the Long Island Railroad, and of the strident thoroughfares that reach their ultimate horror in Jericho Turnpike, which bangles the North Shore like a honky-tonk charm bracelet made of topless dives, lonely bars, gas stations, hamburger drive-ins, and appliance stores.

But I am sick of all the blather I hear from the people who think it is important to be seen at Stella's, and who would probably move to Connecticut if they could swing it. I am sick of all their yammering about the hellishness of places like Levittown and Plainview. Because they don't know what the blue blazes they're talking about.

Not all the developments are unsightly, and there are plenty of individualists among the conformists. There are artists and writers living in the real Long Island, as well as ball-players and prize-fighters. I know a steeplejack who lives on Long Island, and a man who tried to swim the English Channel. True, most of the people on my block have the same kind of split-level, but one man built an airplane in his garage and another is a ham radio operator with a tower in his back yard that looks big enough to catch signals from Saturn. Or take my immediate neighbors. He quit a large company to start his own successful computer business, and she went back to college several years ago and got a bachelor's degree, and then a master's, and now she's teaching on a graduate level.

It is important that people in places like New York City start understanding places like the real Long Island. It is important because the real Long Island is suburbia and the suburbs represent the new America. Consider that the suburbs passed the cities in population in 1970. Or consider that Nassau and Suffolk, the two counties that make up Long Island, have a population greater than that of 24 states and all but three U.S. cities. The real Long Island is an America of power mowers and paneling and model-home come-ons and town dumps. But it is also an America of increasing political power, of busy shopping centers, and of fresh air and room in which to breathe it. It is an America of people searching for the good life and working to meet mortgage payments. And it is also the America of a harried middle class beginning to rebel against high taxes, heavy traffic, imperfect appliances, uncaring corporations, and a lot of other monoliths that have been kicking all of us in the soul for a long time.

It is also a place where there is still a lot of natural beauty some people want to preserve. It is a place of simple pleasures—a place where you can cook outdoors and grow vegetables. I have a backboard in my driveway, and my son, who is 6, can't reach the basket, but he is learning to handle the ball. And even in the winter we can be at Sunken Meadow State Park within minutes and throw flat stones at the water. The real Long Island is a place where you put down new roots.

For Many, Suburbia's Grass Isn't So Green

by Ralph Blumenthal

"I LOATHED IT out there," said Stephen MacDonald, a New Yorker-turned-suburbanite-turned-New Yorker. He was talking about his 17 months of living in New Providence, New Jersey.

"We succumbed to the suburban dream—I mean, who is immune?" said Mrs. Betty Friedan, author of *The Feminine Mystique.* She moved back to New York from Rockland County with her family because, she said, "The nature was idyllic, but I like people better."

"The house was too empty and too big," said Dr. Nathaniel J. Breckir, a former Brooklynite who raised his children in White Plains and returned to the city 18 months ago.

In the face of a continuing exodus to the suburbs by scores of thousands of New Yorkers every year, thousands of suburbanites are coming back.

Left with large, empty houses when their children have grown up and moved out, they are yearning once again for the rich cultural life of the city. Some say they are fed up with "the commute," finding that some of the problems of the city have followed them to suburbs.

Original title: "Many Families Find Suburbia's Grass Isn't As Green." From *The New York Times,* April 8, 1968, copyright © 1968 by The New York Times Company.

These returnees are part of a countermovement to the much-discussed flight to suburbia.

They are not threatening a depopulation of the suburbs, which continue to grow, rippling outward into once-rural areas. Rather, they are showing that what appeared to be an abandonment of the city was actually the first half of a round trip to the suburbs and back, spread over the time it takes children to grow up.

For the Nathaniel J. Breckirs, that period ran from 1945 to 1966. Dr. Breckir, a psychiatrist, moved with his wife, nine-year-old daughter and six-year-old son from their apartment in Brooklyn to a ten-room house in one of the best sections of White Plains.

"We moved," he said recently, "for the better schools and the easier and more pleasurable life. I wouldn't do it any differently now."

But twenty-one years later, with his son a lawyer on the West Coast and his daughter married with a child of her own and living in another suburb, Huntington, Long Island, the parents decided the house was too empty and too far from Lincoln Center and other cultural attractions of the city.

They sold the house and bought a six-room cooperative apartment at 36 East 72nd Street, around the corner from Dr. Breckir's Fifth Avenue office.

"Our social and cultural life is really beginning now," Dr. Breckir said.

For Mrs. Friedan, her husband, two sons, and a daughter, the suburban mystique lasted about eight years. Seeking more space, the family moved from Manhattan to Queens and then, in 1957, to a "dreamy" eleven-room house in Grandview on the Hudson River near Nyack.

Becoming bored ("You don't want to climb a mountain every day," Mrs. Friedan said), they returned four years ago to a seven-room apartment in the venerable Dakota at 1 West 72nd Street. Mrs. Friedan, who has since separated from her husband, [said,] "My roots are in what's happening. And now I don't have to worry about a septic tank."

The dimensions of the movement out and back are not fully known and will not be until the 1970 census or some other comprehensive survey is made. The last census showed that 424,000

New Yorkers moved to the nearby suburbs between 1955 and 1960, while 59,000 people moved from those suburbs to the city.

More recently, the city's Board of Education found that New York continued to be a net loser to the suburbs of families with young children. During the 1966–1967 school year, the board's data show, 16,658 pupils transferred from city schools to schools in Nassau, Suffolk, Westchester and Rockland Counties and in New Jersey, while only 5,582 pupils were enrolled here from schools in those areas.

The city seems to be gaining population again, however, after the 1950-to-1960 falloff from 7,892,000 to 7,782,000 shown by the last census. By 1965, according to an estimate of the Regional Plan Association, the city had 7,991,500 residents, a gain spurred chiefly by the migration of Negroes and Puerto Ricans and by natural increase.

A more recent estimate by the city Health Department's Bureau of Vital Statistics put New York's population at 8,125,000 as of last July.

Mayor Lindsay last January offered an explanation for the return of suburbanites, who make up at least a small part of the city's population gain. He said:

> When the core city declines, the same symptoms inevitably spread to the suburbs. Many who move to the suburbs are, surprisingly, coming back to the city because they find out that there is no place to hide, but that the inner city is where the action is—cultural, recreational, social and exciting.

A number of disquieting facts seem to confirm the outward spread of problems. Last year, for example, the number of burglaries reported to the police rose by 25.1 per cent in Nassau County and by 18 per cent in Suffolk County, rates that approach the 27 per cent increase reported in the city. The rise in burglaries in the first half of the year in Greenwich, Connecticut, was 50 per cent, almost double the rate in the city.

Last year, Westchester County found it necessary to establish an air pollution control agency to begin an attack on the dirty air problem there. The welfare caseload has risen 130 per cent in the past five years in Nassau, Suffolk and Rockland Counties. The rise for the city, which began with a much higher base, was 96.4 per cent.

While the population has risen in the suburban counties, the rise in such things as burglaries and welfare cases has outstripped population growth.

Who are the returnees who make up what some real estate agents call "the return of the natives"?

They include some young people who grew up in the suburbs and who now seek employment in New York and the excitement of city life. They often team up in two's and three's to afford the high rents charged for many apartments.

For the most part, however, the returnees are middle-aged and elderly couples, widows and widowers who can no longer be bothered with large suburban houses and who again want the conveniences of apartment living. Some still retain their suburban houses for weekends and holidays, while others buy country cottages to ease the transition from suburb to city.

Alan B. Friedberg, vice president of Charles H. Greenthal & Co., Inc., which manages 14,000 apartments in ninety buildings in the city, said that a check of 4,000 rentals in seventy buildings during the past year showed that 20 per cent had been taken by persons who once had lived in the city, had gone to the suburbs, and now were coming back.

"A tidal wave it's not," said Alvin Moskowitz, vice-president of Alexander Wolf & Co., another management concern, "but it's a new kind of direction we've been seeing for some time now."

It apparently has been a direction taken chiefly by families and individuals of means. Because nonluxury apartments—those renting for less than $75 a room a month—are in short supply, returnees from the suburbs must be able to afford as much as $300 a month for one-bedroom luxury apartments in midtown Manhattan.

As Mr. Moskowitz explained it, the general philosophy of the returnees was: "Why live in Wantagh and do the 'schlepp' [trek] if you don't have the kids?"

Although one of their three sons was still living at home, Mr. and Mrs. Henry Widrich gave up their "schlepp" last July. After ten years of suburban living in Jericho, Long Island, (they had come from Brooklyn before that), the Widrichs sold their ten-room house and moved to a five-and-a-half-room apartment in Lefrak City in Rego Park, Queens.

"I loved it out there," Mrs. Widrich said, "but when we wanted to go away we had to notify the police and the fire department and the newspaper delivery. Here we just lock our apartment. There we had the Long Island Railroad: one hour and twenty minutes to New York, if the weather was good. Or I was the chauffeur doing all the driving. Here we take the bus or the subway."

She added, "We just felt we wanted city living now."

High on the list of factors that induce people to leave the city is a feeling of insecurity and fear in neighborhoods of racial transition. But the inconvenience of the "commute" and the isolation of suburban living sometimes outweigh even these reasons.

For example, Mrs. Maurice Epstein and her husband, an investment and development consultant, left their Central Park West apartment seven and a half years ago because they felt that the neighborhood was unsafe.

"When I had to go to the corner drugstore, I took a taxi to the corner and had it wait for me," Mrs. Epstein recalled. The Epsteins moved to a thirteen-room house on Cedar Lane in Ossining, on the Hudson River in Westchester. "But after five years," she said, "my husband had enough. He was tired of commuting, even though the chauffeur took him to the station and picked him up every day."

The couple moved back to the city to a five-and-a-half-room apartment in a building at 150 East 61st Street. Is she glad to be back? "No, but my husband is," she said.

Among the returnees may be found even young families with children. Stephen MacDonald, editorial writer for *The Wall Street Journal,* and his wife and baby daughter moved from their Manhattan apartment on West 15th Street in 1966 and into a $27,000 house in New Providence, a town near Summit, New Jersey.

"We just got to the stage where the apartment was too small and we were thinking about the air here and the green grass there," he said.

Last October, the MacDonalds—by then a family of four with the addition of a son—moved back to the city to Brooklyn, bad air, concrete lawns, double-session schools, and all.

"I loathed it out there," Mr. MacDonald said as he paused from sandpapering a mahogany door in his newly bought brownstone at 205 Berkeley Place in Park Slope. "I loathed every minute of it. The people would talk about their lawns and the stock market like it was their sex lives. I felt isolated there. Talk about alienation."

For the MacDonalds and other young families who dislike the congestion of Manhattan yet shun also the sometimes homogenized life of the suburbs, neighborhoods like Park Slope have become an ideal middle ground.

The neighborhood of 144 square blocks is bounded roughly by Flatbush and Prospect Avenues, Prospect Park West, and Fourth Avenue, and has a racially mixed population of 84,000. Most of its streets are lined with brownstones seventy to eighty years old.

Many of the houses are being bought and restored by middle-class families who have found the neighborhood to be to their liking. The MacDonalds paid $27,000 for their four-story house and rent one floor to a tenant. Now, four months after they acquired it, they could sell the restored house for almost $40,000.

Real estate agents say Park Slope is being discovered the way Brooklyn Heights was before it and Greenwich Village before that, and the way the West Side Urban Renewal Area in the West 90's in Manhattan is being discovered now.

These neighborhoods may provide a city alternative to suburban life for the great increase in young families that the Regional Plan Association projects for New York, beginning in 1970.

Part **2**

THE SUBURBAN
SURGE

RACE, CLASS, AND NUMBERS

The White Exodus to Suburbia Steps Up

by Herbert J. Gans

IN THIS unpredictable world, nothing can be predicted quite so easily as the continued proliferation of suburbia. Not only have American cities stopped growing for more than a generation, while the metropolitan areas of which they are a part were continuing to expand lustily, but there is incontrovertible evidence that another huge wave of suburban home building can be expected in the coming decade.

Between 1947 and about 1960, the country experienced the greatest baby boom ever, ending the slowdown in marriages and childbirths created first by the Depression and then by World War II. Today, the earliest arrivals of that baby boom are themselves

From *The New York Times Magazine,* January 7, 1968, copyright © 1968 by The New York Times Company.

old enough to marry, and many are now setting up housekeeping in urban or suburban apartments. In a few years, however, when their first child is two to three years old, and the second is about to appear, many young parents will decide to buy suburban homes. Only simple addition is necessary to see that by the mid-seventies, they will be fashioning another massive suburban building boom, provided of course that the country is affluent and not engaged in World War III.

The new suburbia may not look much different from the old; there will, however, be an increase in the class and racial polarization that has been developing between the suburbs and the cities for several generations now. The suburbs will be home for an ever larger proportion of working-class, middle-class, and upper-class whites; the cities, for an ever larger proportion of poor and non-white people. The continuation of this trend means that, by the nineteen-seventies, a greater number of cities will be 40 to 50 per cent non-white in population, with more and larger ghettos and greater municipal poverty on the one hand, and stronger suburban opposition to open housing and related policies to solve the city's problems on the other hand. The urban crisis will worsen, and although there is no shortage of rational solutions, nothing much will be done about the crisis unless white America permits a radical change of public policy and undergoes a miraculous change of attitude toward its cities and their populations.

Another wave of suburban building would develop even if there had been no post-World War II baby boom, for American cities have always grown at the edges, like trees, adding new rings of residential development every generation as the beneficiaries of affluence and young families sought more modern housing and "better" neighborhoods. At first, the new rings were added inside the city limits, but ever since the last half of the nineteenth century, they have more often sprung up in the suburbs.

Although these trends may not be so apparent to New Yorkers, who live in a world capital rather than in a typical American city, both urban and suburban growth have almost always taken the form of single-family houses, first on large lots and later, as less affluent city dwellers could afford to move out, on smaller lots. Even inside most American cities—again, other than New York and a few others—the majority of people live in single-family homes.

Moreover, studies of housing preferences indicate that the majority of Americans, including those now living in the city, want a suburban single-family house once they have children, and want to remain in that house when their children have grown up. This urge for suburban life is not limited to the middle class or just to America; the poor would leave the city as well if they could afford to go, and so would many Europeans.

The only people who clearly do not want to live in the suburbs are the single and some of the childless couples, and that handful of urban middle-class professionals and intellectuals living in New York and a few other cosmopolitan cities. For everyone else, suburbia means more housing space at less cost, a back yard and an up-to-date community—all of which make raising children significantly easier for the mother, more compatible neighbors, cleaner air, a chance to leave the dirt and congestion behind, and, in recent years, a chance also to escape the expansion of Negro and poor neighborhoods. Even some of the dedicated urbanites move to the suburbs when their children are young, although they—but only they—miss the cultural facilities of the big city and are often unhappy in suburbia.

Obviously, the popular antisuburban literature, which falsely accuses the suburbs of causing conformity, matriarchy, adultery, divorce, alcoholism, and other standard American pathologies, has not kept anyone from moving to the suburbs, and even the current predictions of land shortages, longer commuting and urban congestion in the suburbs will not discourage the next generation of home buyers. Most, if not all, metropolitan areas still have plenty of rural land available for suburban housing. Moreover, with industry and offices now moving to the suburbs, new areas previously outside commuting range become ripe for residential development to house their employes. Thus, for several years now, more than half the suburbanites of Nassau County have been commuting to jobs inside Nassau County; in the next decade, they will probably be joined by new commuters living in Suffolk County. Of course, all this leads to increasing suburban congestion, but most suburbanites do not mind it. They do not leave the city for a rural existence, as the folklore has it; they want a half-acre or more of land and all their favorite urban facilities within a short driving distance from the house.

In some metropolitan areas, or in parts of them, land may indeed be too scarce and thus too expensive to permit another round of old-style suburbanization. There, people will move into "townhouses" and semidetached houses, which have less privacy than single-family houses, but still provide private yards and a feeling of separateness from the next-door neighbors. The recent failure of Reston, Virginia, the much-praised new town near Washington, D.C., suggests, however, that the exquisitely designed communal recreational areas cannot substitute for private space. Most home buyers do not seem to want that much togetherness, and Reston's townhouses, which lacked front or back yards, sold too slowly.

It goes without saying that almost all the new suburbanites— and the developments built for them—will be white and middle-income, for, barring miracles in the housing industry and in Federal subsidies, the subdivisions of the seventies will be too expensive for any family earning less than about $7,500 (in 1967 dollars). Thus, even if suburbia were to be racially integrated, cost alone would exclude most nonwhites. Today, less than 5 per cent of New York State's suburban inhabitants are nonwhite, and many of them live in ghettos and slums in the small towns around which suburbia has developed.

Nevertheless, the minuscule proportion of nonwhite suburbanites will increase somewhat in the future, for, if the current affluence continues, it will benefit a small percentage of Negroes and Puerto Ricans. Some of them will be able to move into integrated suburban communities, but the majority will probably wind up in existing and new middle-class ghettos.

If urban employment is available, or if the ongoing industrialization of the South pushes more people off the land, poverty-stricken Negroes will continue to come to the cities, overcrowding and eventually enlarging the inner-city ghettos. Some of the better-off residents of these areas will move to "outer-city" ghettos, which can now be found in most American cities; for example, in Queens. And older suburbs like Yonkers and Mount Vernon will continue to lose some of the present residents and attract less affluent newcomers, as their housing, schools and other facilities age. As a result of this process, which affects suburbs as inevitably as city neighborhoods, some of their new inhabitants may be almost as poor as inner-city ghetto residents, so that more and more of the older suburbs will face problems of poverty and social pathology now thought to be distinctive to the city.

That further suburban growth is practically inevitable does not mean it is necessarily desirable, however. Many objections have been raised, some to suburbia itself, others to its consequences for the city. For example, ever since the rise of the postwar suburbs, critics have charged that suburban life is culturally and psychologically harmful for its residents, although many sociological studies, including my own, have shown that most suburbanites are happier and emotionally healthier than when they lived in the city. In addition, the critics have charged that suburbia desecrates valuable farm and recreation land, and that it results in "suburban" sprawl.

Suburbia undoubtedly reduces the supply of farm acreage, but America has long suffered from an oversupply of farmland, and I have never understood why allowing people to raise children where other people once raised potatoes or tomatoes desecrates the land. Usually, the criticism is directed to "ugly, mass-produced, look-alike little boxes," adding a class bias to the charges, as if people who can only afford mass-produced housing are not entitled to live where they please, or should stay in the city.

Suburban developments sometimes also rise on recreational land, although state and Federal funds are now available to save such land for public leisure-time use. Even so, I find it difficult to believe that child raising and the at-home recreation that goes on in a suburban house is a less worthy use of land than parks, which people only visit during part of the year. Furthermore, there is no reason why we cannot have both suburbia *and* parks, the latter built farther out, with high-speed expressways and mass transit to bring them closer to visitors.

Suburban sprawl scatters residential developments over large areas because single-family houses take up so much more acreage than multiple dwellings. As a result, highways, transit systems, utility lines, and sewers must be longer and therefore more expensive. These added costs are not a steep price for affluent sub-urbanites; they want low-density housing more than economy, and they do not care that sprawl looks ugly to the trained eye of the architect. There may even be somewhat less sprawl in the future, partly because of townhouse developments, partly because high land costs at the far edges of the suburbs may induce builders to fill up vacant land left in the existing suburban rings during earlier periods of residential construction. Moreover, the next wave of suburbia may finally generate sufficient political support for the building of high-speed mass transit systems, now languishing on the planners' drawing boards, to connect the parts of the sprawling area.

The harmful effects of suburbia on the city are a more important criticism. One charge, made ever since the beginning of sub-urbanization in the nineteenth century, is that the suburbs rob the city of its tax-paying, civic-minded, and culture-loving middle class. Actually, however, middle-class families are often a tax lia-bility for the city; they demand and receive more services, particu-larly more schools, than their taxes pay for. Nor is there any evi-dence that they are more civic-minded than their non-middle-class neighbors; they may be more enthusiastic joiners of civic organiza-tions, but these tend to defend middle-class interests and not neces-sarily the public interest. Moreover, many people who live in the suburbs still exert considerable political influence in the city be-cause of their work or their property holdings and see to it that urban power structures still put middle-class interests first, as slum organizations, whose demands for more antipoverty funds or public housing are regularly turned down by city hall, can testify.

The alleged effect of the suburbs on urban culture is belied by the vast cultural revival in the city which occurred at the same time the suburban exodus was in full swing. Actually, most sub-urbanites rarely used the city's cultural facilities even when they lived in the city, and the minority which did continues to do so, commuting in without difficulty. Indeed, I suspect that over half the ticket buyers for plays, art movies, concerts, and museums, particularly outside New York, are—and have long been—sub-urbanites. Besides, there is no reason why cultural institutions can-not, like banks, build branches in the suburbs, as they are beginning to do now. Culture is no less culture by being outside the city.

A much more valid criticism of suburbanization is its effect on class and racial segregation, for the fact that the suburbs have effectively zoned out the poor and the nonwhites is resulting in an ever-increasing class and racial polarization of city and suburb. In one sense, however, the familiar data about the increasing polarization are slightly misleading. In years past, when urban census statistics showed Negroes and whites living side by side, they were actually quite polarized socially. On New York's Upper West Side, for example, the big apartment buildings are de facto segregated for whites, while the rotting brownstones between them are inhabited by Negroes and Puerto Ricans. These blocks are integrated statistically or geographically, but not socially, particularly if white parents send their children to private schools.

Nor is suburbanization the sole cause of class and racial polarization; it is itself an effect of trends that have gone on inside the city as well, and not only in America. When people become more affluent and can choose where they want to live, they choose to live with people like themselves. What has happened in the last generation or two is that the opportunity of home buyers to live among compatible neighbors, an opportunity previously available only to the rich, has been extended to people in the middle- and lower-middle-income brackets. This fact does not justify either class or racial segregation, but it does suggest that the polarization resulting from affluence would have occurred even without suburbanization.

Class and racial polarization are harmful because they restrict freedom of housing choice to many people, but also because of the financial consequences for the city. For one thing, affluent suburbia exploits the financially bankrupt city; even when payroll taxes are levied, suburbanites do not pay their fair share of the city's cost in providing them with places of work, shopping areas and cultural facilities and with streets and utilities, maintenance, garbage removal and police protection for these facilities.

More important, suburbanites live in vest-pocket principalities where they can, in effect, vote to keep out the poor and the nonwhites and even the not very affluent whites.

As a result, the cities are in a traumatic financial squeeze. Their ever more numerous low-income residents pay fewer taxes but need costly municipal services, yet cities are taking in less in property taxes all the time, particularly as the firms that employ suburbanites and the shops that cater to them also move to the suburbs. Consequently, city costs rise at the same time as city income declines. To compound the injustice, state and Federal politicians from suburban areas often vote against antipoverty efforts and other Federal funding activities that would relieve the city's financial troubles, and they also vote to prevent residential integration.

These trends are not likely to change in the years to come. In fact, if the present white affluence continues, the economic gap between the urban have-nots and the suburban haves will only increase, resulting on the one hand in greater suburban opposition to integration and to solving the city's problems, and on the other hand to greater discontent and more ghetto rebellions in the city. This in turn could result in a new white exodus from the city, which, unlike the earlier exodus, will be based almost entirely on racial fear, making suburbanites out of the middle-aged and older middle-class families who are normally reluctant to change communities at this age and working-class whites who cannot really afford a suburban house. Many of them will, however, stay put and oppose all efforts toward desegregation, as indicated even now by their violent reaction to integration marches in Milwaukee and Chicago, and to scattered-site public housing schemes which would locate projects in middle-income areas in New York and elsewhere.

Ultimately, these trends could create a vicious spiral, with more ghetto protest leading to more white demands, urban and suburban, for repression, resulting in yet more intense ghetto protests, and culminating eventually in a massive exodus of urban whites. If this spiral were allowed to escalate, it might well hasten the coming of the predominantly Negro city.

Today, the predominantly Negro city is still far off in the future, and the all-Negro city is unlikely. Although Washington, D.C.'s population is already about 60 per cent Negro, and several other cities, including Newark, Gary and Richmond, hover around the 50 per cent mark, recent estimates by the Center for Research in Marketing suggest that only five of the country's twenty-five largest cities and ten of the 130 cities with over 100,000 population will be 40 per cent or more Negro by 1970. (New York's Negro population was estimated at 18 per cent in 1964, although in Manhattan, the proportion of Negroes was 27 per cent and of Negroes and Puerto Ricans, 39 per cent.)

Moreover, these statistics only count the nighttime residential population, but who lives in the city is, economically and politically, a less relevant statistic than who works there, and the daytime working population of most cities is today, and will long remain, heavily and even predominantly white.

Still, to a suburbanite who may someday have to work in a downtown surrounded by a black city, the future may seem threatening. A century ago, native-born WASP's must have felt similarly, when a majority of the urban population consisted of foreign-born Catholics and Jews, to whom they attributed the same pejorative racial characteristics now attributed to Negroes. The city and the WASP's survived, of course, as the immigrants were incorporated into the American economy, and suburban whites would also survive.

Today's nonwhite poor play a more marginal role in the urban economy, however, raising the possibility that if the city became predominantly Negro, many private firms and institutions, which hire relatively few Negroes, would leave to build a new downtown elsewhere, a phenomenon already developing on a small scale in Arlington, Virginia, just outside Washington, D.C., and in Clayton, Missouri, just outside St. Louis. If this trend became widespread, someday in the distant future only public agencies and low-wage industries, which boast integrated work forces, would remain in the present downtown area.

Many white suburbanites might welcome this development, for it would cut their remaining ties to the city altogether. Some Negroes might also prefer a predominantly black city, partly because they would be able to move into the good housing left by whites, and partly because they would take over political control of the city, thus promising the rank-and-file ghetto resident more sympathetic if not necessarily better treatment than he now gets from the white incumbents of city hall.

Nevertheless, the predominantly black city is undesirable, not only because it would create apartheid on a metropolitan scale, but because it would be a yet poorer city, less able to provide the needed public services to its low-income population, and less likely to get the funds it would need from a predominantly white Federal government.

Unfortunately, present governmental policies, local, state, and Federal, are doing little to reverse the mounting class and racial polarization of city and suburb. Admittedly, the strong economic and cultural forces that send the middle classes into the suburbs and bring poor nonwhite people from the rural areas into the city in ever larger numbers are difficult to reverse even by the wisest government action.

Still, governmental policies have not been especially wise. The major efforts to slow down class and racial polarization have been these: legislation to achieve racial integration; programs to woo the white middle class back to the city; plans to establish unified metropolitan governments, encompassing both urban and suburban governmental units. All three have failed. None of the open housing and other integration laws now on the books have been enforced sufficiently to permit more than a handful of Negroes to live in the suburbs, and the more recent attempt to prevent the coming of the predominantly black city by enticing the white middle class back has not worked, either.

The main technique used for this last purpose has been urban renewal, but there is no evidence—and, in fact, there have been no studies—to show that it has brought back a significant number of middle-class people. Most likely, it has only helped confirmed urbanites find better housing in the city. The attractions of suburbia are simply too persuasive for urban renewal or any other governmental program to succeed in bringing the middle class back to the city.

Even most older couples, whose children have left the suburban house empty, will not return; they have just paid off the mortgage and are not likely to give up a cheap and familiar house for an expensive city apartment, not to mention their gardens, or the friends they have made in the suburbs. At best, some may move to suburban apartments, but most American cities other than New York have too few downtown attractions to lure a sizable number of people back to the center.

Metropolitan government is, in theory, a good solution, for it would require the suburbs to contribute to solving the city's problems, but it has long been opposed by the suburbs for just this reason. They have felt that the improvements and economies in public services that could be obtained by organizing them on a metropolitan basis would be offset by what suburbanites saw as major disadvantages, principally the reduction of political autonomy and the loss of power to keep out the poor and the nonwhites.

The cities, which have in the past advocated metropolitan government, may become less enthusiastic as Negroes obtain greater political power. Since the metropolitan area is so predominantly white, urban Negroes would be outvoted every time in any kind of metropolitan government. Some metropolitanization may nevertheless be brought about by Federal planning requirements, for as Frances Piven and Richard Cloward point out in a recent *New Republic* article, several Federal grant programs, particularly for housing and community facilities, now require a metropolitan plan as a prerequisite for funding. Piven and Cloward suggest that these requirements could disfranchise the urban Negro, and it is of course always possible that a white urban-suburban coalition in favor of metropolitan government could be put together deliberately for precisely this purpose. Under such conditions, however, metropolitan government would only increase racial conflict and polarization.

What, then, can be done to eliminate this polarization? One partial solution to reduce the dependence of both urban and suburban governments on the property tax, which reduces city income as the population becomes poorer, and forces suburbs to exclude low-income residents because their housing does not bring in enough tax money. If urban and suburban governments could obtain more funds from other sources, including perhaps the Federal income tax, parts of the proceeds of which would be returned to them by Washington, urban property owners would bear a smaller burden in supporting the city and might be less opposed to higher spending. Suburbanites would also worry less about their tax rate, and might not feel so impelled to bar less affluent newcomers, or to object to paying their share of the cost of using city services.

Class polarization can be reduced by rent- or price-supplement programs which would enable less affluent urbanites to pay the price of suburban living and would reduce the building and financing costs of housing. But such measures would not persuade the suburbs to let in Negroes; ultimately, the only solution is still across-the-board residential integration.

The outlook for early and enforceable legislation toward this end, however, is dim. Although election results have shown time and again that Northern white majorities will not vote for segregation, they will not vote for integration either. I cannot imagine many political bodies, Federal or otherwise, passing or enforcing laws that would result in significant amounts of suburban integration; they would be punished summarily at the next election.

For example, proposals have often been made that state and Federal governments should withdraw all subsidies to suburban communities and builders practicing *de facto* segregation, thus depriving the former of at least half their school operating funds, and the latter of Federal Housing Authority (F.H.A.) insurance on which their building plans depend. However desirable such legislation is, the chance that it would be passed is almost nil. One can also argue that Washington should offer grants-in-aid to suburban governments which admit low-income residents, but these grants would often be turned down. Many suburban municipalities would rather starve their public services instead, and the voters would support them all the way.

The best hope now is for judicial action. The New Jersey Supreme Court ruled some years back that builders relying on F.H.A. insurance had to sell to Negroes, and many suburban subdivisions in that state now have some Negro residents. The United States Supreme Court has just decided that it will rule on whether racial discrimination by large suburban developers is unconstitutional. If the answer turns out to be yes, the long, slow process of implementing the Court's decisions can at least begin.

In the meantime, solutions that need not be tested at the ballot box must be advanced. One possibility is new towns, built for integrated populations with Federal support, or even by the Federal government alone, on land now vacant. Although hope springs eternal in American society that the problems of old towns can be avoided by starting from scratch, these problems seep easily across the borders of the new community. Even if rural governments can be persuaded to accept new towns in their bailiwicks and white residents could be attracted, such towns would be viable only if Federal grants and powers were used to obtain industries—and of a kind that would hire and train poorly skilled workers.

Greater emphasis should be placed on eliminating job discrimination in suburban work places, particularly in industries which are crying for workers, so that unions are less impelled to keep out nonwhite applicants. Mass transit systems should be built to enable city dwellers, black and white, to obtain suburban jobs without necessarily living in the suburbs.

Another and equally important solution is more school integration—for example, through urban-suburban educational parks that will build up integrated student enrollment by providing high-quality schooling to attract suburban whites, and through expansion of the busing programs that send ghetto children into suburban schools. Although white suburban parents have strenuously opposed busing their children into the city, several suburban communities have accepted Negro students who are bused in from the ghetto; for example, in the Boston area and in Westchester County.

And while the Supreme Court is deliberating, it would be worthwhile to persuade frightened suburbanites that, as all the studies so far have indicated, open housing would not mean a massive invasion of slum dwellers, but only the gradual arrival of a relatively small number of Negroes, most of them as middle-class as the whitest suburbanite. A massive suburban invasion by slum dwellers of any color is sheer fantasy. Economic studies have shown the sad fact that only a tiny proportion of ghetto residents can even afford to live in the suburbs. Moreover, as long as Negro workers lack substantial job security, they need to live near the center of the urban transportation system so that they can travel to jobs all over the city.

In addition, there are probably many ghetto residents who do not even want suburban integration now; they want the same freedom of housing choice as whites, but they do not want to be "dispersed" to the suburbs involuntarily. Unfortunately, no reliable studies exist to tell us where ghetto residents do want to live, but should they have freedom of choice, I suspect many would leave the slums for better housing and better neighborhoods outside the present ghetto. Not many would now choose predominantly white areas, however, at least not until living among whites is psychologically and socially less taxing, and until integration means more than just assimilation to white middle-class ways.

Because of the meager success of past integration efforts, many civil-rights leaders have given up on integration and are now demanding the rebuilding of the ghetto. They argue persuasively that residential integration has so far and will in the future benefit only a small number of affluent Negroes, and that if the poverty-stricken ghetto residents are to be helped soon, that help must be located in the ghetto. The advocates of integration are strongly opposed. They demand that all future housing must be built outside the ghetto, for anything else would just perpetuate segregation. In recent months, the debate between the two positions has become bitter, each side claiming only its solution has merit.

Actually there is partial truth on both sides. The integrationists are correct about the long-term dangers of rebuilding the ghetto; the ghetto rebuilders (or separatists) are correct about the short-term failure of integration. But if there is little likelihood that the integrationists' demands will be carried out soon, their high idealism in effect sentences ghetto residents to remaining in slum poverty.

Moreover, there is no need to choose between integration and rebuilding, for both policies can be carried out simultaneously. The struggle for integration must continue, but if the immediate prospects for success on a large scale are dim, the ghetto must be rebuilt in the meantime.

The primary aim of rebuilding, however, should not be to rehabilitate houses or clear slums, but to raise the standard of living of ghetto residents. The highest priority must be a massive anti-poverty program which will, through the creation of jobs, more effective job-training schemes, the negative income tax, children's allowances, and other measures, raise ghetto families to the middle-income level, using outside resources from government and private enterprise and inside participation in the planning and deci-sion-making. Also needed are a concerted effort at quality com-pensatory education for children who cannot attended integrated schools; federally funded efforts to improve the quality of ghetto housing, as well as public services; some municipal decentralization to give ghetto residents the ability to plan their own communities and their own lives; and political power so that the ghetto can exert more influence in behalf of its demands.

If such programs could extend the middle-income standard of living to the ghetto in the years to come, residential integration might well be achieved in subsequent generations. Much of the white opposition to integration is based on stereotypes of Negro behavior—some true, some false—that stem from poverty rather than from color, and many of the fears about Negro neighbors reflect the traditional American belief that poor people will not live up to middle-class standards. Moreover, even lack of enthusi-asm for integration among ghetto residents is a result of poverty; they feel, rightly or not, that they must solve their economic prob-lems before they can even think about integration.

If ghetto poverty were eliminated, the white fears—and the Negro ones—would begin to disappear, as did the pejorative stere-otypes which earlier Americans held about the "inferior races"— a favorite nineteenth-century term for the European immigrants —until they achieved affluence. Because attitudes based on color differences are harder to overcome than those based on cultural differences, the disappearance of anti-Negro stereotypes will be slower than that of anti-immigrant stereotypes. Still, once color is no longer an index of poverty and lower-class status, it will cease to arouse white fears, so that open-housing laws can be enforced more easily and eventually may even be unnecessary. White suburbanites will not exclude Negroes to protect their status or their property values, and many, although not necessarily all, Negroes will choose to leave the ghetto.

Morally speaking, any solution that does not promise immediate integration is repugnant, but moral dicta will neither persuade suburbanites to admit low-income Negroes into their communities nor entice urbane suburbanites to live near low-income Negroes in the city. Instead of seeking to increase their middle-income population by importing suburban whites, cities must instead make their poor residents middle-income. The practical solution, then, is to continue to press for residential integration, but also to eliminate ghetto poverty immediately, in order to achieve integration in the future, substituting government antipoverty programs for the private economy which once created the jobs and income that helped poorer groups escape the slums in past generations. Such a policy will not only reduce many of the problems of the city, which are ultimately caused by the poverty of its inhabitants, but it will assure the ultimate disappearance of the class and racial polarization of cities and suburbs.

There is only one hitch: This policy is not likely to be adopted. Although white voters and their elected officials are probably more favorable to ghetto rebuilding than to integration, they are, at the moment, not inclined or impelled to support even the former. They lack inclination to rebuild the ghetto because they do not want to pay the taxes that would raise ghetto incomes; they are not so impelled because neither the problems of the ghetto nor even its rebellions touch their lives directly and intimately. So far, most of them still experience the ghetto only on television. Until many white Americans are directly affected by what goes on in the ghetto, they will probably support nothing more than a minuscule antipoverty program and a token effort toward racial integration.

Suburban Families on the Move

by Clarence Dean

AT A cocktail party on Frogtown Road the other night, the talk got around to how long those at the party had lived in New Canaan, Connecticut. To nobody's surprise, it developed that the couple of longest residence had been there five years. It also appeared that most of the twenty persons had moved their homes four or five times since marriage. Some of their paths had crossed before.

One woman told a story.

"When we were living in Toledo," she said, "my daughter met a boy in the second grade. We were transferred to Switzerland, then to England, and finally we came to New Canaan. Here my daughter met the same boy again, this time in high school."

The New Canaan discussion reflected a trend that is increasing in the New York suburbs—a high degree of mobility in the population. It is distinct from the movement that occurs when new housing is built. This is a movement from one existing house to another, either from within or outside the immediate region.

New Canaan, a picture-book suburb in the rocky ridges north

of Stamford, dramatizes the trend for a special reason. Its colonial clapboard charm, old stone walls, the smart specialty shops along Elm Street, and the excellent school system make it a favored stopping-off point for well-paid, transient executives. Transferred to the East from Toledo or Dallas or Los Angeles, these executives, who work for organizations like I.B.M., Johns-Manville, or General Foods, seek out New Canaan's $60,000 homes or its $39,500 barns with exciting prospects for conversion.

Most of them stay for only a few years—sometimes for as little as six months—before transferring to another point. It is commonplace for the same house to be on the market three or four times in ten years. The New Canaan branch of the Fairfield County Trust Company estimates the average turnover in mortgages at seven and one-half years.

"They come and they go," said the manager of a fancy foods store pensively. "You miss them one day and then you learn they've moved to Dallas."

"Different faces all the time," said the conductor of a New Haven commuter train.

To a lesser degree, this form of mobility prevails in other attractive suburbs—Scarsdale in Westchester County, Great Neck in Nassau and Teaneck in Bergen County, New Jersey.

There is another kind of population movement that has become even more widespread in the suburbs. This is the move from one house to another, usually within the same general area, when income or family status changes. In a typical instance, the suburban resident who bought a house for $13,000 six years ago sells it for $16,000 and buys another house for $22,000. The motivation may be merely the desire for a more pretentious home, or it may be the need for more room. Four-bedroom houses, a rarity a dozen years ago, now are in the greatest demand. Conversely, there is a movement of older couples into smaller homes.

Surveying 1,000 mortgages in Nassau County, the Dime Savings Bank of Brooklyn found the average turnover to be six and one-half years. The Long Island Home Builders Institute estimates that two-thirds of the demand for houses comes from second- or third-time home buyers.

All these factors—plus, of course, the construction of new housing—combine to give the New York suburbs a greater population mobility than the city itself. The 1960 census showed that, for the suburban region, only 54.8 per cent of the population was living in the same house occupied five years earlier. For the city, the figure was 58 per cent.

Even more striking was the percentage of population living in 1960 in the house they had always occupied. For the suburbs as a whole it was merely 5.8 per cent, and for the city, 5.9 per cent. But for New Canaan and Scarsdale, it was 3.5 per cent. New Canaan's turnover in occupancy from 1955 to 1960 was 53.5 per cent.

The pattern of population change can be seen in such a long-established and so apparently a stable suburb as Greenwich, Connecticut. In the last year, according to Welcome Wagon International, 508 families moved into the town. They came from thirty-four states and eight foreign countries.

The Allied Van Lines, Inc., with headquarters in Chicago, one of the country's largest long-distance movers, reports that the East Coast has become its second-largest destination point, the West Coast being the first. In the last year, 14 per cent of all Allied moves were to the New York–New Jersey area. Allied's experience indicates that 20 per cent of the country's population moves annually.

Suburban school registrations reflect the mobility. In the Greenburgh 8 school district in Westchester, the enrollment of 2,700 this year included 253 new registrants. Of these, seventy-five were from New York City, thirty-six from other parts of the state, and sixty-seven from outside the state. In New Canaan, the figures are even more striking. Here, 431 new enrollments in a total of 3,718 pupils included 205 from another state or country. The 431 contrasted with 280 in 1958–1959.

While the newcomers are active in community life—the president of the New Canaan League of Women Voters came here from England two years ago—they tend to have their own dinner and bridge sets.

Despite their mobility, they do not appear to suffer from any sense of rootlessness. "You'd be surprised," said one, "when you're making the circuit and you're transferred to Dallas, say, you find other people there in the same position. It's a kind of a society."

"You mean," said another, a little tartly, "it's a kind of Army and Navy life."

The Exodus
of Newark Whites

by John Darnton

"EVERYBODY THAT CAN get out, gets out. Nobody in their right mind stays. It's a dying city, and you don't want to die with it." Thus, a newcomer to this tranquil suburban town summed up his feelings about Newark, his home for the last seventeen years. He is one of a vast army of whites who have abandoned that beleaguered city over the past decade, in numbers that are unknown but could run as high as 100,000. They flee their city environment, as more and more blacks come in, out of fear and prejudice. The movement is accelerated by high crime statistics, rising tax rates, and racial disorders, such as the riots of July 1967, and—perhaps—the current bitter school dispute.

Livingston is one of the towns they come to, among scores of other New Jersey towns that fan out for miles—primarily west and south—some an hour and a half away from Newark. Livingston is only ten miles west of Newark, but that ten miles includes a mountain range, three densely populated towns that serve as a buffer, and a psychic distance that cannot be computed on an odometer. The distance is in the contrast: between open spaces and congested streets, tree-lined avenues bordered by clipped lawns and sidewalks speckled with grease spots and broken glass. In Livingston, the schools function, boys can be seen carrying tennis raquets, and the streets have simple rustic names like Oak and Sycamore. The shopping centers glisten like the new station wagons that pull into their parking lots, and the Weight Watchers Center could be mistaken for the town hall.

The town, like Caldwell, Cedar Grove, and others nearby, has been growing since World War II, especially in the nineteen-fifties. In 1950, there were 9,932 residents; in 1960, 23,870. Today there are 31,000. More than 25 per cent of them are school-age children.

Virtually all the residents are white, except for maybe 1 or 2 per cent, mainly representing black domestics who live in. The barriers to blacks would appear to be economic. Although the highest minimum lot zoning is only three-quarters of an acre, the average new home value last year was $61,881. Lately, there are signs that the population boom is leveling. Last year, for example, building permits for new homes were down, from 124 to ninety-two. The decrease is attributed to the uncertain economy and high mortgage rates.

Although many newcomers to Livingston are corporation executives, transferred from as far away as California, a good proportion are from Newark. According to records from the Welcome Wagon organization, thirty out of eighty-one families who moved in from October to March 1971 came from Newark or the immediate Newark area, including the Oranges.

Many of them continue to work in Newark. Many are in their thirties, and moved here when their children reached school age, sometimes after spending several years in an apartment in a closer suburb. Many are of Italian extraction.

"We just didn't see any future in Newark," explained Mrs. Carmine Scialfo, balancing her four-month-old daughter, Lisa, on her knee. The Scialfo family moved from the Vailsburg section to their split-level home on Hampton Terrace here last September. Their reasons were multitudinous, ranging from a desire for "open spaces" and good schools to a growing anxiety about city streets that were unseemly to look at and unsafe to walk. "If Newark was like it was ten years ago, I would never have moved," said Mr.

Scialfo, a twenty-four-year-old metal worker, who still misses the city and makes frequent trips back to visit his parents.

Others have memories of Newark that are more harsh. A number refused to be interviewed and of those that consented, most asked to have their names withheld. As one put it, "The colored could come up here and get us."

"It was a nightmare and I prefer not to think about it," remarked one store owner, whose shop on Prince Street was among the first to be burned and looted four years ago. "The only time I ride through Newark is when I go to New York, and even then I try to avoid it." Occasionally, he said, a former black customer in Newark, now working for a white family, walks into his new store. "They never apologize," he muttered angrily.

The exodus of whites from Newark, whose population of 380,-000 is now roughly 60 per cent black, follows an ethnic pattern, according to some observers. Jews, many from the Weequahic section of Newark in the South Ward, have tended to settle to the south, in places like Maplewood, South Orange, and Millburn. The Irish are among the considerable numbers who have moved to Monmouth and Ocean County on the shore. The Italians have moved west. Northern communities, such as Belleville, Kearny, and Harrison across the Passaic River, are already thickly settled with a stable population and have not opened to new settlement.

Belleville has a pocket of blacks situated mainly in a factory section known as "the Valley," but their numbers have not grown significantly. The town is separated from the Negro sections of Newark by the predominantly Italian North Ward.

Among those who have followed the downtown street signs pointing the way to the suburbs are a considerable number of middle-class blacks. The vast majority have been funneled west, into Orange and East Orange, where blacks make up 40 and 50 per cent of the populations. In the public school system, the figures run closer to 90 per cent.

East Orange has also seen a recent influx of poor blacks, pushed out of Newark by a housing shortage and drawn to a locale within reach of public transportation. Many of them have been relocated by the Essex County Welfare Board, according to Mayor William Hart, who is black. As the city spreads westward, the demarcation between Newark and East Orange and between East Orange and Orange, which was scarcely more than a change in street names, appears to have vanished altogether, turning them into satellite cities with their own exodus.

Leroy Jones, assistant director of the Orange Community Development Program, who is not related to the well-known playwright and black activist, said that, in fact, some blacks were already leaving the Oranges for places like Scotch Plains. "There's a joke going around," he said. "First we chased you from the city to the suburbs. Now from the suburbs to the second suburbs. Soon the only place left will be the moon. And when you get there, they'll be a sign saying, 'Guess who's coming?' "

The Exodus
of Newark Blacks

by Fox Butterfield

"WE'RE NO LONGER a suburb—we've become part of the central city," said Mayor William S. Hart of East Orange, a once all-white suburb just west of Newark that now has a majority of blacks. "What's happening is Newark is spilling over into East Orange." Mr. Hart, the city's first black mayor, added. "Eighty-seven per cent of our public-school children are black. One-quarter of them come from families on welfare. Our tax rate is confiscatory, $9.24 per $100 of assessed evaluation—higher than Newark's."

East Orange's transition from a white, bedroom community into a largely black urban center of 75,000 people is part of the general transformation taking place all along Newark's perimeter as Newark itself has become an increasingly black city, beset by soaring property taxes and rising crime and welfare rates.

As Newark's population has gradually declined from a peak of 442,000 in 1930 to 382,000 today, the number of black residents has increased from a mere fraction to over 60 per cent of the total, with 10 per cent more Spanish-speaking.

Some nearby communities, by accident or design, have remained largely white and isolated themselves from the turmoil around

Original title: "Newark Transforms Once-White Suburbs." From *The New York Times,* September 27, 1971, copyright © 1971 by The New York Times Company.

them. In Glen Ridge, a quiet, residential town of 8,518 just up Bloomfield Avenue from Newark, the biggest controversy this summer has been over whether to build a municipal swimming pool. In Fairfield, farther north, a Newark businessman is running for the Town Council on the slogan, "Keep the city in Newark, put the town back into Fairfield."

Montclair and Irvington have also had major influxes of black residents, and Montclair, like East Orange, now has a black mayor.

Black leaders in the Newark area feel that zoning ordinances have often been used as a weapon to keep black residents out of some white communities. "In places like Short Hills there's no way many black people are going to buy homes," said a black real estate dealer in East Orange. "They're too expensive, and zoned for too big a piece of property."

But despite Newark's problems—they include the highest crime rate in the nation, the largest percentage of slum housing, and one of the largest welfare rolls, with nearly one out of three residents on welfare—Newark remains the vital center of its own metropolitan area. In this area, which the Census Bureau defines as all of Essex, Union and Morris Counties, with a total population of 1,856,556, Newark serves as a center of jobs, finance and commercial distribution.

Newark's downtown business community, which includes such major corporations as the Prudential Insurance Company, the First National State Bank, and New Jersey Bell Telephone, remains prosperous and largely committed to staying in the city. Some companies stay because of Newark's excellent location in the rapidly growing northeast New Jersey market. Others stay because of tradition and sentiment about being founded in Newark.

Newark has good communications—the New Jersey Turnpike and the Garden State Parkway run through it. Port Newark is now one of the busiest parts of the Port of New York, and work is almost completed on a new $200-million terminal complex for Newark Airport.

Newark's complex relationship to its suburbs can be seen in the local saying that "The people who work in Newark don't live there and the people who live in Newark don't work there." Alan D. Levine, research director of the Newark Chamber of Commerce, said he believed Newark was the first city in the country with more of its work force made up of commuters from the suburbs than from its own residents, 55 per cent to 45 per cent.

In addition, he points out that according to the 1960 census, the last one for which figures are available on the subject, 41 per cent of Newark's residents travel to work outside the city. And currently 15 per cent of Newark's residents are unemployed. Every morning an army of commuters, almost all white, troops into the city on the Penn Central, the Jersey Central or Erie-Lackawanna Railroads, by car or commuter bus lines. After 5 P.M., when they leave, the downtown section of the city closes up tight and only black residents walk the largely deserted streets.

One of Newark's major problems has long been its small size, only twenty-four square miles, more than 60 per cent of which is tax-exempt land occupied by Newark Airport, Port Newark, and the downtown university complex of Rutgers, Newark College of Engineering, Newark College of Medicine and Dentistry, and Essex County College.

In addition, Newark's small tax base has necessitated a high property tax—it is now $9.19 on $100 of assessed valuation, triple what it was at the end of World War II. And as more and more property owners have left the city—often because of the high property tax—the total value of land in the city has actually declined over the last 25 years, forcing the tax rate up still higher.

Many of Newark's suburbs have the same ethnic composition as the sections of the city they border on, suggesting that Newark's ethnic groups have been moving outward as a bloc. Belleville, Bloomfield, and Nutley, for example, which extend out from the Italian-dominated North Ward, are largely Italian.

To the south and west, South Orange, West Orange, and Livingston have heavy Jewish populations, reflecting the once predominantly Jewish community in the South Ward. And East Orange, bordering on the all-black Central Ward, is becoming largely black.

Some Newark residents, both white and black, resent what they consider the suburbanites' condescending attitude toward them. "All those commuters think the city is just a place to be used, then you go home at night and forget about how awful it is," said Stephen N. Adubato. "They don't think about how it is all interconnected, and if they won't help now it will spread to them, too."

In Glen Ridge, a town of quiet, tree-lined streets and large houses with well-tended lawns, the city's major impact has been in rising county taxes to help pay Newark's welfare bills. Glen Ridge's tax payments to Essex County, 19 per cent of which go for welfare costs, have doubled in the last five years. But Glen Ridge's property tax is still only $6.35, and its residents appear content.

"We don't have any of those problems up here like in Newark," a woman in the town clerk's office remarked. "This is a good town. We have a few colored families, a doctor and a lawyer."

In Fairfield, William E. Kean, who was born and raised in Newark and who still owns the Gemini Travel Service there, is running for the Town Council under the slogan, "Keep the city in Newark, put the town back into Fairfield." Mr. Kean said in an interview that he had put his home in Newark up for sale the day in June 1970 when Kenneth A. Gibson was elected mayor. Mr. Gibson is Newark's first black mayor.

"We tried to live in Newark," Mr. Kean said. "But my wife was a teacher in a ghetto school. We saw how bad things were getting, the corruption and all. You don't want children growing up in an atmosphere like that. Fairfield is a very good town. The streets are safe and the schools are good. Taxes are only $3.87 per $100," Mr. Kean said.

"I guess maybe we ran away from Newark's problems, but we couldn't afford to stay."

More Blacks in the Suburbs

by Jack Rosenthal

CONTRARY TO all expectations, migration to suburbs by American Negroes appears to be sharply increasing.

Each year since 1964, it is now becoming clear, an average of 85,000 black parents and children have made the move. Throughout the nineteen-sixties, the number of black migrants totals more than 800,000.

That is small compared with the 14 million whites who poured into the suburbs in the same period. But what is striking about the black migration is that it is apparently rising rapidly, while the growth of the black population in central cities appears to be tailing off just as fast.

If the change continues, it could alter, perhaps decisively, the nature of the nation's urban-racial concerns.

In 1968, the National Advisory Commission on Civil Disorders estimated that the black population of cities was growing at least eight times faster than that of suburbs. Now, recent studies show, it is growing only three times faster, in part, because of accelerating black outward movement.

No one is sure whether the result of the emerging pattern will be for better or for worse. The rising black migration could provide the first contradiction to a widely shared despairing fear that the nation is splitting into separate societies, one white suburban, the other black urban.

In its final report in 1968, the Advisory Commission on Civil Disorders, known as the Kerner Commission, had warned: "This is our basic conclusion: Our nation is moving toward two societies, one black, one white—separate and unequal."

Or the black migration could mean that central city slums are spilling out over city lines into aging, inner suburbs, less able to provide services to the poor. Or it could mean both.

A confident answer must await detailed 1970 Census data, still a year away. In the meantime, a new study now offers a tentatively optimistic conclusion.

"Blacks finally appear to be moving throughout the metropolitan region in something like the way that other immigrants did before them," says the study, which is to be published later this month.

"We can anticipate a gradual decline of the younger black generation in the central city, its emergence in the inner suburbs, and, as black income increases still further, its entry in today's outer, wealthier suburbs."

The new study, by David L. Birch of the Harvard Business School, was commissioned by the Committee for Economic Development, a business and academic research body.

The study, called "The Economic Future of City and Suburbs," notes the current imbalance of the black population in cities, as opposed to suburbs. While about 12 per cent of the American population is black, about 21 per cent of central cities and only about 5 per cent of suburbs are black.

The 21 per cent city figure has been rising and the 5 per cent suburban figure has remained steady.

"If this pattern were to continue," Mr. Birch writes, "the central cities would become dominated by a black population isolated from the rapid expansion of economic activity in the suburbs and requiring great financial assistance.

"But if this pattern is being broken and blacks are beginning to follow other ethnic groups before them—first into the less desirable neighborhoods and eventually into the better ones—then the trend of black concentration could well slow down and ultimately reverse iself."

Recent Census Bureau surveys on which Mr. Birch relies show that, in the early nineteen-sixties, central cities gained in black population at the rate of 400,000 a year, while suburbs gained at the rate of 52,000. Late in the decade, central-city gains dropped to 262,000 a year, while suburban gains rose to 85,000.

These figures show "a continuous and sharply increasing black migration into suburban towns," Mr. Birch says, and cities find that much of this movement is in the twenty-to-thirty age bracket. Detroit's total population under twenty and over thirty is about 45 per cent Negro but only 15 per cent of those twenty to thirty are Negro, he notes.

Sketchy available information suggests that suburban blacks are somewhat better educated and are able to find somewhat better jobs than those in the central city, the study says.

Mr. Birch also raises some more pessimistic possibilities, noting "the effect of these shifts on the inner suburbs and, eventually, on the outer suburbs, may be quite dramatic. Already, inner-suburb densities are approaching those of central cities, and increasingly this density growth is attributable to the poor and the blacks."

Inner suburbs, he says, may soon be experiencing the same social problems now associated with central cities. "They may be forced into new forms of government, whether they intended to move in this direction in 1970 or not," he says.

Another student of Negro migration to the suburbs, Reynolds Farley of the University of Michigan, offered a similar view in a paper published earlier this year.

Blacks are indeed moving outward, he wrote, citing examples around New York City.

Using old census data, compiled even before migration rates had climbed so sharply, he concluded that, in each suburban area, except the outer towns of Suffolk County, the Negro population increased at a faster rate than the white, "producing a small rise in the proportion of blacks within the New York suburban ring."

Mr. Farley doubted the development of many integrated suburban neighborhoods—at least in the near future. "In the meantime," he wrote, "we can be certain that the residential segregation patterns of central cities are reappearing within the suburbs."

Like Mr. Birch, however, he concluded that "Negroes, similar to European ethnic groups, are becoming more decentralized throughout the metropolitan area after they have been in the city for some time and improved their economic status."

The Problems
of a Black Suburb

by Earl Caldwell

ONCE THEY CALLED this city the Hub. Little signs around the town boasted of it. Politicians always said it. And just about everyone believed it.

At the time, it seemed appropriate. In the sprawling suburbs south of Los Angeles, Compton was right there in the center of everything. It was just off the Harbor Freeway, it was middle-class and white and it was surrounded by the fancy little bedroom towns of Lynwood, Downey, Inglewood, Torrance, Gardena, Hawthorne, South Gate, Paramount, and Carson.

But Compton has changed and nobody calls it the Hub any more. It is a black town now. In fact, there is no town west of the Mississippi more black than Compton. In this city the mayor is black, the city manager is black, the schools are run by blacks, and most of the people who live here are black.

Compton is a city that never figured to be black. It did not want blacks. It even tried to keep the blacks out. But it failed.

The city sits on the line twelve miles south of Los Angeles. It is just below the black communities of Willowbrook and Watts.

As recently as 1950, its black population was only 4 per cent. But by 1960 it jumped to 40 per cent and when the 1970 census was taken, 72 per cent of the 80,000 residents were black. The blacks came spilling out of south-central Los Angeles, out of Watts, and out of Willowbrook. First came the affluent blacks, following their white counterparts to suburbia. But as the blacks came, the whites began to drift away.

For a time no effort was made to stabilize the population. And later, when attempts were finally made, it was too late. Whites began selling their homes and moving off in droves. And the blacks kept coming. As the town approached a black majority, something else happened. The affluent blacks who moved here began to move on, too. Housing, once hard to find, became easily available and cheap. And that made it available to poorer blacks.

Compton lost its bedroom-community atmosphere and became an urban city locked in white suburbia. It found it had all of the problems of a city, too. Crime was on the rise, drugs swept through it, welfare rolls climbed, unemployment swelled, and the downtown district deteriorated. The quiet suburban community was gone and a new Compton was born. It was this city that blacks took firm control of in 1969, when their candidate swept their municipal elections.

Compton's City Hall is on a quiet street behind the railroad tracks. It is an old building and officials want to tear it down. But the problem is money. Compton needs many things, but more than anything else it needs money.

In City Hall, the mayor's office is a small, dark room almost hidden in a rear wing. The black mayor is forty-eight-year-old Douglas F. Dollarhide, a man who at a glance looks white.

"We're going to make it," he say confidently. "We have people, plenty of grass-roots people who are working hard. I say we're going to make it."

Compton's population is not only black, it is also young. The average age is said to be 19. "That means that most of our people are not working," the mayor says. "They are not in the labor force. They are in schools and they are costing us money."

Consequently, Compton has a higher municipal tax rate than any of the towns around it. The rate here is $1.54 per $100 of assessed valuation. In Downey, it is $1.54. It is $1.13 in Torrance, $0.75 in Lakewood, $0.67 in South Gate, and $0.70 in Gardena.

"We just can't raise our property taxes any more," the mayor concedes.

Mr. Dollarhide talks of the enthusiasm of the people, of the necessity for blacks to show what they can achieve, but even he admits that the problems facing Compton are formidable. These problems, he says, were born twenty-five years ago when other men were in charge here. "We're paying now," he says, "for what they did not do."

Industry is a prime example. Back when Compton was white it wanted no industry. It was a bedroom community, and the people who ran the government wanted it that way, so they kept industry out. Unemployment in Compton is now so high that industry is what the city needs most. The city has just opened a large industrial park, but tenants are slow in coming.

Mr. Dollarhide sees Compton as more than just another city trying to cope with its problems. He calls it a test tube. He points out that central cities are becoming black all around the country. "Now people are saying we can't do it." He continued, "They are saying that we can't govern ourselves. Here we can prove it can be done."

Compton's business center has all but ceased to exist. The mayor says that the city's rising crime rate led to the deterioration of the downtown. "We can't get any major department stores to come in here," he says. "There's money here but, with the crime problem, they just don't want to take the chance. Probably the only real solution is revenue sharing. We must have more Federal help."

When the whites fled, many middle-class blacks left, too. Compton now needs its base of middle-class blacks. "It's a shame," the mayor says, "but we have a lot of black people who come here —professionals—and they work and make big salaries, but at night they are gone to Baldwin Hills. They don't want to live here, either."

Compton wants to build with blacks, but many of the blacks it wants do not want any part of Compton. "To tell you the truth," Theodore Baskerville said, "I had my house up for sale not too long ago, but they talked me out of it." Mr. Baskerville is black and a long-time resident of Compton. He wanted to move because the taxes and the crime rate were too high. But he stayed. "You may as well stay here and fight it out," he said. "You don't win battles running." And there was another reason. "You know," he said, "there are still a lot of people who don't want Negroes in their town." At least in Compton he knows that being black does not make a difference.

Compton is an unusual city in many respects. It has no exclusive neighborhoods. Some, of course, are better than others, but it is not uncommon for doctors and lawyers and other professionals living here to have homes next door to laborers and municipal employees. And, while most of the fancy shopping centers in this area are outside Compton, the city now is getting some new ones of its own.

But the emphasis here is on new ideas. One of the most unusual is Dr. Hubert Hemsley's plan for cooperative ownership of medical facilities. His idea is to provide people with a stake in institutions. "People who have a stake in their community don't burn it down," he reasons. His plan is designed to not only help solve Compton's health problems but also to strengthen the community's economic base by providing health jobs that would stay in Compton.

Others offer additional new ideas, and slowly now the view is growing here that Compton can make it. "The only problem," Dr. Hemsley says, "is that we are not quite certain just how much time we have."

COMMERCE AND INDUSTRY

The Suburbanization of the Corporation

THE EXODUS of major corporations from the city appears to be increasing, and at least twelve concerns are currently considering moving their headquarters to the suburbs, according to Ken Patton, the city's economic development administrator.

Mr. Patton suggested yesterday that the real reason behind the corporate exodus might not be widely discussed economic factors but more personal factors, such as the desire of corporation presidents to work close to their suburban homes. Referring to studies under way within his agency, the administrator said, "We have yet to find a significant case where the company did not move in the direction of the chief executive's home."

Mr. Patton discussed the operations of his administration yesterday with reporters and editors of *The New York Times* in one of a series of interviews with city and state officials.

Mr. Patton, whose agency is charged with attracting and keeping business and industry in the city, was philosophical about his chance to reverse the recent movement of corporate headquarters away from New York.

But he contended that his agency was having "real success" in other areas, particularly the development of industrial parks and Operation Main Street, which seeks to renew fifteen of the city's largest commercial streets.

The movement of business headquarters to the suburbs in recent years—about a dozen have moved out while perhaps half as many have moved in, according to the agency—was discussed by Mr. Patton for an hour. There was little emphasis on the economic arguments that attended the suburban moves of a number of companies.

The thirty-eight-year-old Administrator said he was negotiating with twelve companies that are "reviewing" their location in New York. "There are some more we don't know about—more often than not we don't know," he said, adding that he did not think the number was as high as the forty-two companies Governor Rockefeller said three months ago were considering moving from the city.

"The economics of the companies that move generally show a trade-off—they gain something by moving and they lose something else," he said. "Taxes are not that decisive. . . . They move to places with less labor supply—northern Westchester, where there's an outmigration of people between eighteen and twenty-seven— turnover and reliability of employes is the same or worse in the suburbs."

Mr. Patton said preliminary studies by his agency and his own personal experience had convinced him that the controlling factor in corporate moves was something he called "social distance."

"The executive decision-maker lives in a homogenized community, ethnic and class community," he continued. "Increasingly, his employes in the city are from communities very different in class and ethnicity. Maybe I'm getting to the ethnic question. . . . The decision-maker can't relate to the city kid, that kid doesn't look the same as him. It's an older generation in charge trying to reestablish a setting that seems to be more comfortable, more the old way."

Mr. Patton's analysis was somewhat similar to the private views of some other members of the city administration, including Mayor John Lindsay. They have reacted bitterly to some corporate moves by complaining that company presidents leave the city after they realize that a large percentage of their office help is black or Puerto Rican.

But Mr. Patton emphasized that the complaints he heard from chief executives were highly personal—they have no desire to live in the city and are frustrated with commuting by railroad or bus from New York, New Jersey, and Connecticut suburbs.

"When these executives talk to me," Mr. Patton said, "they say 'I've had it with the cocktail parties and the opera, I don't need it any more.' They always stress the word 'I'—I've heard it over and over again. They're forcing their own semiretirement on their company."

"The bad city services—telephone and everything—may prompt a corporation to review its position," Mr. Patton continued. "But once the review begins, the decision-maker says, 'I live in Greenwich, we're going to Greenwich.' Then he calls in consultants or his controller and says, 'Going to Greenwich is cheaper, isn't it?' "

But then Mr. Patton argued that many corporations would regret their move to the suburbs because younger men they want to recruit would rather live in the city. "We have good information that some companies that have moved out are losing their creative edge," he said. "Their best young people are leaving them."

The "boundary condition" of the corporate exodus from New York, Mr. Patton suggested, might be when companies find they can no longer "recruit young people into the corporation."

The administrator said that two patterns seemed to be developing in the movement of businesses away from the city—the favored new location appears to be southern Connecticut, and companies seem to move in cycles related to mayoral elections.

"We're in an accelerating part of the cycle now, and the last big move was in late 1966," he said. "That suggests that companies may review their situation here after the problems of the city are brought to prominence during city election campaigns."

Mr. Patton's judgment about Connecticut seemed to be underscored yesterday when the Xerox Corporation, formerly headquartered in Rochester, announced that it had found a new headquarters site in Greenwich, Connecticut, on the Westchester County border.

The administrator also said that the companies now reconsidering their New York locations could jeopardize one of the city's proudest statistics—that it least 125 of the nation's 500 largest corporations have their headquarters in New York. He said that five of the twelve companies now considering relocation were in the top 500 listed by *Fortune* magazine.

While conceding that any significant loss of companies would hurt the city's efforts to provide more jobs for its residents, Mr. Patton said the city's economic status was still optimistic when compared with the nation and the region.

"From January to November of last year, we had an increase of 20,000 jobs, although I've sensed some slippage in the past month or two," he said. "Our unemployment remains 1.5 per cent below the national average and 2 per cent below the regional average."

WHEN THE General Dynamics Corporation announced two months ago that it was moving its national headquarters out of the city, New York's loss appeared to be St. Louis's gain as the company announced:

"St. Louis is well-located, offers excellent facilities at reasonable cost and provides major living advantages for our people."

But St. Louis gained almost nothing.

General Dynamics has since decided to move to Clayton, Missouri, a St. Louis suburb of 16,000 people that has been pulling business out of the Missouri city for ten years, just as Greenwich, Connecticut, has pulled business from New York and as Southfield, Michigan, has pulled business from Detroit.

The exodus of business from downtown to suburb—a subject much discussed here because of corporate moves in recent months —is not a New York phenomenon, but a national pattern, according to reports from correspondents of *The New York Times* in ten cities.

In fact, in Detroit the exodus has reached such proportions that two prime symbols of civic identity, the Detroit Lions football team and *The Detroit News,* are moving out, the Lions to a new stadium in Pontiac and *The News* to a new satellite printing plant in Sterling Heights.

With that, a banner at the last banquet of the Detroit Press Club facetiously made one request: "Will the last company to leave Detroit please turn off the lights?"

In St. Louis, which like other cities has a local group—Downtown St. Louis, Inc.—trying to hold or expand downtown business, the number of merchant licenses has decreased from 6,302 in 1969 to 5,608 this year, and manufacturing licenses from 1,270 last year to 1,210 this year.

There are breaks in the pattern, however, especially on the West Coast. The economic development agencies of Los Angeles and Portland, Oregon, for example, report no visible movement of business away from their cities.

"We are still bringing industry in," said Howard Chappell, president of the Los Angeles Economic Development Board. And John Kenward, executive secretary of the Portland Development Commission, added: "We just have a freshness and vitality in the central city that is refreshing when compared to the Midwest and East."

Kansas City, Missouri, has also managed to hold its position as the unchallenged business center of its area, by extending city boundaries into unincorporated suburbs. The area of the city has grown from sixty square miles to 317 in the last 25 years.

Thus, at the moment, Kansas City has something that the mayors of New York or Detroit will never have again—100 square miles of undeveloped land.

The need for land to expand is a primary factor that drives corporate offices, manufacturing and assembly plants, and even athletic teams, out of central cities.

"We've contacted firms and asked why they moved," said a spokesman for the Boston Economic Development Industrial Commission. "The prime reason is lack of space and the high cost of space. Only a handful—less than 10 per cent—even list crime, vandalism, congestion or taxes."

But, in other cities—particularly Detroit—city officials and businessmen do tend to talk about the spectrum of urban problems. The vice-president of a Detroit insurance company who asked not to be identified said several major moves had been based on "insidious institutional racism."

The insurance executive reported:

"A vice-president of [he named a prominent organization] told me that they wanted to move for one reason—to get rid of low-echelon workers, like file clerks and typists. These days in Detroit those workers have to be black."

Some urban spokesmen—New York's economic development administrator, Ken Patton, is one—believe the decisions of companies to move to the suburbs often reflect the feelings of one or two men at the top of the business.

They point to the General Dynamics move and the fact that the company's new chairman, Donald S. Lewis, is moving the headquarters a few minutes driving time from his home near Clayton. When he resigned as president of McDonnell-Douglas, Inc., in St. Louis last year to join General Dynamics in New York, Mr. Lewis's family stayed in the St. Louis suburbs, and now he will be rejoining them.

Clayton itself is an example of what older downtown areas, with all their problems, are competing with. The St. Louis suburb, which calls itself "the Executive City," has aggressively recruited business to its grassy land since World War II. It now has offices with jobs for more than 40,000 people, and its 16,000 residents have not had local taxes increased since 1954. The business that has left St. Louis pays the tax bill.

The situation in other cities surveyed by correspondents of *The New York Times* follows:

NEW ORLEANS

"This is a very serious problem for us, if for no other reason than because it reduces our city sales-tax collection," says Robert E. Develle, the city's finance director.

New Orleans does not compile statistics on its suburban exodus, but it has lost the Elmer Candy Company, the Diebert-Bancroft Machinery Works, automobile dealers and numerous distributors of national products. Most companies have moved to Tangipahoa Parish, which offers tax-exempt bonding for industrial construction.

ATLANTA

Despite the construction of 10 million square feet of office space in downtown Atlanta in the last ten years, the city has lost many major corporate offices to suburban office parks, including Sinclair Oil, Shell Oil, the Continental Can Company, Avon Cosmetics, the Piedmont Life Insurance Company, and Monsanto Chemical Company.

CHICAGO

"A lot of industries have moved out, but they've been replaced with commercial-type businesses," says Dever Scholes, director of research for the Chicago Association of Commerce and Industry.

The association compiles industrial and commercial development statistics, which show that the number of new industrial projects and industrial expansions have steadily decreased in the city and now total only 24 per cent of similar suburban projects.

But office-building, warehouse, and financial-institution projects have increased in Chicago in recent years, and are now growing at about the same rate as similar suburban projects.

BOSTON

The Mayor's Economic Development Industrial Commission reports business loss is a "serious, but manageable, problem." As in many other cities, Boston officials say that they are losing small and medium-sized manufacturing concerns—perhaps 100 in the last five years—but that new office jobs have helped the city "weather the storm."

MILWAUKEE

"We've lost very few companies to the suburbs," says Harvey Hohl, chief economist of the Division of Milwaukee Development.

"When we lose them, they normally go to the South or West; they pull out altogether."

Mr. Hohl estimates that his city has gained as much business as it has lost, even though the Jos. Schlitz Brewing Company and other major local companies are building new facilities in the suburbs, because they have run out of space to expand their city operations.

The Service Industries Follow the Corporations

by John Darnton

FOLLOWING THE MIGRATION of major corporations to the suburbs, a new migration has begun—that of the small, independent concern engaged in specialized business services.

To some degree, these satellite enterprises—ranging from management consulting to office interior decorating—feed off the larger corporations. But they are also thriving in the general atmosphere of suburban commercial growth.

They are sometimes as small as one man, and their reasons for relocation are sometimes as singular as a crumpled commutation ticket.

Their move to the suburbs does not gain the headlines that moves by corporate headquarters do. But as representatives of a business world hitherto concentrated in Manhattan, it is perhaps as significant.

The phenomenon is typified in the experience of Herman P. Taub, a forty-three-year-old entrepreneur who describes his field as "communications."

Mr. Taub believes that highly paid executives are precious commodities, damageable in transport. Accordingly, he went about constructing a six-story office building here to provide harried commuters with an office-away-from-the-office.

The idea, aside from saving the executive railroad time, was to offer him an environment conducive to creativity by isolating him from the hurly-burly of his Manhattan skyscraper office.

Lest the executive become too rusticated, Mr. Taub included optional installation of a direct telephone—"the hot line" he called it—and a transmitter for sending copies of documents of immediacy.

An additional selling point to his prospective tenants was the fact that they would not be liable for New York State or city income taxes for work clocked up in a suburb fifty miles away.

But in September when Mr. Taub opened his spanking new $1 million structure—the Connecticut Office Building—it did not attract the expected clientele.

Instead of top corporate executives seeking a part-time retreat from the city, those on the waiting list were mostly the smaller, independent businessmen who no longer wanted to work in the city at all.

Mr. Taub blames the economic recession for cutting down on his corporate recruits. "It was a poor year to introduce the concept because their interest was in maximizing short-term income," he observed.

But his building is nonetheless a going concern, thanks to the influx of the smaller, business-oriented concerns.

Such concerns are filling similar structures, many of them built in the plate-glass image of Park Avenue, that are rising in key suburbs, as near as the new Greenwich Plaza building in Greenwich and as far away as the Franklin National Bank building in Westbury, Long Island.

The trend is part of a larger picture, in which the national economy as a whole is moving toward a service-oriented economy, and the suburbs of New York in particular are feeling the spread of "paper-pushing" industries like insurance, finance, and real estate.

"It's a secondary effect of the major corporations moving out here," said Mark Feinberg, managing director of the Connecticut Development Commission. "We're now getting all the service businesses that look to the major corporations for their livelihood—public relations, printing services, everything."

Mr. Feinberg, in charge of an agency whose job is to lure industry into the state, said that forty-four corporate or executive offices had moved in since 1968, most of them from New York. Within the next eighteen months, he said, thirty to forty more are expected, including several from the top 500 listed by *Fortune* magazine.

There is no count of the smaller, service businesses that have come. But for those already here, a continued in-migration of major corporations could mean only greener pastures.

"Corporations are finding out that they don't have to be located in New York to do business, and I think individuals are beginning to find that out, too," said David Thompson, president of Thornhill Thompson Associates, a tenant in the Westport building.

His one-man business, which he described as a marketing, promoting, and consulting service, handles everything from racing car drivers in search of a commercial sponsor to a promotional device called "discovery cards" inside cereal boxes.

Mr. Thompson is enthusiastic over his suburban location. He finds that there is a pool of highly skilled talent he can draw upon on a short-term basis, and an extended working day, from 8:30 A.M. to 6:00 P.M.

"I live fifteen minutes from here," he said. "At night I can come into the office and just think if I want to. On weekends, I can stop in for an hour or so while my wife is shopping."

The sole disadvantage, he noted, was in losing "that convenience of being able to walk two blocks or jump in a cab to make a sales call."

As seems to be the case with the major corporations, the tenants who have moved into the Connecticut Office Building explain the relocation with professional reasons that soon lapse over into personal ones.

There is the family man who wants to spend more time at home, the nature-lover who wants to live even farther out in the country, and the executive who is looking for an "alternate life-style."

For many tenants, it was the time and hardship of commuting that pushed them from the city. Their new building is midway between the Penn Central Railroad tracks and the Connecticut Thruway, and its occupants regard these transportation arteries as the Scylla and Charybdis of their former lives.

"You have to be crazy to take that daily beating," commented one, whose office looked out upon a vista of parked cars clustered around the railroad station.

"It was the lost time that prompted me to move," said another, Henry C. Roehr, who runs a building construction firm. "You've got to figure it at three hours a day."

Equally decisive, it appears, was the pull of family life, and a collection of almost unarticulated strivings lumped into the category called "quality of life."

"Society is changing," said Mr. Thompson. "The question of how a man relates to his job is changing. People are saying 'My kid is thirteen now and I want to be around, even if it only means eating breakfast with him in the morning and tucking him in at night.' "

Another businessman agreed, and carried the thought further: "Business is primarily the way I express myself. My child has got to see me doing what is most important to me. He's got to know me," he said.

Malcolm Shaw, president of a consulting concern called Educational Systems and Designs, Inc., put it this way: "A guy is all of one piece. He's not one thing in the office, and another thing at home.

"It's not unusual here to have a six-year-old child run up and jump on his father's lap during a board meeting. The first reaction is: 'My God, this is happening in a business office?' The second reaction is : 'My God, this is great!' "

Mr. Shaw, whose firm aids in organizational changes in large corporations and institutions, finds his Westport office more "exciting" than the fifteenth floor of Rockefeller Center where he worked before.

"There's a subtle difference in attitude. There's a tightness in New York in every way—the way you dress, the way you cram into a subway—that detracts from the capacity of an organization to create a better atmosphere and life-style.

"Clients love to come out here to discuss business. The first time they wear a shirt and tie, the second time something else," he said, tugging at the sleeve of a combination suede and green knit pullover.

Some of the dozen or so tenants listed in the building's directory stand to gain in personal taxes because there is no state income tax in Connecticut and no city tax. Corporate taxes are roughly the same in the tri-state area.

Mr. Taub, the building's owner, keeps the figures handy. An executive with four dependents who earns $25,000 in taxable income, for example, will save approximately $2,100 by earning it in Westport instead of New York City, he says.

Since the New York State tax is steeply graded, the savings would be greater the higher the income bracket. Tax experts, however, point out that top metropolitan executives are adept at tax deductions and tend to travel and work outside the city frequently anyway.

What's more, city and state taxes from one year are deductible from the Federal taxes of the next. And Connecticut and New Jersey both, according to a widely held consensus, cannot long forestall a state income tax of their own.

In any case, the tax situation does not seem to loom overly large in the thinking of the newcomers here. Instead, the thoughts are how to maximize profit and how the business services can get services of their own—an extra stenographer for the day, a messenger to deliver a dummy of a promotion pamphlet.

As a partial solution to the problem, Mr. Taub, sensing a vacuum, has saved one office in his building for an enterprise of his own. It is called Business Serve, and it operates throughout Fairfield County, providing secretarial help, foreign language translation and a plethora of other minor functions.

"It's quite a good organization," he said, standing in the reception room of his building. "You know what happened yesterday? We got our first order from New York."

The Rapid Growth
of Suburban Employment

by Jack Rosenthal

THE MUSHROOMING SUBURBS of America's major metropolitan areas, which already have more population than the cities that produced them, are fast approaching an even more striking milestone in urbanization. They have equaled, and perhaps by now surpassed, the central cities as providers of jobs.

According to a *New York Times* analysis of new data from the 1970 Census, half of all employment in the fifteen largest metropolitan areas is now outside city limits. And of all the enormous number of workers who live in the suburbs, only one in four still commutes from a suburban home to a city job. The others both live and work in the suburbs. . . .

It is a time of the suburbanization of almost everything. Potato fields and tract developments have been joined by poverty (for every three poor people in the cities there are two in the suburbs) and wealth (all fifty of the nation's richest counties cover suburban areas); by crime and culture; by pro football and French cuisine.

Still, for all the development and diversity, the conventional view of the suburbs has remained mired in what John F. Kain, a Harvard economist, calls "the monocentric trap." This is that at root, suburbs remain "sub" because their residents commute to cities to earn their livelihood.

The first finding of *The Times'* new analysis of suburban work patterns—drawn from 1970 and 1960 Census reports for each of the fifteen largest metropolitan areas—demonstrates that this view is now decisively obsolete.

HOW JOBS HAVE SHIFTED TO THE SUBURBS
[In the fifteen largest metropolitan areas]

Metropolitan area		Reported metropolitan area workers	Those who work in the city	Those who work in the suburbs	Those who live and work in the suburbs	City's share of metropolitan area jobs
		(*Figures in thousands of workers*)			(*Number*)	(*Per cent*)	(*Per cent*)
New York	1970	4,943	3,172	1,771	1,593	77.7	64.1
	1960	4,929	3,511	1,418	1,267	74.9	71.2
Los Angeles—	1970	2,483	1,133	1,350	1,053	78.6	45.7
Long Beach	1960	2,432	1,270	1,162	947	68.8	52.2
Chicago—Gary	1970	2,737	1,438	1,299	1,065	73.2	52.5
—Hammond	1960	2,460	1,670	790	674	65.4	67.8
Philadelphia	1970	1,597	772	825	744	77.8	48.2
	1960	1,381	870	511	459	69.8	63.0
Detroit	1970	1,393	537	856	695	76.3	38.6
	1960	1,223	693	530	433	65.1	56.7
San Francisco	1970	1,113	557	556	500	70.4	50.0
—Oakland	1960	1,008	555	453	448	73.8	55.1
Washington,	1970	1,089	492	597	544	66.7	45.1
D.C.	1960	757	483	274	238	52.8	63.8
Boston	1970	988	374	614	564	74.2	37.8
	1960	920	409	511	467	70.8	44.5

HOW JOBS HAVE SHIFTED TO THE SUBURBS (*cont.*)
[In the fifteen largest metropolitan areas]

Metropolitan area		Reported metropolitan area workers	Those who work in the city	Those who work in the suburbs	Those who live and work in the suburbs	City's share of metropolitan area jobs	
		(*Figures in thousands of workers*)			(*Number*)	(*Per cent*)	(*Per cent*)
Pittsburgh	1970	786	286	500	465	76.2	36.3
	1960	762	274	488	465	83.0	36.0
St. Louis	1970	809	340	469	426	70.0	42.0
	1960	661	401	260	239	59.9	60.7
Baltimore	1970	723	368	355	282	67.3	50.1
	1960	591	390	201	164	61.4	65.9
Cleveland	1970	726	392	334	273	56.9	54.0
	1960	646	463	183	159	47.7	71.7
Houston	1970	714	537	177	135	76.2	75.6
	1960	427	360	67	53	54.1	84.3
Minneapolis	1970	694	409	285	227	56.7	58.9
—St. Paul	1960	534	408	126	125	51.7	76.4
Dallas	1970	587	417	170	133	50.1	71.0
	1960	401	303	98	89	63.1	75.6
Totals	1970	21,382	11,224	10,158	8,699	72.3	52.4
	1960	19,132	12,060	7,072	6,227	67.8	63.0

Source: *The New York Times* analysis of Census Tract Reports.

In 1960, the suburbs of these areas contained about 7 million jobs and their cities contained about 12 million. That is, the central cities provided nearly two-thirds of the jobs in their metropolitan areas.

But during the nineteen-sixties, the suburbs of these areas gained more than 3 million jobs—a rise of 44 per cent. Meanwhile, the central cities lost 836,000, a 7 per cent decline.

By census day, April 1, 1970, the central cities had only 52 per cent of total metropolitan area jobs—11,224,000 as against 10,158,000 in the suburbs. And if, as is likely, the rates of change of the last decade have continued, one day in the next month or two the suburbs will draw ahead.

In some individual areas, notably New York, that day may never come. New York City still provides two-thirds of the jobs in its broad metropolitan area. Cities like Houston, which can still readily annex developing suburbs, provide three-fourths of metropolitan employment.

But in nine of the fifteen largest metropolitan areas, the milestone has already been passed: the suburbs have already equaled —and even far exceeded—the cities as the principal location of jobs.

The single most dramatic example is Washington, D.C. Even here in the nation's capital, with its heavy city concentration of government employment, at least 55 per cent of all jobs are now suburban.

In 1960, there were 483,000 city jobs and 274,000 suburban jobs. In 1970, after a momentous 118 per cent jump in the suburban category, there were 492,000 city jobs and 597,000 in the suburbs.

Much of the explanation for such striking changes lies in the development of most new jobs in the suburbs. But there is another explanation more ominous for the economic future of the central cities.

Of the fifteen cities covered in *The Times'* study, only two had significantly more jobs at the end of the nineteen-sixties than at the decade's start. And both of these were in Texas, where state law facilitates city annexation of growing fringe areas.

Total employment in the fifteen areas went up 11 per cent in the decade. But nine of the central cities lost jobs. The largest numerical loss was in New York City, whose total dropped 10 per cent to 3,172,000. By far the largest proportionate loss was in Detroit, where city employment dropped 23 per cent.

And the other four cities barely held their own.

The second major finding of *The Times'* analysis is of a massive increase in the number of workers who both live and work in the suburbs.

There was a rise in the number of conventional "monocentric" commuters—from suburbs to city. They increased 13 per cent, to 3.3 million. But meanwhile, the number of people who commuted from a home somewhere in the suburbs to a job somewhere in the suburbs shot up 40 per cent, to 8.7 million.

Overall in the fifteen metropolitan areas, 72 per cent of workers who live in the suburbs also work in the suburbs. For some areas, the figure is significantly higher. In New York suburbs, for example, it is 78 per cent. In other words only 22 per cent of suburban workers commute to the city.

The pull of suburban employment is evident also from a sharp rise in reverse commuters, those who travel from homes in the city to jobs in the suburbs. Overall, the number rose from 845,000, or 4 per cent of metropolitan employment, in 1960 to 1,460,000, or 7 per cent.

The same pattern of suburban preeminence appears in each of the major types of employment covered by a Census Bureau analysis of the economic censuses of 1958 and 1967.

For example, the suburbs accounted for three-fourths of all new manufacturing and retail jobs that developed in this period. As a result, by 1967, they had 45 per cent of all metropolitan area manufacturing jobs and 41 per cent of all those in retail trade.

By now, as with other measurements, the suburbs may have pulled even and perhaps gone ahead. For all these measures are reflections of an "outward movement" in this century that ranks in importance with the westward movement of the last.

This outward movement overshadows even major shifts in the nineteen-sixties. The South, for example, the most populous region, grew by 7.8 million during the decade, to a total of 63 million. The West gained 6.8 million, a 24 per cent increase, reaching 35 million.

But the movement to the outer cities of America was greater still, and it affected every region. As of 1970, there were 76 million suburban Americans, compared with 64 million in the cities and 63 million outside metropolitan areas.

The force of those totals is evident from a comparison with the 1950 census. In the intervening twenty years, cities added 10 million people. Suburbs added 85 million.

Suburban "Downtowns": The Shopping Centers

by Seth S. King

SHUFFLING LANGUIDLY along the marbled walkway, under the taut gaze of a white capped security officer, the teen-agers were already making the afternoon scene in the Monroeville [Pennsylvania] Mall.

On the level beneath them, ice-skaters were wheeling cautiously around the shopping mall's large rink, while other people circulated among 129 boutiques, restaurants, snack shops, department stores, professional offices, a reference library, a night club, a Roman Catholic chapel, and a personal counseling service headed by a Protestant minister.

Like scores of other elaborate shopping centers in the nation's mushrooming suburbs, the forty-two-acre Monroeville Mall has become, by design and by accident, a new downtown and away-from-home center for many of the one million people who now live within a fifteen-minute drive of it.

And the mall's developers, like their counterparts in scores of other metropolitan areas, are finding they have inherited, along with the teenagers and their shopping parents, such social prob-

Original Title: "Supermarkets Hub of Suburbs." From *The New York Times,* February 7, 1971, copyright © 1971 by The New York Times Company.

lems as drug abuse, problems that now beset the cities and small towns.

"In these suburbs around here there just aren't any more street corners where the kids can hang out or their parents can gather," said the Rev. Lyndon Whybrew, a young Presbyterian minister with sideburns who directs a counseling service called Ministry in the Mall at South Hills Village, another enormous enclosed shopping center in south suburban Pittsburgh built for the company that developed the Monroeville Mall.

"These malls are now their street corners," Mr. Whybrew said. "The new shopping centers have killed the little merchant downtown, closed most movies, and are now even supplanting the older shopping centers in the suburbs."

In the Monroeville area, twelve miles east of midtown Pittsburgh, hundreds of acres of new houses and suburban apartments have covered the crumpled hillsides in the last five years, sweeping around and over the tiny communities that existed here before.

With no traditional attachment for the "downtowns" of the old villages, the residents of these communities—and their sons and daughters—have gravitated to the action, to the shopping center's easy parking and air conditioned comfort, to its concentrated shopping facilities, and, with growing frequency, to the center itself as a place to go for many of the functions once held downtown.

The International Council of Shopping Centers, the trade group for developers of these enterprises, says there are now nearly 13,000 large scale shopping centers in the country, many of them built within the last decade.

In twenty-one of the nation's largest metropolitan areas, shopping centers now get more than 50 per cent of all the retail trade. In some communities, like Paterson and Passaic (79 per cent), or Hartford (68 per cent), or St. Louis (67 per cent), or Boston (70 per cent), the proportion is even higher.

The progression in many localities has now become familiar. As hundreds of families moved to the suburbs, the large department stores followed with branches. Then the developers saw the appeal of grouping these branches physically in vast centers and adding scores of smaller establishments.

As the suburbs continued to grow outward, these centers became the only identifiable collecting point for the rootless families of the newer areas. And many shopping centers have responded, or led them in, by including facilities they would have sought downtown in their city or village.

Last week the 10-degree weather in north suburban St. Louis did not deter the crowds now accustomed to roaming the vast Northwest plaza shopping center.

Especially not the long-haired, blue-jeaned teenagers, some of whom were wheeling their girlfriends around in grocery carts as they congregated among the snack bars, record stores, and mod clothing shops.

This week the new Eastwood Mall near Youngstown, Ohio, another elaborate under-one-roof development, was providing almost everything once found downtown, including three banks, a dozen eating places, a night club, a luxury movie theater, and a Catholic chapel.

As long as the weather permits, the South Shore Plaza in the Boston suburb of Braintree has been offering art shows, youth and musical festivals, an auto show, and free jazz concerts.

At San Jose, California, Town and Country Village (145 establishments) crowds gather almost nightly in a discothèque, a posh restaurant, or two movie theaters, one of which has sponsored lectures during the last year (one by Ralph Nader), industrial conferences, charity benefits, and broadcasts by the Radio Church of God.

South Hills Village, the enclosed mall on the south side of Pittsburgh, also periodically offers its walkways free of charge to church, civic, and school groups for their charity bazaars and fairs.

"This, of course, helps bring them in by the thousands day and night," said Mr. Whybrew, the young Presbyterian minister who directs the Ministry in the Mall.

Mr. Whybrew, whose principal mission is to offer counseling service at the mall to patrons, mall employees, and more often, to the Mall's teenagers, believes the shopping centers have also inherited many of the community's social problems and the developers no longer either want them or are willing to cope with them.

Two years ago the Don-Mark Realty Company, which developed the South Hills and Monroe malls, agreed to let the community room at South Hills be used Saturday nights as a coffee house for area youngsters.

"It's been a place where we could go by ourselves, like you know, playing our instruments and rapping with other kids from around here," said Denny Hamrick, a seventeen-year-old high school junior from neighboring Bethel, who fingered a mandolin as he stood talking in Mr. Whybrew's office.

"But now they've gotten upset over a little confusion, like, and they've closed it. I don't know where half the kids around here can go now," he said.

The teenage problem at South Hills, at least in the view of Don-Mark officials, has ballooned out of control.

"When we started to develop these malls, we thought they should be like the old Roman forums, where people could not only buy but be entertained and meet their friends," Joseph Chotiner, general manager of the Don-Mark malls said.

"But when they also come to loaf and use us as a place to hang out, we've had trouble. They've been pushing dope, loitering in the walkways, and using obscene language. I had no choice but to close that coffee house, I'm sad to say," he added.

James Johnson, advertising manager for Seattle's Southcenter Shopping Center, went even further.

"There used to be a day when shopping centers would do anything to draw people," he said. "We don't take that approach anymore. We don't try to duplicate the downtown community. Now we don't do anything unrelated to our main purpose, which is merchandising."

Mr. Whybrew does not agree.

"But even those malls that try to duck it really can't avoid these problems," he said. "These are suburban kids, whose fathers have often been moved around the country by their companies. These youngsters don't know anything else but the shopping center as a gathering place. Even if you don't do anything for them here, they'll come anyway. I don't think the developers have any moral right to turn away the kids when they're pushing so hard to get their parents in here to spend their money."

The Cultural Boom in the Suburbs

by Jack Rosenthal

THE KENNEDY cultural center, Washington's new marble monument to the arts, is 27 miles away [from Manassas]. The Great White Way is an era away. But out here, where the new rows of town-less townhouses curl ever farther across the fields, stands a symbol of a new form of American cultural life, culture in the suburbs.

This symbol in the Washington area, where suburbanites now outnumber city residents three to one, is an old barn and toy factory called the Hayloft, a new dinner theater. Rustic name and setting notwithstanding, it serves up such offerings as faison galantine at 7 and "Cabaret" at 8:30 six nights a week every week of the year.

But the Hayloft is only one symbol in one area.

When the Israel Chamber Orchestra visits the San Francisco area, it appears in San Rafael, in a new $3.5 million auditorium holding 2,000.

In South Huntington, Long Island, the reading room of the new $800,000 public library quickly converts into an arena theater used by four different dramatic companies.

Original title: "Cultural Boom is Carrying Urbanity to the Suburbs." From *The New York Times,* September 7, 1972, copyright © 1972 by The New York Times Company.

Two suburbs of Dallas—Richardson and Irving—each have full symphony orchestras with annual concert series. Around Chicago, there are community symphonies in at least twelve suburbs.

In Miami, a distributor estimates that a film earns five times as much in small multiple-screen suburban theaters as it does downtown. Indeed, movie "twins" are already passé. In places like Daly City, California, Houston, and Landover, Maryland, suburbanites now attend complexes with six screens operating at once.

In every region, the outward rush of higher-rise towers and hospitals, of law offices and factories, now is paralleled by the development of fine restaurants, ballet schools, lecture series, and drama.

Beyond populating their new suburban outer cities, Americans now are civilizing them. The geographic movement of the arts to suburbia and even exurbia is undisputed. But there is sharp disagreement as to its significance.

"To many people, 'culture in the suburbs' is a contradiction in terms," says Jack Herman, a Washington art dealer, "—unless by culture you mean mindless, pretty landscapes marked Now! $19.95."

But to others, the rapid emergence of the arts outside central cities is further proof that the suburbs have become urban.

"The suburbs are beginning to share in the civilizing function, the acculturation, that has traditionally been a central role of cities throughout Western history," says Donald Canty, editor of *City,* a leading urban affairs periodical.

The clearest evidence of both views, the scorn and the optimism, is now given by the suburban agglomeration of civilities called the dinner theater.

From a variety of origins, the dinner theater has, in five years, mushroomed into a major entertainment phenomenon. Last year, there were nineteen professional dinner theaters around the country. At last count, there were forty-two, plus some fifty more that operate without Equity contracts.

The rapidity of their growth is typified by the Washington area. The first one here, the Burn Brae Dinner Theater, opened in June 1968, on an investment of about $40,000 in a country club building in the Maryland suburbs.

It has begun a major expansion and has already sent traveling companies to inaugurate dinner theater in Dallas, Philadelphia, and Charlottesville, Virginia.

Hayloft, the seventh such theater in the area, opened last December. By then, its organizers were convinced that a specially designed facility was necessary. By the time they had thoroughly remodeled the old barn and factory, installing, for example, a rotating stage, their investment had reached $650,000.

Typically, a dinner theater's patrons come for a cocktail, a lavish buffet dinner, the play, and free parking, all for a single ticket costing from $6 to $12, depending on the season and location.

Audiences range between 200 and 400 and seats are almost always within thirty or forty feet of the stage.

"They don't come for the meal. They don't come for the show. They don't come because of parking. They come for the whole package," says Frank Johns, artistic director of Hayloft.

The format varies from theater to theater. In some, patrons never leave their tables. In others, they walk from a restaurant to a separate theater. In some, actors conform to Equity rules. In others, they wait on tables. At Burn Brae, patrons were once surprised to find themselves being served by nuns—actually costumed members of the cast of "The Sound of Music."

But the major variation is in the nature and quality of the productions.

Some dinner theaters insist on producing only wholesome shows, restricting profanity, let alone obscenity. Others welcome ribaldry. Some feature musicals, with sizable orchestras. Others rarely venture beyond small bedroom comedies. It is the latter kind of production that generates the sneers of purists.

"Any amateurish production of something like *Natalie Needs a Nightie* hurts the rest of us, doing quality stuff," says Bernard T. Levin, co-owner of Burn Brae.

So far, the general audiences do not seem to care much. Suburbanites pack the dinner theaters even on summer week nights. And in their indiscriminate popularity rests both the strength and weakness not only of the dinner theaters but also of suburban culture in general.

"Something fascinating is going on here," says Mr. Johns. "We're not just the nightclub of the seventies. We're not just meeting a new geographic market. We're developing an entirely new audience. I would guess that a third, maybe half, of our audiences have never before seen a professional dramatic production."

The result, at least for the time, is an outside limit on the sophistication of dinner theater productions.

"You've got to remember where this part of our audience comes from—television comedies. You just can't take people from sitcoms [situation comedies] to Genet's *The Balcony* in one jump," says Mr. Johns.

Sally Jane Heit, a well-known Washington comedienne, challenges a contemptuous attitude about dinner theaters she has often experienced among professional theater people:

"Whatever else one can say about dinner theaters, they create real jobs for real actors. Even if they're bad, they're better than not working. And there are now a few magnificent examples of first quality.

"The audiences are still too struck with the dinner-theater medium to be very selective. But they're going to be. The theaters themselves are educating their audiences. And that is culture."

The Suburbanization
of Professional Sports

by William N. Wallace

THE TREND in stadiums, as in corporate headquarters, is to locate in the suburbs. The Giants, bound for New Jersey, helped to open the newest suburban site, the New England Patriots' Schaefer Stadium in Foxboro, Massachusetts eleven days ago. On October 11, the Giants will play in another new suburban facility when they meet the Cowboys in Texas Stadium at Irving, outside Dallas. William Clay Ford has accepted an invitation from the city of Pontiac to move his Lions into a new stadium there and out of the old baseball park in downtown Detroit. Carroll Rosenbloom, wealthy owner of the Baltimore Colts, had plans to build his own football stadium in Columbia, Maryland, 30 miles away. But public indignation in Baltimore has caused him to pause.

For the moment, plans for a much-needed stadium in Buffalo lie dormant. When it does go up it will be in a suburb.

The owners of the Minnesota Vikings have talked about a new stadium next door to the present facility they share with the baseball team in Bloomington, outside Minneapolis and St. Paul.

Schaefer Stadium, which is plain, and Texas Stadium, which is

Original title: "U.S. Trend in Stadiums Is Away from the Cities." From *The New York Times,* August 27, 1971, copyright © 1971 by The New York Times Company.

fancy, have in common private rather than governmental financing. Where tax funds or government funds are involved, city stadiums continue to arise. Two were opened last year, in Cincinnati and Pittsburgh, one was opened this year in Philadelphia, and one is planned next year in Kansas City.

In San Francisco and Chicago, existing stadiums have been renovated or improved, as was the plan for Yankee Stadium. The city of San Francisco is enlarging its Candlestick Stadium, while Chicago refurbished Soldier Field for the football Bears. Ground was broken recently for New Orleans' Superdome Stadium, an ambitious project that will shatter all records for cost. It will cost at least $130 million, with the state of Louisiana standing behind the bonds.

That price is a far cry from the $6.1 million that Schaefer Stadium cost. Texas Stadium's cost came to $27 million. These facilities are for football only. Philadelphia's Veterans Stadium for football and baseball had a price of $60 million while Pittsburgh's Three Rivers came in at $53 million. These sums include land acquisition, the structure, parking lots, and access roads.

Parking space is essential, especially for suburban stadiums, where most of the customers all come by car or bus. Texas Stadium will have space for 16,000 cars. It is near one interstate highway and an eight-lane highway. Schaefer Stadium is in between two interstate highways.

Tickets for professional football games are not inexpensive and are going up. The average price is now $7, which better suits a suburbanite's budget than that of an inner-city slum resident,

Part **3**

THE EXCLUSION
OF "UNDESIRABLES"

THE ISSUES

The Attack
on "Snob Zoning"

by David K. Shipler

ZONING LAWS that tend to exclude poor and working-class families
from affluent suburbs ringing the major cities are shaping up as a
key battleground in efforts to improve the nation's housing. The
head of Operation Breakthrough, the Nixon Administration's program to develop assembly-line construction techniques, says that
such zoning patterns must be broken to open up suburban land
for apartment buildings if a mass market is to be provided for such
prefabricated housing.

Harold B. Finger, assistant secretary of housing and urban development, said in an interview in Washington that the Federal
agency planned to create incentives for towns to relax such zoning
laws. Meantime, the controversial zoning practices are coming

under increasing attack in the courts, from civil rights groups, and from legislators.

Suburban towns, often "bedrooms" for commuters who work in the cities, usually adopt zoning to preserve a certain style of life, to keep school costs down, and to protect and perpetuate communities of spacious, single-family homes surrounded in some cases by vast lawns. The "snob zoning" ordinances, as they are called by their opponents, may require that each lot be a minimum of one, two, three, or four acres in size. Or the laws may permit small lots, but ban apartment houses. The result is to make housing in those towns too expensive for families of low and moderate incomes. Some city planners and civil rights groups see this as a form of racial discrimination.

An examination of the problem around the nation by *The New York Times* has shown that the decay and congestion of the central cities and the inaccessibility of much suburban land close to blue-collar jobs have produced enormous pressures and bitter fights over zoning in such diverse places as Union City, California, a small town with a Mexican-American population, and Philadelphia, where whites have blocked public housing in their neighborhoods.

Among the main developments are the following:

• The Department of Housing and Urban Development plans to give first priority in sewer, water, and open-space grants to towns that relax their zoning laws. If that fails, Mr. Finger said, he favors cutting off the agency's aid to communities that keep out apartment houses.

• A bipartisan bill mandating this harsher penalty has been filed in the Senate by Senators Jacob J. Javits of New York and Hugh Scott of Pennsylvania, Republicans, and Philip A. Hart of Michigan, a Democrat.

• At least four constitutional challenges to restrictive zoning are in the Federal courts. Last week, the National Association for the Advancement of Colored People announced the preparation of a fifth as the start of a nationwide drive.

• A Federal court ordered the Chicago Housing Authority to build 75 per cent of its new low-income apartments in white neighborhoods.

• The Massachusetts legislature recently enacted a law creating a state committee empowered to overrule local zoning upon appeal by a nonprofit or limited-profit developer.

• Builders, also looking for space, are joining civil rights groups in seeking ways to break down the zoning.

"State and city action can remedy the effects of unduly restrictive local zoning regulations," George Romney, secretary of housing and urban development, said in a recent speech. "All too generally, these exclusionary practices foster and perpetuate artificially isolated enclaves, distort the natural and needed balanced development of metropolitan areas, and prevent the efficient and effective use of land."

Some civil rights lawyers think their cases will reach the Supreme Court and may result in a landmark decision as important as the 1954 school desegregation ruling, *Brown v. Board of Education.* According to Mr. Finger, an objective of the Federal agency in seeking a relaxation of zoning laws is to create a housing market large enough to induce private corporations to invest in factories to turn out prefabricated parts for housing.

New York's Regional Plan Association has estimated that a family earning less than $15,000 a year could not afford to live in most suburbs around New York City, which means that nearly 90 per cent of the metropolitan area's population does not have access to most of the region's land.

Simultaneously, the plants with blue-collar jobs are moving away from the low-income people who need them but are locked in the central cities, the planners contend. A Census Bureau study found that from 1952 to 1966 the entire New York region gained 888,000 jobs, of which only 111,000 were in the city.

Many industries in the Chicago suburbs send shuttle buses to the ends of municipal transportation lines to pick up workers from the central city and take them to suburban factories. In St. Louis during those years, employment dropped by 50,000 while it rose 193,500 in the surrounding suburbs, a pattern typical of other large cities.

"The jobs are in the suburbs, but the unemployed are in the ghetto. It's ironic," said Edward L. Holmgren, head of the Leadership Council for Metropolitan Open Communities, a nonprofit agency in Chicago.

The Federal court order against the Chicago Housing Authority last summer directed the authority to stop concentrating low-income, government-subsidized housing in the slums. Although that case did not deal directly with zoning, there are several pending that do. The National Committee Against Discrimination in Housing has filed Federal suits against Union City, California; Lawton, Oklahoma; and Montclair, New Jersey. The N.A.A.C.P. Legal Defense and Educational Fund has a case in Lansing, Michigan, and the N.A.A.C.P. plans a court test of zoning in Oyster Bay, Long Island, as the first step in its nationwide drive.

Union City, once an agricultural settlement ten miles southeast of Oakland, has grown quickly in the last few years to a suburban town with a population of 13,550. Last spring a group of Mexican-Americans from the town's rundown neighborhoods won from the City Council a rezoning of a 23.4-acre parcel of land for 279 apartments under a Federal subsidy program for low-income families. But residents of Westview Estates, a new development of single-family houses across a tree-lined creek from the proposed apartment site, circulated a petition and collected 800 signatures requesting a reversal of the rezoning. Arguing that the project would become "an instant slum" and would overcrowd the schools, the Westview residents persuaded the City Council to hold a referendum on the matter. The rezoning lost, 1,049 to 845, and the project was blocked.

According to Richard F. Bellman, an attorney for the Committee Against Discrimination in Housing, the irony is that the Mexican-Americans have lived in the town much longer than the whites in Westview Estates. And tracts of land, he maintains, have been rezoned numerous times without any referendums as the town has grown. A suit has been filed contending that the rezoning procedure was a violation of the equal protection clause of the Constitution's Fourteenth Amendment. Mr. Bellman said that because the project was to be financed by the Department of Housing and Urban Development, the Federal government was asked to enter the case as a friend of the court, but it refused.

A spokesman for the department said last week that there had been "some talk" among the department's legal staff about going to court, but that only the Justice Department could do it. He said his agency had made no request for action by the Justice Department.

A similar case emerged in Lansing recently, when white home-owners managed to get a referendum scheduled for next month on a rezoning action by the City Council that would permit government-subsidized apartments. The Legal Defense Fund has filed suit in Federal court.

In Lawton, the Committee Against Discrimination joined in a suit by the Roman Catholic Archdiocese of Oklahoma City and Tulsa, which had been rebuffed in an attempt to build a moderate-income project. The town of Montclair, Mr. Bellman said, made a zoning change for a builder on the condition that with his garden apartments he erect two single-family houses costing not less than $35,000 each. The committee contends that legislating cost minimums is unconstitutional.

A week ago the N.A.A.C.P. announced that it had asked the town of Oyster Bay, Long Island, to rezone 20 per cent of its vacant land for low-density apartments, the least expensive type of housing now produced. If the town fails to act by January 1, the association plans a broad court test of Oyster Bay's zoning. Neil Newton Gold and Paul Davidoff, two planners whose organization, the Suburban Action Institute, is acting as consultant to the N.A.A.C.P., say that Oyster Bay is especially vulnerable to a law suit. They cited the fact that it is close to large industrial plants such as Grumman Aircraft Engineering Corporation and Republic Aviation Division of Fairchild-Hiller, where more blacks could work if they could live nearby. Furthermore, they cite a Bi-County Planning Board study showing that the town is getting more whites and fewer blacks. From 1960 to 1965, the study shows, the white population rose to 348,000 from 309,000, while the number of nonwhites fell to 3,000 from 4,600. In this period, New York City gained half a million nonwhites, Mr. Davidoff said.

"It's an improper use of the police power of the state," Jack E. Wood, Jr., codirector of the Committee Against Discrimination, said in reference to exclusionary zoning.

But whether the courts will think so is another question. Lawyers observe that the Supreme Court has not heard a zoning case since the nineteen-twenties. And lower court decisions have repeatedly stressed that each case must be decided on its peculiar and specific circumstances, that the courts are not supraplanning commissions.

Nevertheless, Mr. Bellman and other civil rights lawyers are putting their chips on the Supreme Court decision in 1926, *Euclid, Ohio v. Ambler Realty Company,* in which the Court upheld the town's right to zone out industry, but also concluded: "It is not meant by this, however, to exclude the possibility of cases where the general public interest would so far outweigh the interest of the municipality that the municipality would not be allowed to stand in the way."

There is some fear among planners that successful court challenges will simply destroy certain aspects of zoning. They believe that zoning is clearly a tool that must be used to give some order to development. Mr. Bellman believes this, too, and says his court action is aimed to get the judiciary to set standards by which zoning can be measured. In fact, his associate, Mr. Wood, criticized the N.A.A.C.P.'s Oyster Bay action as "precipitous."

The New York State Urban Development Corporation has the power to ignore local zoning ordinances, condemn property, and build new structures. It is the only such public corporation in the country, and Mr. Finger, of the Department of Housing and Urban Development, remarked, "We'd like to see that kind of organization in more places." But both Mr. Gold and Mr. Wood have charged that the corporation has been too timid about using its power. Edward J. Logue, who heads it, says he plans to move "quietly and carefully." The political climate apparently does not permit him to do much more. Nineteen bills were filed in the Legislature to dilute the corporation's power. And Governor Rockefeller is running for reelection next November.

Observers in the suburbs say there is no more highly emotional issue than zoning, not only because there are racial overtones to it but also, and perhaps more compelling, because apartment buildings mean that the city and all its problems have come a little closer. There is a little less green and a little less sunlight, more of a burden on the roads and the schools, and a little less place for escape.

The U.A.W. Contests Class Zoning

by Ronald Sullivan

THE UNITED AUTO WORKERS and the National Committee Against Discrimination in Housing filed a complaint here [Mahwah, New Jersey] today charging that local zoning laws are depriving union members—many of them low-income blacks—from living near their jobs at the Ford Motor Company assembly plant in Mahwah. The complaint, which was filed with the State Division on Civil Rights, represents the first legal challenge in the country by a major American labor union of local land-use restrictions that effectively exclude low-income residents, a committee official said.

The fight to abolish such zoning practices shows every sign of becoming a burning public issue in the nation's suburbs, which face new population pressures and rising local property taxes. Because New Jersey is the most densely populated state and is a microcosm of virtually every form of urban and suburban crisis, state officials and civil rights activists believe that New Jersey will be the country's major battleground on zoning practices. And because many communities regard families with low or moderate incomes as a financial drain on limited municipal resources,

Original title: "U.A.W. Maintains a Jersey Suburb Keeps Out Poor." From *The New York Times,* January 29, 1971, copyright © 1971 by The New York Times Company.

they are expected to oppose any changes that encourage additional population.

In today's complaint, which was filed as a class action in behalf of a number of Ford workers, the auto union and the committee against discrimination charged that Mahwah's one-acre minimum zoning requirement served to bar most of the nearly 5,000 Ford workers in Mahwah, an isolated Ramapo Valley community, from building homes there. As a result, it is argued, many Ford workers have to drive long distances every day to get to work. The complaint also alleged that Mahwah's opposition to new apartment construction effectively "confined" the community's small black population to a dilapidated neighborhood in the downtown section, or else "was driving it out of town."

Region 9 of the United Auto Workers in New Jersey has set up a housing corporation prepared to build Federally subsidized low-rent housing in Mahwah, provided that it can get community approval.

The complaint did not surprise Mahwah officials. They already have vowed to resist any attempt to introduce low-income housing in a community that got its big push forward in the early part of this century as a company town for the American Brake Shoe Company.

"We have nothing to hide, nothing to be ashamed of," said Mayor Morris E. Ruddick, a works manager at the Abex Corporation, which is Brake Shoe's new name. Abex, with Ford and Mahwah's other industries, combines to pay nearly half of the community's $3.7 million in annual property taxes. However, Mahwah has no sewers and its school costs are rising faster each year. Any substantial increase in its 11,000 population, Mahwah officials contend, will result in higher taxes as well as in higher crime rates and welfare costs, which the officials associate with low-income housing.

Up to now, most attacks on local zoning have taken place in the courts. But Jack E. Wood, Jr., the executive codirector of the committee against discrimination said that the courts had generally been slow and that the State Civil Rights Division had been granted broad power to assure equal housing opportunities.

At a recent news conference he said: "Mahwah symbolizes the

sickness and the vicious form of rascism that exist in the width and breadth of this country, and we believe that New Jersey is an appropriate place to begin the development of a model action for civil rights agencies in other states."

If the division finds enough substance to the complaint, it can order a public hearing on the charges. If it rules in favor of the plaintiffs, it can issue a directive requiring Mahwah to provide equal housing opportunities. In turn, Mahwah can contest any division order in the state courts. In any event, the complaint promises to arouse the kind of racial animosity that was generated during a battle to place low-income housing in Englewood, but outside its predominantly black section.

After fighting local opposition for more than ten years, advocates of mixed housing were successful in getting the approval of two new apartment developments in Englewood, which is in Bergen County, as is Mahwah. One of the developments will rise in a predominantly white section of the city. Although the resolution of the housing controversy in Englewood is believed to have eased racial tensions there somewhat, some bitterness apparently remains.

At the site of the development in the city's white section, someone demolished a construction trailer by running a bulldozer through it.

The act was described as sabotage by the Rev. Walter S. Taylor, a minister who heads the organization that sponsored the development.

"We haven't been frightened," Mr. Taylor asserted. "We didn't give up the fight in court, and we won't give up now. We'll build." A similar vow has been made by supporters of a low-income housing project in Blackjack, Missouri, a community that has incorporated itself for the sole purpose of enacting a zoning ordinance that would prohibit low-income apartments.

In other parts of New Jersey, the Suburban Action Institute, which favors low-income housing in the suburbs, is secretly acquiring options on nearly 2,000 acres of land in a number of communities that have large-acre zoning requirements, that prohibit apartment construction or that require through building codes that new homes be costly.

The strategy of Suburban Action is to confront each community where it has acquired land with a comprehensive plan for mixed-income housing. If the community refuses to grant a zoning or building code variance, Suburban Action will take the community to court.

Neil Gold, a codirector of Suburban Action, contended that the state could no longer afford a system in which "the rich people get together and keep out the poor." He declined to identify the communities involved, saying that premature disclosure would hurt his initial chances of success. Other housing experts, however, suggested some possible targets.

The wealthy community of Far Hills in Somerset County, for example, has a ten-acre zoning requirement that Gov. William T. Cahill, a Republican, called "unconstitutional." Other Somerset communities—such as Bedminster and Bernardsville—that enjoy riding to hounds over lush, rolling hills require five-acre minimums. No Somerset community now allows apartment construction. Only 2 per cent of the available houses cost less than $20,000, while 55 per cent cost more than $40,000.

A state study of eight counties shows that 60 per cent of the land available for housing has one-acre zoning restrictions. In Monmouth County, which has seen a vast expansion of home building in recent years, most of the remaining land is zoned for at least one acre. In addition, local building codes in the county require at least 1,200 feet of floor space, assuring that virtually every new home will cost more than $30,000.

State officials contend that zoning and building requirements have inflated housing costs to the point that only 15 to 20 per cent of the state's families can afford the homes now being built in New Jersey.

Suburban Action was involved in a recent zoning dispute in Bedminster, where New York City opposed a zoning variance that would have allowed the Western Electric Company to move part of its headquarters there from New York. Bedminster zoning officials ultimately rejected the variance. But they acknowledge privately that, sooner or later, Bedminster will be forced to give way to the urban sprawl that will be accelerated in its direction by the construction of Interstate Route 78 from Newark.

In Trenton, Governor Cahill said he would introduce a comprehensive estate land-use proposal in the Legislature with a warning that if "perversions" at the local level are not abolished, "the day will come when local zoning and planning will be nonexistent."

The Cahill administration has recognized that any outright attempt to eliminate local zoning power undoubtedly would be defeated in the Legislature. The reason is that legislators are keenly sensitive to strong local political support for zoning as a defensive measure to screen out residents who cannot pay their way or industries that pollute the air or disfigure a community. As a result, the Cahill proposal is not expected to challenge continued local sovereignty over zoning.

At the same time, Mr. Cahill has appointed a task force to draft a statewide building code with an eye toward superseding local codes that inhibit the introduction of new types of low-cost housing in the suburbs. New Jersey now requires 100,000 new housing units each year, but only 40,000 are actually being constructed.

The lag has already resulted in a lack of housing for an estimated total of 1 million people. New Jersey, which has 7.2 million residents, is expected to have 10 million by 1985.

Mr. Cahill outlined his plans for opening outlying suburban areas to a more equitable racial and economic housing mix.

"We're going to try to get new housing built without arousing emotions," he said. "If that doesn't work, I'm going to have to jab a little harder," he added as he feigned a right cross. "Ultimately," he concluded, "I'll have to resort to harsher measures if nothing else works."

According to Mr. Cahill and other state officials interviewed, the primary reason for community efforts to zone out new residents is that increasing local education, welfare and municipal costs simply cannot be met by the property taxes on low-cost housing.

New Jersey has the fourth highest per capita local property tax rate in the country—$236 in 1969. Local property taxes produced $1.7 million in that year, $1.1 million of which went for education. Nevertheless, state figures clearly show that local taxes are failing to keep up with rising education costs. As a result, communities do not want more families that produce more pupils.

However, a number of opponents of restrictive zoning contend that the battle against them should be fought primarily against the revenue system that has made communities rely on property taxes to support their schools. With the imposition of a state income tax, they contend, the state could pick up the major cost of local education and thus free local taxes for municipal services. By eliminating the fear that new families will create higher local education costs, communities would no longer feel compelled to zone them out.

In addition, they contend that any tax reform also should eliminate the competitive advantages of zoning out people entirely, as was done in the Bergen County community of Teterboro, which was conceived as an industrial tax haven that would offer low taxes and virtually no residents to support. Today, Teterboro, with $75 million in industrial wealth, still has only twenty-two residents, no schools or welfare costs and the second lowest tax rate in the county.

Ernest Erber, the research director of the National Committee Against Discrimination in Housing, contends that tax reform will take too long and that the only way to compel communities to reform their tax base is to confront them with an influx of residents. However, hardly any opponent of restrictive zoning wants to abolish zoning. Assemblyman John J. Fay, a Democrat from Middlesex County and a resident of Woodbridge, can find some sympathy for Bedminster residents.

"I don't want to be dramatic," he said, "but just look what suburban sprawl has done to my town. Woodbridge is a mess because it clawed its way to get industrial ratables to pay for its schools."

Another Assemblyman, John H. Ewing, a Republican who lives on ten acres in Bedminster, agrees. But for now, Mr. Ewing and most of Bedminster's other prosperous residents are willing to pay the price to remain exclusive and isolated.

"We want to still make sure around here that you can't buy a Cadillac at Chevrolet prices," he said.

Subsidized Housing

by John Herbers

INVESTORS AND BUILDERS in the growing subsidized housing field are increasingly sponsoring projects in the suburbs and avoiding the troubled inner cities, according to a broad range of authorities on the subject.

This development, along with the government's newly tightened policy against building in areas of the poor and minority groups, points up an accelerating trend away from building in central-city neighborhoods, many of which are experiencing extensive housing failures and abandonment.

There are two distinct views of the trend, one hopeful and the other alarmed.

Those involved say that the extensive construction of subsidized suburban housing may at long last provide an escape to stable neighborhoods and job opportunities for families of marginal means who have been confined to areas of social and physical decay.

But mayors and other urban officials with jurisdiction over the central cities are expressing alarm at what is happening. They say they are left holding vast areas of cleared land for planned housing that may not materialize. The National Association of Housing and Redevelopment Officials has charged that guidelines promulgated by the Department of Housing and Urban Development

Original title: "Subsidized Housing Rise in Suburbs Alarms Cities." From *The New York Times,* January 24, 1972, copyright © 1972 by The New York Times Company.

show "a definite bias toward assisted housing in suburban and rural areas."

A recent statement by the association said that the final version of the guidelines, published January 6 in the *Federal Register,* go even further than earlier versions against building new housing in urban renewal and model cities areas.

The guidelines are in the form of a grading system that local H.U.D. offices apply to applications for authority to build or rehabilitate subsidized units. A project could fail to meet the test if it tended to increase substantially the number of minority poor in an area of great minority concentration.

High ratings are provided for projects that would meet an acute housing need, would be in areas offering good job opportunities and a favorable environment.

However, the decision of many investors to build outside the central cities whenever possible may be as important as government policy in the matter.

These findings are based on interviews in recent weeks with Federal and local officials, private experts and investors in the housing field. Some officials interpret the trend to mean an even faster migration from the central cities during the next few years than was experienced in the nineteen-sixties.

At the same time, these developments have raised new questions about the controversial housing programs that have mushroomed in the last three years. Not only are investors awarded enormous tax writeoffs to provide low- and moderate-income housing, the critics say, but also their decisions are having an enormous impact on the structure of urban areas.

Last year, more than 500,000 units of subsidized housing— about 25 per cent of the total production—were built, and the figure is expected to be higher this year. The government subsidizes interest on mortgages, provides rent supplements and other benefits, and maintains one of the most lucrative tax shelters in the Federal law for high-income groups in order to attract investments.

The housing programs were enacted during the sixties with the understanding that they would provide housing opportunities throughout a metropolitan area and be a big factor in renewing the decaying central cities. This was to be particularly so in model-city and urban renewal areas, where the authorities were making an effort to raise both the physical and social environment.

One of the largest components, the home ownership program known as Section 235, which provides interest subsidies and guaranteed mortgages, has gone largely to the suburban ring in single-family homes because of land availability outside the cities and has done little to change traditional racial patterns. Blue-collar whites have been the chief beneficiaries.

However, a substantial percentage of subsidized apartments, both new and rehabilitated, has gone into the central city as non-profit groups and local public bodies have sought to improve housing conditions in the urban slums.

A large proportion of these are now in trouble, in default of their mortgage payments because of a combination of factors: The subsidized system frequently produced a poorly constructed, poorly managed property in areas where little had been done to halt spreading crime, vandalism, poverty, and abandonment.

As a result, investors and developers are staying away from such areas and the new Federal guidelines give them an advantage in doing so. In almost every city, there is a backlog of applications for subsidized housing, and the grading system set out in the guidelines favors suburban construction.

What is involved can be seen through American Housing Partners, a real estate operation set up last August under Kaufman & Broad, Inc. The operation, based in Washington, invests money provided by high-income persons seeking tax shelters in subsidized housing.

William B. Dockser, the president, is a thirty-four-year-old graduate of Harvard College and Yale Law School who has held several positions in the Department of Housing and Urban Development in the Nixon administration, most recently assistant commissioner for subsidized housing. In other words, he ran the subsidized housing programs.

Now Mr. Dockser is making his expertise available to investors who want the tax shelter—generally people with incomes of $50,000 or more—but who also want some assurance that their investment is sound.

The attractiveness of the tax shelter is indicated by a statement by Henry B. Schecter, senior specialist in housing for the Library of Congress.

For a person in the 50 per cent income tax bracket, he said, it has been estimated that the return on equity investment in Section 236 housing would range from 30 per cent in the first year down to 26 per cent in the fourth year, 15 per cent in the eighth year, and so on, because of rapid depreciation and other deductions permitted in the law.

Mr. Dockser said that in the first year or so the tax shelter was so appealing that many investors put their money in projects where the risks were great. But now, after the high incidence of failures, they are more cautious.

His own company has projects under way across the country, mostly in the suburbs and none in the central cities, except under unusual conditions such as a stable neighborhood or where an entire section is being upgraded.

Essentially, the money is going where the growth is, he said.

There is still great opposition to subsidized projects in the suburbs, Mr. Dockser said, but this is being overcome by better construction and lower rents.

For example, a typical project is in a stable neighborhood of Las Vegas, a city where a high percentage of working people is eligible for housing subsidies because many work for tips and do not report their full income.

"The whites don't want to live in a development with blacks," Mr. Dockser said, "but they will live with a few if they can rent an apartment for $110 that would cost over $200 otherwise."

Subsidized housing increasingly is going for families earning between $6,000 and $10,000 a year.

"Look what is happening in Baltimore," said M. Jay Brodie, Deputy Commissioner of the Baltimore Department of Community Development.

"A builder looking around for land does not buy here in the central city. He goes out in the suburbs where his investment is more secure and puts up housing that will be mostly for whites."

Most subsidized housing in the suburbs is going for service workers and others on marginal salaries, and many authorities question whether it will ever be open to the central-city poor.

Some subsidized housing is being built within the boundaries of the major cities, but usually it is in outlying neighborhoods or in stable areas in the core of the city. Cities across the country vary widely in the degree and location of decay.

The National Housing Partnership, a private corporation established by Congress to attract new money into subsidized housing, has a social mission and thus is promoting some inner-city projects. But an examination of its projects shows that only a small percentage is in troubled inner-city neighborhoods.

Typical of central-city projects now being approved by the partnership is one called Battery Park, to be built on filled land on the Lower East Side of Manhattan to serve the financial district, where thousands of workers are demanding moderate-priced housing.

The government, in approving applications, is now stressing quality over quantity—another factor that will favor the suburbs because that is where the best builders are active.

The new government guidelines on site selection were drawn up after a series of court rulings against the continued concentrations of the poor and minority groups in the central city. The guidelines give only slight consideration to projects in inner-city neighborhoods, where concerted efforts at renewal are supposedly under way but where in many cases decay is still rampant.

"What worries us," said a spokesman for the United States Conference of Mayors, "is that in many cities urban renewal is at last beginning to work. Land is cleared for housing and the residents have been promised that it is coming. What are we going to tell them when it doesn't?"

Suburban Resistance to Subsidized Housing

by John Herbers

BECAUSE OF PRESSURE by the Federal government in 1969, the white Boston suburb of Stoughton has a new subsidized housing development for low-to-moderate-income families. The Interfaith Housing Corporation, a nonprofit sponsor, was able to build garden apartments, which are working out quite well for 100 families, because the government quietly withheld water and sewer grants from the town until it cleared the way for the development.

But in March 1971, in the wake of President Nixon's repeated statements against forced integration of the suburbs, the residents of nearby Canton and Randolph decisively voted down zoning changes that would have brought subsidized apartments there. Rejection of the proposals for garden apartments came in emotionally charged town meetings even though Interfaith leaders noted that the Stoughton development did not precipitate a rush of blacks and poor from the slums of Boston, as many Stoughton residents had feared.

The controversy surrounding the efforts of Interfaith in the Boston area point up what is involved in tense suburban housing

Original title: "Suburbs Resist New Demands for Subsidized Housing." From *The New York Times,* April 10, 1971, copyright © 1971 by The New York Times Company.

struggles across the country. Towns such as Stoughton, Canton, and Randolph, which once were self-contained and economically integrated, are now bedroom communities in the path of urban growth. They are becoming increasingly exclusive as housing where the poor have lived gives way to commercial development and lower-salaried people are priced out of the conventional housing market. And home owners are becoming more resistant to the efforts of nonprofit and private developers, as well as public housing authorities, to construct subsidized apartments that are now in great demand.

The resistance clearly is based largely on a fear of an influx of blacks and welfare families and lowered property values. Stoughton, Canton and Randolph contain a mixture of white-collar and blue-collar families. The three communities are a few miles south of Boston, along an extension of Blue Hill Avenue, the main street of the Boston slums. There is also a suspicion of different life styles associated with the central part of Boston and the large youth culture that thrives there. The staff of Interfaith includes long-haired conscientious objectors who were said to have aroused the resistance of some residents. The sea of angry faces at the Canton town meeting, at which the zoning change was voted down, was white and middle-aged.

What concerns some residents of the communities, however, is that the effect of the votes is to drive out many whites who work in the area. Interfaith has documented that there is not a concerted push by central-city blacks of Boston to move into suburbs, and there is a widespread belief among housing experts that the same is probably true of other large cities.

Canton residents who sought the Interfaith development did so because young people who were growing up in the community and working at relatively low-paying jobs could not find homes in Canton. And the small black population there has declined to a tiny percentage—sixty-six blacks in a population of 17,000—as substandard housing has been torn down. When Interfaith applied for the Canton zoning change, it offered assurances that there would be less density than with single-family homes, that the apartments would provide more tax revenue, that there would be only a sprinkling of poor and blacks, and that property values would not be endangered.

"It's a problem of credibility," said Joseph G. Gilligan, Jr., a highly respected Canton lawyer and former town-meeting moderator who worked in behalf of Interfaith. "We would cite all these assurances to them and they would say, quite simply, 'We don't believe you.' "

Federal policies play an important role. The Department of Housing and Urban Development was able, through the leverage of Federal funds, to affect the Stoughton development. In the past, the Department of Housing and Urban Development quietly withheld funds from a few communities across the country for excluding federally subsidized housing, but just as the department was preparing a stronger stance, the issue was taken up by the White House. President Nixon made it clear that his administration was opposed to using Federal funds as a leverage for bring subsidized housing to the suburbs.

A few days after Randolph rejected the Interfaith project, Representative James A. Burke, Democrat of Massachusetts, announced in Washington that the Federal housing agency had approved a $780,000 water and sewer grant for Randolph. The application had been pending since July 1970.

Aside from the relaxation of Federal pressures, some residents said that Mr. Nixon's recent statements against "forced integration" of the suburbs seem to harden the opposition to the Interfaith developments in both Randolph and Canton.

It is a long fifteen miles from the town centers here to the Boston Common and to Boylston Street, where Interfaith, formed in 1965 by a group of Protestant, Catholic, and Jewish leaders, has its offices. Interfaith, determined to build in Canton and Randolph if it can, may fall back on a unique Massachusetts law called "anti-snob zoning." The law, enacted in 1969, was intended to stimulate construction of low- and moderate-income housing in the suburbs by providing relief from local zoning and building codes found to be unreasonble.

Public and nonprofit corporations denied building permits may appeal to a statewide Housing Appeals Committee. The law has not been fully tested, however, and the procedure could be long and costly. Interfaith, after several years of struggles, is running short of operating money.

Interfaith is one of a number of nonprofit sponsors that have sprung up across the country as the government has increased its housing subsidies. In addition to the Stoughton development, the corporation is building apartments in Framingham and is rehabilitating and managing several developments in the central city. The Rev. Roland S. Larsen, director of Interfaith, who has ten years of experience in housing, said it took four years to overcome the objections in Stoughton to building Presidential Courts, a 104-unit development on a ten-acre tract across the street from a high school. When the project was opened with advance notice that it would be racially and economically integrated, there was no rush from Boston's blacks to get in.

Of 217 applications, only thirteen came from Boston. The vast majority, who came from Stoughton and surrounding towns, were white and were employed. Those selected followed a similar pattern. In the first ninety-six units occupied, there were thirteen black families and nine mothers receiving aid to dependent children. There is a mixture of young and old—waitresses, barbers, blue-collar workers, technicians, clerks, and students. There are 161 children under nineteen.

Presidential Courts is a cooperative built with Federal subsidies so that persons in the lower income brackets can move in with a $200 down payment and pay between $114 a month (for one bedroom) to $156 a month (for four bedrooms). The project is attractive and has a sense of community and order. Several occupants said in interviews that they had come from crowded, substandard quarters. For example, Richard Stone, a taxi driver, moved with his family from a flat over a meat market. Until Presidential Courts opened, he could not find a better place that he could afford.

Less than five miles from Presidential Courts is the fifty-seven-acre site where Interfaith wanted to build its next development. Canton is a community of single-family homes. But Mrs. Edward Clasby, president of the local League of Women Voters, said that because of rising costs Canton is in danger of becoming an unbalanced town, a town in which only the well-to-do can live. She added, "Many of us are fortunate we came to Canton when we did, because we might not be able to do so today."

Philip Zlochiver, an organizer of Human Concerns Committee, which asked Interfaith to come in, said: "Our first concern was for the young people of our community. They would grow up and leave home and get a job. But then, when they would look for a place to live, there was nothing they could afford."

Rev. Larsen hoped that the presence of Presidential Courts nearby would help in getting the zoning changed from single-family to general residential. To further ease fears, the project was designed so that it would be less of a burden on the schools and other public facilities than would single-family homes, which would eventually be built if the zoning remains the same.

The Suburbs Have to Open Their Gates

by Linda and Paul Davidoff and Neil N. Gold

A FEW years ago, socially conscious residents of the New York suburbs joined in a project that occupied several spring weekends: they chose blocks in the East Harlem and Bedford-Stuyvesant ghettos and traveled to them in teams, equipped with paint, brushes, buckets, and mops, for cooperative cleanup, fixup sessions with the residents. This was a way for middle-class people to experience and, at the same time, try to help solve the neighborhood problems of the ghettos.

A few weekends and some paint had little effect on the crumbling structures and festering economic and social problems of the ghetto neighborhoods. But these efforts, worthy enough in themselves, skirted the reality: that it is the exclusionary practices of the suburbs themselves that help create the poverty and ugliness of the slums, and that well-motivated suburbanites could do more for poor and working-class people trapped in the inner cities by opening up their land, job markets, and tax resources to them.

The 1970 Census revealed what had begun to dawn on urbanists in the nineteen-sixties: that the suburbs contain the largest share

From *The New York Times Magazine,* November 7, 1971, copyright © 1971 by The New York Times Company.

of America's population. In 1970, 36 per cent of the people lived in suburban parts of metropolitan regions, 30 per cent in the central cities, and 34 per cent in rural areas. Sometime in the current decade, more people will be employed in the suburbs than in either the cities or rural areas. And according to all predictions, the suburbs will continue to have the largest number of Americans for a long time.

Although the suburbs have provided housing and jobs for millions of new families since 1950, many suburban communities have maintained controls over the kinds of families who can live in them. Suburban values have been formed by reaction against crowded, harassed city life and fear of threatening, alien city people. As the population, the taxable income, and the jobs have left the cities for the suburbs, the "urban crisis" of substandard housing, declining levels of education and public services, and dried-up employment opportunities has been created. The crisis is not urban at all, but national, and in part a product of the walls that have been built by the suburbs to discourage outward movement by the poor and blacks in the cities.

Opening the suburbs will not only reduce race and class tensions in our society but bring economic gains to all our people—through better use of the resources these communities have to offer: *land* for housing (and with it the opportunity for a decent public education), *jobs* and *tax revenues*. To bring this about, we need *action* to convince the communities—as well as Federal and state courts and legislators—that change must come, plus imaginative *planning* for an era of housing construction that will meet the needs of an expanding suburban population.

The new ecological consciousness in America and the cityward movement of our population have led to a widespread belief that we are exhausting our most precious resource: the land. Nothing could be further from the truth. America is land rich. "Megalopolis," the concentration of population along the Eastern seaboard from Boston south to Washington, consists largely of unbroken expanses of open space. Settlements along the Boston-Washington corridor are mostly thin strips along major roads and railroads; off the beaten path, woods and farms predominate. Outside the great metropolitan complexes, the land is open and unused, and places that once were farm land or villages are losing their populations and returning to the wilds. Out of 3,000 counties in the United States, 1,000 have had a net loss in population during the last thirty years; the move from country to city and the mechanization of agricultural production are leaving larger and larger portions of the continent's land to open space.

Within metropolitan areas, population growth has exhausted the supply of developable open land only within the older inner cities. Vacant land is plentiful within twenty to thirty miles of the centers of every major city in the nation. Without restrictive laws, it would be possible to develop commercial and industrial properties at relatively low land costs in the outer suburbs of metropolitan regions. Moreover, only restrictive zoning, building codes, and other antidevelopment legislation prevent the construction of a large number of housing units in these same areas.

The zoning laws cover a large proportion of vacant developable land in the suburbs. In the New York region, 90 per cent of all such land is zoned for single-family residential use; in eight counties of New Jersey, 82 per cent of it is zoned for lots of a half-acre or more; in the portion of Connecticut closest to New York City, three-fourths of the open residential land is zoned for an acre or more. While many older suburban towns either have no significant tracts of vacant land or already have a large population of working-class and minority families, the communities that control the bulk of the vacant land have enacted exclusionary laws.

If housing could be built in an open-market situation in the suburbs, the structure of the housing market in metropolitan America would change sharply. It would be possible to build many more houses on quarter- and half-acre lots, the accepted pattern of construction in the nation since World War II. And it would be possible to build row houses and garden apartments, the least expensive form of housing for families of moderate means.

The land supply in metropolitan areas is being kept off the market not by private acts, but by public enactment. In creating private preserves for the wealthy, law has become the instrument of those who want to keep out moderate- and low-income families. This leads to a paradox that has been called "Ivy League Socialism": excessive government intenvention on behalf of not the poor but the rich. The protected property owners are precisely those most able to protect themselves from undesired neighbors by their own wealth. They can buy large tracts of land, build high fences around them and put their houses in the middle of their estates at the end of long driveways. They do not need the help of the law.

The exclusionary laws are not completely explicit: there are no zoning maps divided into racially or economically restricted areas, so labeled. But there are thousands of zoning maps which say, in effect: "Upper-Income Here"; "Middle-to-Upper Income Here"; "No Lower-Income Permitted Except as Household Employees"; "No Blacks Permitted." The practical effect of the maps and codes is to prohibit all but the most costly forms of housing development.

Why do we call the result *de jure* segregation? Because the racial consequences have been understood for a decade or more by anyone familiar with patterns of population movement. *It is a certainty that the planners and public officials who draft and enact zoning ordinances restricting land development to single-family, detached structures on plots of an acre or more do so in full awareness that, as a consequence, almost all blacks will be excluded from such zones.*

In many areas, acreage zoning is the preferred exclusionary device. The bulk of the land in a municipality is held off the market except for purchasers who are able to afford a house on a tract of one, two, three, or more acres of land. Since a single-family home on an acre or more of land cannot be constructed in most suburban areas for less than $35,000, including the lot, families with incomes under $17,000 cannot afford to buy a house built on this land (under the generally accepted rule of thumb that a family can afford to buy a house that costs twice the annual household income). Thus the housing market in the community is effectively closed to the 80 per cent of the population which earns under $17,000—and to 90 per cent of the blacks.

In other areas—and in some communities that also have acreage-zoning regulations—housing-construction codes have been devised reforms [*sic—ed.*] of residential development: wide lot frontages, costly materials and equipment, square-footage requirements for house interiors—all beyond what is needed for health and safety.

In almost all suburban municipalities, tax laws undergird the structure of land-use controls and provide a rationale for exclusion. The real-property tax pays the bulk of local costs for public education, the biggest item in the budget and a major factor in maintaining the status of the community. If a dozen houses are built at costs within the reach of low-income families, the entire community suffers because the taxes realized from the new houses will tend to be below the additional expense to the school system of educating the children from the new families.

In New Castle, a Northern Westchester community, a 1968 League of Women Voters study showed that school costs were so high that a new house would have to cost $58,500 in order to yield enough taxes to educate the average number of children per household—$1,688 in taxes for 1.6 children.

As expenses for education have become the last straw on the suburban taxpayer's back, the impetus toward ever-higher barriers to moderate-cost housing construction has been almost irresistible. Even if motivated by the best and most democratic public instincts, a community must finance its schools; and the easiest way to make the burden bearable is to keep the community costly and exclusive.

What would happen if the exclusionary land-use controls were eliminated? In the private market, the effect would be to dramatically increase the supply of building lots, both for single-family homes and for garden apartments and row houses. The increase in supply would lower the price per lot; the result would be a sharp reduction in the cost of a new home and an increase in the number of families that could afford one. The construction industry would boom, and lower-cost housing could be produced as the market demands.

Putting aside for the moment the moral questions raised by suburban exclusion, regulations adopted over the past decade or more by suburban communities is that they have stifled the natural development of the home-building industry. Today most of the vacant residential land around New York and in other metropolitan areas is zoned for homes on lots five to ten times larger than Levittown's. Zoning has operated to slow down and spread out development. In a nation that has highly valued growth, it is strange to find growth disdained as a matter of policy. Particularly at a time of recession, the multiplier effect of a sustained form of new community development—which would require large capital investment—cannot be ignored. A reinvigorated residential building industry would not only create jobs for unemployed construction workers but lead to enlarged investment in all industries required to serve new suburban developments—and to other urgently needed jobs.

Even if a construction boom produced mostly middle-income or luxury housing, it would help to ease the pressures throughout the housing market that keep moderate-income housing consumers bottled up in city neighborhoods. This is because the "filtering" process—lower-income consumers moving into housing left behind by more affluent consumers moving into bigger and better homes—could begin to operate again. The result would be some improvement in the housing situation for low-income families. The favorite argument of real estate operators against government housing subsidies to the poor used to be that "filtering" would satisfy this group's needs. In fact, filtering alone will never provide enough used housing to meet the needs of the lowest-income families. But the current virtual halt in the construction of new, moderately priced housing in suburbia has made the absence of a normal used-house, or "filtered," market acutely noticeable to moderate-income families who would normally be able to afford such homes.

When, in the late nineteen-forties and fifties, it was possible for a family earning a moderate income to buy a new small house in Levittown or its equivalent, the houses and apartments these families vacated went on the market at reduced prices to families earning below the median level. Now that no Levittowns are being built, mobility in the housing market has been sharply reduced and families that should have been able to move are staying put. Obsolescent housing that should have been torn down decades ago is still in use, often at exorbitant prices; city neighborhoods that should have been torn down for urban renewal are still desperately needed for families that have nowhere else to go. It is as true as it ever was that the private market in housing, whether in new or used units, cannot provide housing for the families at the bottom of the income ladder. Subsidies, either in the form of cash to families or government outlays for housing construction, must be provided. But the cost of such programs has become exorbitant because the private construction market for new housing has been closed off in the suburbs by artificial means.

Since the Industrial Revolution began dumping rural families into big-city slums, housing planners have recognized that public subsidy is needed to enable working-class families to live decently. Every industrial nation provides some form of subsidy for workers' housing; the United States has been in the housing business on a large scale since the thirties.

The nineteenth-century English garden-city movement laid down the principle that the cheapest—and most wholesome—form of housing for working-class families was the attached cottage, or row house, built so that each unit would have access to common open space. But in America, housing built for low-income and moderate-income families has generally been "projects" in the central cities: massive apartment towers built on the sites of destroyed ghettos, on land that is close to the city's hub and therefore so expensive that building at lower densities is not possible. In the nineteenthirties the housing pioneers Henry Wright and Lewis Mumford decried the trend to housing for the poor in the inner cities; they pointed out that cheap housing at livable densities requires cheap land, and they urged public-housing authorities to build at the city's fringes. Urban-Renewal experts in the Federal Government and city authorities ignored the experts. Suburban land was locked up, and housing for the poor built at choking densities on the sites of the old ghettos.

Opening up suburban land would mean that Federal money, rather than being used to build absurdly expensive high-rise structures in inner cities, could be spread to a far larger number of units. In New York City, it costs more than $30,000 per unit in Federal and local funds to build public housing. Row houses and garden apartments could be built in the suburbs for well under $20,000 per dwelling unit, if the land costs were reasonable and if lot-size and square-footage requirements were not excessive. Not the least of the savings in time and money would come from working through the manageable governments of the towns instead of the tangled and near-paralyzed bureaucracies of the cities.

If the growth of the suburbs in sheer numbers of people has not yet been fully recognized as a fact of national life, suburban dominance of the metropolitan—and national—job markets has been barely noticed. Yet in "bedroom" suburbs like Westchester County in New York, as many workers now commute into the county each day as travel to the city in the customary pattern.

The service sectors of the job market—the shopping centers and colleges, for instance—have followed the roads and the population. One example is the Cherry Hill Mall shopping center in Philadelphia, which employs 2,000 workers and occupies eighty acres of land about eight miles from the center of the city (accessible via three major highway bridges).

The demand for cheaper land for single-floor assembly-line and warehousing operations has brought more companies—and jobs— to the suburbs. The long, low building requires land; parking lots for employes' cars and for truck storage require land; and land that is far from the streets of the central city costs less. In Mahwah, New Jersey, for example, the Ford Motor Company purchased about 200 acres just off a New York State Thruway interchange, about twenty-five miles from the center of New York City and about the same distance from downtown Newark, for a plant which now employs 4,200 workers.

Traditionally, companies that are prestige-conscious or need a communications network near their headquarters have occupied space in downtown skyscrapers. Increasingly, however, they have been able to enhance their prestige and satisfy the residential preferences of their executives by moves to long, low buildings in parklike settings in far-out suburbia. For instance, Pepsico, Inc., has just completed a corporate headquarters in Purchase, New York, which employs 1,250 people on a 112-acre site.

The decentralization of the metropolitan job market means that the working population must be permitted to decentralize too, if workers are to be matched with jobs. The unemployment rate in this recession period may be hovering around 6 per cent for the society at large, but inside the urban ghettos it has been at the Depression level of 12 per cent for years. To end the acute problem of unemployment and underemployment, ghetto workers must be permitted to follow the blue-collar jobs out of the central cities.

The remoteness of the job market for relatively low-skilled workers from the ghetto areas aggravates the employment problem. So does the lack of coordination between job-finding agencies in the cities and the suburbs, which makes it difficult for the low-skilled worker living in the ghettos to find out about and apply for low-skilled but decently paid jobs in suburban manufacturing plants. The United States Employment Service and other job-finding agencies must be reorganized along metropolitan lines, so that information about openings can be transmitted to the unemployed in the ghettos. But this will not be enough. Workers must be able to travel to the jobs, which means in the case of blue-collar jobs that they must be permitted to find homes near enough to the jobs so that commuting does not take an excessive bite out of their incomes.

If the ghettos are viewed as underdeveloped areas—an approach that became fashionable in the sixties—the need for movement of workers to jobs in suburbia is even more sharply evident. Economists who were once captivated by the notion of pouring capital investment into depressed regions in order to create new factory jobs are now beginning to recognize that by far the cheapest solution to the problem is to give unemployed workers information about jobs in thriving industrial areas, help them to learn about the unfamiliar customs and housing patterns of the new area, pay them resettlement allowances and get them moved. Only in rare cases does it pay to invest heavily in declining areas rather than help families left behind by changing patterns of industrialization to move into the economic mainstream.

Of the 4,200 workers employed at the Ford plant in Mahwah, many live in Newark and New York, and only eighty-eight, or 2 per cent, in the town where they work. Despite the important role that this factory plays in the metropolitan economy, the local property taxes paid by Ford benefit only Mahwah residents. Taxes on industrial and commercial property that are paid to suburban communities are another example of a metropolitan resource that could be—but is not—used to help solve inner-city problems.

The tax rate on business property reflects the needs only of the suburban jurisdiction that levies it. If the suburb has a relatively small public-school enrollment and few low- and moderate-income families, its local tax rate will be much lower than the rate that would be necessary if the business property were situated in a poverty-ridden central city. The tax rate is further reduced when, as in the case of Mahwah, the suburb uses its zoning powers to keep out children and to exclude low- and moderate-income households, including those whose breadwinners work in the plant.

Mahwah's successful effort to lure new companies and to exclude the companies' employees has resulted in a 1970 tax rate on industrial and commercial property of 1.55 per cent of full value. By comparison, the city of Newark, which houses and educates nearly 1,000 of Ford's black workers and their families, is compelled to tax business property at the rate of 7.14 per cent of full value.

Mahwah's tax base included $104 million of business property and yielded $1.6 million in revenues. If this $104 million were taxed at the rate levied on similar property in Newark, it would bring $7.4 million in added funds to the city. The comparison, of course, is a rough one, since a bigger tax rate in Newark might permit the city to lower its rate somewhat. But it does demonstrate the fiscal gains that induce corporations to relocate from poverty-ridden central cities to restrictively zoned suburbs.

Suburban towns and cities use the taxes generated by the coming of large new business properties to reduce residential property taxes or to increase the quality of public services, or both. On the other side of the coin, the movement of industry to the suburbs weakens the tax bases of central cities, requires an increase in their tax rate, and cripples their capacity to respond to the social and educational needs of the disadvantaged groups, many of whose members are forced to commute at great cost in money and time to the very suburban plants which are no longer on the city's tax rolls.

The movement to open the suburbs has begun. The thorny legal, financial, and moral questions will be settled not only by debate but by legislative and court action and by economic pressure.

The first step may well be the establishment of a clear connection, in the public mind and in public law, between jobs and housing for workers. The decentralization of the job market is, as we have noted, one of the least appreciated phenomena of metropolitan life; it is time that voters and public officials became aware of it and acted accordingly. Rather than assuming that a corporation moving its plant or offices from the central city to the suburbs is a tax bonanza for the lucky municipality that succeeds in attracting it, we must require that the company have a clear policy of relating jobs to workers' housing and commuting patterns. The rule must therefore be: no corporation hiring a significant number of workers can move to a location in a suburban community where the housing market is closed to families earning what the plant workers in the plant will earn.

In effect, this will mean that the tax benefits to a town which welcomes new industry will be balanced by the costs to that community of educating the workers' children, policing their neighborhods, providing them with municipal services. If a community has all its vacant land zoned for single-family houses on five acres of land, then if it permits a zoning variance for the construction of Jones Corporation's new international headquarters, it must also rezone land for sufficient new garden apartments to house Jones's 300 janitorial, service, and lower-level clerical workers, create sufficient quarter-acre plots so that Jones's 250 executive secretaries and junior managerial personnel have a chance of buying homes, and make sure that land and construction costs do not make housing prohibitively expensive in the five-acre zones for its 100 middle-management people.

Both state and Federal action will be needed to promote the rule. In Washington, Senator Abraham Ribicoff is working for just such an approach by reintroducing the proposed Government Facilities Location Act of 1970, which provides that no Federal installation may move to a community which refuses to provide land for workers' housing. Though it does not cover private industry, the bill would have significant impact on communities bidding for Federal largess in the form of shipyards, research facilities and other economic jackpots. (The bill did not emerge from committee in 1970; hearings are scheduled for late fall of 1971.)

If a community enforces zoning laws which in effect keep out blacks, can the Federal government continue to provide water and sewer grants, open-space acquisition loans, and other forms of aid to them? Does not such aid violate the antidiscrimination guidelines imposed by the Civil Rights Act of 1964? The clamor against suburban exclusion has led to sharp questioning of the president on this point, and a now-famous statement issued by the administration last June was meant to answer the questions by establishing a distinction between economic and racial discrimination. A community cannot be punished, in the administration's view, for keeping out the poor, only for overtly keeping out the black. This distinction is, to say the least, far from firmly established; and lawsuits will soon be brought to challenge the point. The suits will argue that the racial discrimination in the suburbs is the direct and calculated result of zoning laws.

In New York State, Assemblyman Franz Leichter has introduced a package of antiexclusionary bills which include a prohibition against establishing state facilities in exclusionary communities. Such a prohibition would affect the location plans of state university branches, hospitals, state schools, and other major service installations, as well as—under some interpretations of the bill—state assisted elementary and secondary schools (meaning all schools, now that the barriers to state aid to parochial schools have largely fallen).

Massachusetts enacted in 1969 its "antisnob zoning law," which provided that at least 0.3 per cent of every community's vacant land must be made available for the construction of low- and moderate-cost housing in each of five years. Other states, including New York, New Jersey, and Connecticut, are considering similar legislation to exempt at least a portion of suburban land from the exclusionary regulations.

Our own organization, Suburban Action Institute, is seeking to induce Federal regulatory agencies to act against corporations planning moves to exclusionary suburbs. We have filed complaints with three agencies—the Federal Equal Employment Opportunity Commission, the Federal Communications Commission, and the Office of Federal Contract Compliance—against R.C.A., American

Telephone and Telegraph and General Electric for taking steps to relocate to the acreage-zoned communities of New Canaan, Connecticut; Bernards Township, New Jersey; and Fairfield, Connecticut.

By moving to communities within which their minority-group employes cannot find housing, we charge, these corporations are creating conditions of employment discrimination. We believe that they are not simply acquiescing in a discriminatory situation, but affirmatively aiding the creation of segregated employment. (Because of the complaint against R.C.A. before the Equal Employment Opportunity Commission, the company has temporarily withdrawn its proposal to build offices in New Canaan for 1,000 people.)

Making laws to restrict corporations from moving jobs to exclusionary communities will not remove the basic incentive for such moves: the tax laws. As long as the costs of educating suburban children are borne by the local real-property tax, a community will try to enhance its tax base by luring industry and will try to keep out housing developments that attract families with children. A radical restructuring of the tax system for financing education is needed, both to end exclusion and to assure every child, whether born in a rich or a poor community, equal educational opportunity.

A statewide income tax for education is the remedy now advocated by the Regional Plan of New York, by the Lindsay administration, and even by suburban taxpayers who can no longer pay educational costs in newly developing communities. Governor William G. Milliken of Michigan, a Republican, has moved to establish a statewide tax for education. New York State's Fleischman Commission is about to conclude a study of school financing by calling for "full state assumption" of the cost of educating children. Political pressure to relieve local property owners of the burden of school costs is building up around the country as record numbers of local school budgets are defeated.

A recent decision in the California Supreme Court may signal the beginning of the end of the present system of financing local schools. In *Serrano v. Priest,* the court said that the local property tax "invidiously discriminates against the poor because it makes the quality of a child's education a function of the wealth of his parents and neighbors. Recognizing, as we must, that the right to an education in our public schools is a fundamental interest which cannot be conditioned on wealth, we can discern no compelling state purpose necessitating the present method of financing."

The Supreme Court has not ruled on the fundamental issues raised by zoning since 1926 when, in the case of *Euclid v. Ambler,* it declared that comprehensive zoning ordinances are a reasonable and constitutional method of controlling land use. But the lower courts have begun to rule on the contention that the zoning frequently denies racial minorities the equal protection of the law guaranteed by the Fourteenth Amendment. In one recent Pennsylvania Supreme Court case, the justices declared:

"We fully realize that the overall solution to [housing and growth] problems lies with greater regional planning; but until the time comes that we have such a system, we must confront the situation as it is. The power currently resides in the hands of each local governing unit, and we will not tolerate their abusing that power in attempting to zone out growth at the expense of neighboring communities."

The Justice Department and the American Civil Liberties Union have raised questions of suburban-exclusion with their suit against Blackjack, Missouri, on behalf of a group of black residents in St. Louis who wanted to build housing in the town. The group charged that Blackjack incorporated itself into a municipality for the purpose of denying the needed zoning change.

Court cases challenging exclusionary laws are in preparation against a number of suburban communities around the nation and the biggest initial victory has just been won in New Jersey. Judge David Furman of the Middlesex County Supreme Court recently declared invalid an ordinance in Madison Township, New Jersey, that called for one- and two-acre lots, required a minimum floor area that was excessive and placed limitations on multifamily dwellings. The ordinance, the judge said, had the effect of preventing 90 per cent of the people in the area from living in the township and directly contributed to the ghettoization of neighboring cities. The suit was brought in behalf of a group of black and Spanish-speaking residents of Elizabeth, Plainfield and New Brunswick.

The judge did not reach the constitutional questions, basing his ruling instead on the state zoning law, which says that localities must zone for the public welfare. Under this law, he said, a community when it passes land-use regulations must in the future take into account not only its own needs but those of the region.

The direction the U.S. Supreme Court may take has been hinted at in recent rulings on the need for school busing to achieve integration. Despite the negative decision in the recent Valtierra case in California, which dealt with a referendum that was designed to prevent construction of housing for an economic minority, the record of the court on matters relating to *racial* discrimination has been quite uncompromising. It is fair to expect that proof of the racially discriminatory effects of exclusionary zoning will carry great weight with the court.

The massive spurt in suburban housing construction which followed World War II occurred at a time when new young families were desperate for homes—in a full-employment economy and following the end of war-related restraints on building. The decade of the seventies has brought the beginnings of another market of this kind (as those born in the postwar baby boom come into their own child-rearing years), but without the economic conditions which made the housing surge possible after the war.

Housing construction is now at a low ebb. Even if the vise of exclusionary zoning is removed, government subsidies and controls will be required to see to it that the combined public-private housing market actually produces the needed housing. The Kaiser Commission has called for the construction of 600,000 units of Federally assisted housing each year for the next decade, at a cost of $2.8 billion per year. Aid to the housing market of this magnitude, *combined with* the opening up of vast acreages of suburban land, can insure the construction of the housing that is neded to eliminate the slums and ghettos of the central cities and to permit rebuilding on their land at decent densities.

If suburban land resources do become available, new residential development can be of a far higher quality than that of the nineteen-fifties, which gave rise to fears about "urban sprawl," Levittowns, and endless identical rows of shoddily built bungalows. Critics of America's suburbs have led us to fear the terrible sterility of look-alike suburbs. But the suburbs have offered a very satisfactory form of life to those who live in developments that do look alike in many respects. Of course, suburbs have many problems; what form of human community does not?

We should not prohibit development because it may have some undesirable aspects, unless we develop alternatives that provide suitable housing for all classes of the population.

The garden-city movement and the new towns of Europe as well as the best examples of new development in this country—Columbia, Maryland, and Reston, Virginia—have demonstrated that amenable communities open to all classes can be constructed at far higher standards than those of today's expensive suburban developments, in which each house sits on a plot of one, two or more acres. Present acreage development saves no open space for the public. It calls for cookie-cutter development writ large. It demands that every inch of space be devoted to a private lot—even land not suitable for development.

But if new housing in the suburbs need not follow the pattern of Levittown, it also need not conform entirely to the rules of the garden-city movement in Europe and America. Housing can be built in small developments in existing towns, or in new towns, or in larger developments around highway interchanges and commercial projects. Towns, moreover, can assure the preservation of large amounts of open space through such devices as "cluster zoning" and "planned-unit development," which permit higher densities on portions of a tract if a certain amount of acreage is set aside for public recreational use. Nor would elimination of suburban exclusion prevent those who wish to own large amounts of land from doing so—a privilege guaranteed them by our economic system.

As the prospect of intensified development of the suburbs comes closer, private groups, sniffing profits, are investing in land for eventual massive building. One hopes that these developers will be guided by the principles of balancing industrial and commercial growth with new housing, and of a wide mixture of housing types and costs in open neighborhoods.

Nonprofit groups and public agencies should also be preparing for the future by negotiating for tracts of suburban land on the theory that when the exclusionary laws are struck down, they had better be ready with plans for construction of low- and moderate-cost housing or they will risk leaving the whole ball game to the private developers.

THE FEDERAL GOVERNMENT'S ROLE

Nixon: No "Forced Integration"

by Robert B. Semple, Jr.

PRESIDENT NIXON'S reaffirmation at a news conference last week of his opposition to the "forced integration" of suburban housing not only shed a bit more light on what he means by that term, but also sent nervous ripples through the two Federal agencies that have tried the hardest to open the suburbs to low- and moderate-income housing—the Department of Housing and Urban Development and the Department of Justice. Mr. Nixon has spoken twice before about "forced integration," leaving others to speculate on his meaning. Last Wednesday, he clarified himself on the following essential points:

• He said, without equivocation, that he would continue to

defend black plaintiffs who believe they have been discriminated against by suburban developers who rent and sell housing.
• But he also said, with equal clarity, that he would resist efforts to use the legal and financial leverage of the Federal government to compel suburbs to accept low- and moderate-income housing against their wishes.

"I think what the law does require is that there be open neighborhoods," the president said. "The law does not require that the Federal government step in and provide in a neighborhood the type of housing that an individual could afford to move into."

Mr. Nixon said further that the civil rights laws now on the books required nondiscrimination in the sale or rental of housing, but did not require a policy of "economic integration."

The distinction may have seemed confusing at first, but in effect the President was only restating his basic premise. It is that while the black man who has the money to buy a house in the suburbs— can confidently expect the administration's support, the millions of blacks now trapped in the slums should not expect the government to build the kind of suburban housing that most blacks are likely to move into and that the suburbs—knowing full well the racial consequences—have vigorously resisted.

The percentage of blacks in the suburbs of the sixty-seven largest metropolitan areas of the country rose only slightly, from 4.2 per cent in 1960 to 4.5 per cent in 1970, despite the enactment of the Civil Rights Act of 1968 requiring "affirmative" government action to open the suburbs to all races. Federal intervention in behalf of individual black clients, in other words, appeared not to be doing the job. The answer, some officials believed, was to provide new housing outside the central city that blacks could afford to move into.

One who held that view was the secretary of Housing and Urban Development, George Romney, who decided last year that the "affirmative responsibility" clause of the 1968 act allowed him to threaten several small towns with the loss of valuable water-and-sewer grants, and the suburban city of Warren, Michigan, with the loss of its urban renewal money, if these communities did not accept low-income housing. The Romney effort collapsed when administration conservatives rebelled and Mr. Nixon's comments on Wednesday were hardly calculated to revive it.

In a parallel effort to Mr. Romney's the Justice Department has been joining or initiating suits against communities that use zoning laws, local referendums and other devices to prevent the construction of low income housing. One purpose of this effort has been to give Mr. Romney a legal mandate to carry out the construction of low-income housing in white suburbs where he has been prevented from doing so on his own administrative initiative.

Federal appeals courts in five circuits covering about half the country have ruled that devices used to prohibit construction of inexpensive housing violated the Civil Rights Act of 1968 or the equal protection clause of the Constitution, or both. What worries some Justice Department lawyers now is that Mr. Nixon's prohibitions against Federal efforts to change the "economic pattern of a neighborhood"—which public housing assuredly does—may inhibit them from intervening in such cases in the future.

"I don't know if we would bring the Second Circuit case now," one Justice Department official said. He referred to a case that involved an attempt by Lackawanna, New York, to prevent construction of a housing project for blacks in an all-white section of town.

What the president appears to be saying, in words reminiscent of his approach last year to certain Federal court decisions requiring racial balance in the public schools, is that he wishes to go one way while the courts go the other.

How and in which direction Mr. Nixon will ultimately move on the housing question is still unclear, in part because he is awaiting advice from Attorney General John N. Mitchell on whether to bring suit in the controversial case of Blackjack, Missouri, which barred a moderate-income housing project. But judging by his comments last Wednesday, his instinctive legal and political response to the problem is that neither the equal protection clause nor the Fair Housing Act of 1968 requires him to force change in the racial composition of the suburbs.

H.U.D.'s Failure
in Warren, Michigan

GEORGE ROMNEY, secretary of Housing and Urban Development, has run into an uproar in his home state of Michigan over Federal efforts to press for desegregation in suburban housing. Mr. Romney hurried to the Detroit suburb of Warren in July 1970, to try to stem some of the controversy that has developed in the predominantly white, working class suburb of 180,000 people, many of them Roman Catholics of Polish descent.

The controversy arose over reports that Federal housing experts had selected Warren as one of the first targets in what could become a national drive to crack suburban zoning laws and local attitudes that have the effect of keeping blacks out of housing beyond the central cities. The secretary, who came to reinforce his department's denials that Warren had been selected as such a target, suffered much abuse at the hands of white suburbanites. And the dispute itself has provided important insights into the emotional nature of the issue in suburbs around the country.

The trouble began when an expert in Mr. Romney's department

Original title: "Michiganites Jeer Romney and Suburbs' Integration," by Jerry M. Flint. From *The New York Times,* July 29, 1970, copyright © 1970 by The New York Times Company.

said that the Nixon administration was planning to take steps to reduce housing segregation in the suburbs and that Mr. Romney was moving to implement the idea in the Detroit area. The *Detroit News* then said in a series of articles that Warren had been picked as the spearhead community. That in turn set off an uproar in Warren and other mostly white Detroit suburbs that brought Mr. Romney to Warren to address representatives of forty suburbs and subjected him to abuse.

Secretary Romney said that the suburbanites had been "inflamed" by newspaper articles and that the uproar over integration was threatening the department's programs nationally. He repeatedly told the officials that he was against any "forced integration" and favored only "affirmative action" by the community toward desegregation as the price of getting Federal renewal grants. But it was clear that many in Warren could see no difference. When he left, hundreds of persons jeered him and some banged against his car, as the police cleared a path for the former Michigan governor.

The Warren councilmen who spoke at the meeting made it clear they wanted the Federal money but not black residents from the city. When Warren's mayor, Ted Bates, asked the secretary if any acceptance of affirmative action programs would be tested by looking for an increase in black residents, Mr. Romney did not answer directly, but said the program would depend only on "good faith" of the suburbanites.

In a compromise, Mayor Bates decided to continue to seek Federal money for renewal in Warren, and Secretary Romney agreed to approve it. Mr. Romney's aides apparently believe local acceptance of the grants gives them a foot in the door in their fair housing efforts.

There are no laws that keep blacks from buying homes in Warren or similar suburbs. Federal and Michigan law bar such discrimination. But suburbs such as Warren make it clear that blacks are not welcome—the crowds that shout or picket without sharp criticism from local officials are one sign. The open housing laws are weakly enforced, and zoning and building codes may be used to keep low income projects out. The Civil Rights Act of 1968 empowers the secretary of Housing and Urban Development to with-hold the programs administered by his agency from communities that pursue discriminatory housing practices.

Despite the denials, there is the following evidence to indicate that Mr. Romney's department has made Warren an integration target:

• Secretary Romney had made a major point of the importance of breaking the white suburban circle that encloses the blacks and the poor in the cities.

• A departmental memorandum that came to light said Detroit suburbs present an unparalleled opportunity for the application of a fair housing strategy.

• Mrs. Romney, a candidate for the Republican Senate nomination from Michigan, first said and then denied that the city must have a 1 per cent quota of black residents to get the renewal money. Warren at last count had twenty-eight black families, most of them living on Federal property.

Under Secretary Richard Van Dusen said there was nothing wrong with the newspaper reports of the department's policies to push integration in Warren. Mr. Romney said he had told his top aides he was wrong. . . .

A fast retreat by the government shows how touchy the desegregation issue is. At first the Department of Housing and Urban Development suggested a dozen steps that Warren might take to show good faith in open housing. Later this was cut to five items and later to two—passing an open housing ordinance and appointing a human relations commission.

In 1967, when a Negro with a white wife bought a house in Warren, mobs threw rocks and garbage at the house and shouted obscenities for days. In 1969, a 100-unit low-income housing project was rejected in the city because of fear that blacks might live there.

But not all Warren residents are so vehement. As the crowd faded away after Secretary Romney left, a teenager on a bicycle ripped down an anti-Romney sign. "I didn't like what it said," the boy explained as he wheeled away.

[Editors' note, based on article, "Suburb Rejects Housing Pro-

On November 7, 1970, Warren became the first city in the United States to reject a Federal urban renewal project at the polls.

"It's going to be a long time before any politician will have the guts to propose urban renewal," a Warren official said after voters had rejected a $10 million program.

Mayor Ted Bates attributed the vote to "innuendos and untruths," referring to stories that the Federal government was trying to force blacks into the white suburbs.

George Romney said the vote "made very clear there's no such thing as forced integration" in the Nixon administration. The nation "can't keep the black and the poor bottled up in the central cities," Mr. Romney said, but he added that the suburbs can't set integration quotas, either.

After Mr. Romney spoke in Warren and called for "affirmative action" by the community toward desegregation, a community relations commission was established but its members were never named.

"He only confused things," said Mayor Bates, speaking of Mr. Romney's appearance in Warren to explain the issues.

Warren residents, many of whom felt that they were escaping the city's racial problems by moving to the suburbs, reacted with a petition to put the rejection of urban renewal on the ballot.

The urban renewal program already under way was to improve older parts of the suburb, which has more than doubled its size in the last decade. Many new residents who moved from Detroit into their new ranch homes do not know about the rundown sections of the suburbs, Mayor Bates asserted.

"It's a tremendous loss for the city," the Mayor continued. "You just don't go out and get $10 million." Federal funds are now cut off, and there are no state funds—in the recent election, Michigan voters turned down a $100 million bond issue for low-income housing.

---

gram," from The New York Times, *November 8, 1970; copyright © 1970 by the New York Times Company.*]

The Justice Department vs. Blackjack, Missouri

UP UNTIL about five years ago, the rolling Missouri hills crept right up to the back door of the general stores and the handful of clapboard farm houses scattered around the crossroads here. Life in Blackjack was very quiet and very pleasant.

Then the bulldozers and the builders came, and suddenly Blackjack was just another link in the chain of "bedroom" suburbs that ring St. Louis. Life grew hectic and confusing as some 4,000 strangers moved into new $30,000 split-levels and sought out new friends and a new rhythm of life.

But in time, things settled, and Blackjack once again became a very nice—if different—place to live in. Husbands bragged about the easy half-hour drive to their $14,000 jobs at McDonnell Aircraft or Emerson Electric. Wives liked the low-pressure salesmanship and the friendly banter of local merchants. Children discovered tree lines, ditches, and abandoned barns.

Then, a few months ago, the bulldozers returned, tearing once

Original titles: "Bulldozers Turn Up Soil and Ill Will in a Suburb of St. Louis," by Drummond Ayres, Jr., and Jack Rosenthal. From *The New York Times,* January 18, 1971. "U.S. Sues Suburb on Housing Bias," by Jack Rosenthal. From *The New York Times,* June 15, 1971. "Suit on Integrated Housing Upsets a St. Louis Suburb." From *The New York Times,* June 20, 1971. Copyright © 1971, by The New York Times Company.

again at Blackjack's heavy dark soil and its way of life. Never in the century-long history of this town, which was named for two huge oaks, has there ever been so much bewilderment, unease, and bitterness.

This time, the builders are the St. Louis Inter-Religious Center for Urban Affairs, a group of seventeen faiths interested in providing improved housing for the poor. The Center proposes a $3.5 million, 210-family apartment project for the poor, complete with rent supplements. The Center chose the Blackjack construction site because it wanted to determine the feasibility of providing subsidized housing for people—black and white—just beginning to climb above the poverty line, but still too poor to move to the suburbs.

"This is a pretty new and important concept," says Jack Quigley, the Center's director.

The residents of Blackjack find it an utterly alien concept, and are opposing it determinedly. Blackjack has incorporated itself into a formal community and adopted a zoning law that excludes apartments, thus stopping the religious center's project for the moment. But supporters of the construction say that this is a tactic aimed at keeping out what many local residents term "those people," and the case has become a focal point in the mounting national controversy over efforts to build low-income housing in white suburbs.

George W. Romney, secretary of housing and urban development, has called Blackjack's action a "blatant violation of the Constitution and the law," while the Center has filed a suit charging that the town's zoning action keeps poor blacks in inferior housing and limits their opportunities. But Blackjack residents have sent hundreds of letters to Washington, demanding that the Federal government deny the usual housing subsidy in this case. Eventually, it appears, the courts will have to settle the issue.

In Blackjack, the few residents who support the project have been isolated, and the thousands who oppose it have been tightly bound in friendship by the charges of racism leveled against them.

"This fight has nothing to do with race," says Mrs. Noah Epley, a member of the new Blackjack Town Council. She adds: "It's simply a matter of economics—everything from land and housing values to overcrowded schools and cluttered streets. We have blacks here. They go to our churches and schools and are on our zoning board. Just ask them what life's like here."

When asked, Louis Hughes, a salesman for International Business Machines, said: "I guess my family is one of half a dozen or so black families living in this town. Nobody really bugs any of us. Some neighbors are friendly. But I have one next door who has never spoken to me in over three years."

What about the opposition to the religious center's apartment project? "About 90 per cent racist," Mr. Hughes replied.

One of the handful of Blackjack residents supporting the project is Arthur Repp, a teacher at a nearby Lutheran school. He says: "This fight has cost me some friends, but I've got to stick by my belief. Things got so bad at one point that a few fellows that I know dropped around to talk about the situation and parted by saying something like, 'Sometimes these disputes can get rough.' Maybe I got overexcited, but after that I worked out a fire evacuation plan for the house and taught it to our four kids. I had to consider, too, that my wife had gotten a couple of phone calls from people who refused to identify themselves as they berated her about our position."

Perhaps the only Blackjack resident completely neutral about the project is Gerald Rose, a twenty-six-year-old gas company employee who lives adjacent to the disputed construction site. He says he neither opposes nor favors the apartments, then adds: "I just wish I was back again in the old days when I could go out into the empty fields with my dog and gun and shoot me a mess of rabbits or quail right in sight of my house."

AFTER MONTHS of study, in June 1970 the Nixon administration sued Blackjack, Missouri, charging the St. Louis suburb with illegally blocking an integrated housing development. Filing of the suit in St. Louis was announced by Attorney General John N. Mitchell, thirty-five minutes after the administration disclosed another initiative in the politically volatile field of suburban housing integration. George Romney, secretary of housing and urban development, issued proposed guidelines that would limit Federal grants for community development to those communities that agree to plan for low-income and moderate-income housing.

Previously, President Nixon issued a detailed policy statement on the subject. He called for strong legal action against racial discrimination but said he would not compel suburbs to undergo economic integration.

Filing of the Blackjack suit, first recommended six months earlier, was in accord with Mr. Nixon's policy. And Mr. Mitchell, at a joint news conference with Mr. Romney, said the Department of Justice would soon file eight other housing discrimination cases around the country.

Mr. Romney, praising the presidential policy statement, described his proposed guidelines as consistent with that statement. It is one thing, he said, to force communities to accept low-income and moderate-income housing, but, "It's a very different thing to use the leverage of Federal programs to encourage acceptance" of such housing. In the words of another administration official, "We're not swinging a big stick. We're just saying we can withdraw the carrot."

The Blackjack case was a civil suit asking a Federal court order to "permit the prompt construction" of a multifamily town house development in the St. Louis suburb. The government also asked the court to forbid any racial discrimination in housing. The issue developed when a nonprofit corporation made detailed plans in late 1969 to build the development for persons of limited income. It was widely known that the project would be integrated.

The Federal suit charged that the residents of Blackjack incorporated their community to gain zoning power and then used that power to block construction of the project. This action violated Federal civil rights laws and the Constitution, the suit said.

Mr. Romney's statements related to two areas of his department's responsibility: community development—which includes sewer, water, and urban renewal grants—and Federal housing assistance. On community development, Mr. Romney issued a set of proposed guidelines that would require a community that sought community development funds to provide for low- and moderate-income housing.

Would an unwilling community, he was asked, thus have to pay for its own sewers, without Federal help? "Sure, they don't have to take it. That's leverage, but it's not force," the Secretary replied energetically.

On Federal housing assistance—to home ownership, rentals, and public housing—Mr. Romney proposed a new set of criteria for funding. "If a project doesn't rate at least 'adequate' on the non-discriminatory location criterion," he said, "it will be disapproved." The new criteria were offered on a preliminary basis, to be made final after a thirty-day period for public comment.

Housing experts applauded the clarity of Mr. Romney's elaboration of the Nixon policy. But they questioned whether his new guidelines and criteria would, in fact, encourage much additional lower-income housing in the suburbs. Tying community development grants to planning for such housing could be an effective step, they said, but it is not a new policy. Mr. Romney himself declared that this "is the policy we have followed, are following and will follow."

The Department of Housing and Urban Development now grants about $1.7 billion in community development funds annually. But the bulk of this money goes to urban renewal, primarily relevant to cities, authorities said, so that attaching conditions to these grants is likely to promote only limited new lower-income housing in the suburbs.

As to the new guidelines for Federal housing assistance programs, suburban communities generally shun them in the first place, officials acknowledged. "So this is not much of an inducement to them. The communities that want these programs know they're getting into lower-income housing and don't really need to offer additional guarantees," one official said.

The Blackjack suit and Mr. Romney's proposals coincided with another development in the area of suburban housing desegregation. This was an agreement between Mr. Romney's department and the General Services Administration designed to improve government practices in locating lower-income housing for employees of Federal facilities that move to the suburbs.

BY THE dinner hour, nearly everybody in suburban Blackjack had heard the news, but few were happy about it. The Department of Justice had just filed suit to force their city to allow the construction of a racially integrated housing project that it had blocked by adoption of a zoning code prohibiting multifamily housing.

For most, the reaction was surprise, disappointment, and a feeling they had been abandoned by a friend. Many felt that President Nixon's opposition to "forced integration of the suburbs" meant that the government would not enter the case.

"I feel like I had been led down one path and now, all of a sudden, told I've been following the wrong one," commented Charles Brownfield, an armament engineer, who had moved to Blackjack about two years earlier. Like several other residents, Mr. Brownfield felt that the suit had violated the spirit of suburban housing guidelines announced by the administration on June 11, 1971.

"We're afraid that if they build the project, they'll fill it with a bunch of have-nots who, once they see what we've got, will be walking up the street to take it," said Mrs. Mary Lou Buenger, a school teacher.

The community, named for the large blackjack oak trees that once grew in the area, petitioned to incorporate in June 1970, when the Federally assisted low-to-moderate-income housing project was proposed by an agency representing several churches in the area. Three months later, the City Council blocked the project by passing a zoning code prohibiting multifamily dwellings. City officials said that the area already had an overabundance of apartments.

The question of whether the Federal government would take action caused a dispute within the administration that focused nationwide attention on the suburbs. Blackjack, once a farming village, now consists largely of treeless subdivisions of large modern ranch homes in the $25,000 to $35,000 price range, built among gently rolling hills twenty miles north of St. Louis. Most of its 3,000 residents, predominantly white and economically successful, insist that their opposition to the project is not based on racial discrimination.

"It's more than just race we're talking about, per se," Mr. Brownfield insisted. "It's the discrimination of the neighborhood;

being able to walk the streets at night. It's fighting against the establishment of another Pruitt-Igoe in the suburbs."

Pruitt-Igoe, a complex of forty-two high-rise apartment buildings in St. Louis, has been called by some the worst public housing project in America. Many persons in Blackjack fear that the crime, destruction, and despair of Pruitt-Igoe might be transferred to their community if the project is built.

This is one of the most beautifully racially integrated communities in the country, according to Blackjack's mayor, Keith J. Barbero, a thirty-two-year-old computer service salesman. "We've had no racial problems, and we don't want any," he said. Mr. Barbero said that the suit had made him feel alone but "nervously confident. I'm nervous because the whole country is looking toward tiny little Blackjack to carry the ball for them," he said, "yet I feel confident the allegations are false and we'll be able to prove it in court."

Roy W. Bergmann, the city's special counsel, calls the government's allegation of racial discrimination "a phony issue."

However, his view is disputed by Jack L. Quigley, director of the Inter-Religious Center for Urban Affairs, the project sponsor, who said: "The most common statement we heard at meetings out there was 'we don't want those people, we don't want another Pruitt-Igoe.' If that's not racial discrimination, I don't know what is."

A few Blackjack residents opposed the city's incorporation. One was Oscar C. Williams, a black aerial space engineer whose family is among an estimated total of twenty Negro households scattered throughout the community. "I felt that incorporation was a blatant attempt to exclude people from living here because of their race," he said. Mr. Williams acknowledged that some blacks had worked for incorporation, adding, "but for me to have a nice home here and then close the door on my brothers—well, that wasn't right."

Nevertheless, Mr. Williams opposes the building of the project now. "The atmosphere in the community is not right for it," he said, standing outside his sprawling four-bedroom ranch home. "People moving into it will get the feeling they are not wanted, and there will be trouble, I'm afraid."

The Supreme Court: The Valtierra Case

by John Herbers

THE NATIONAL FORCES that have been pushing for a dispersal of the poor into the suburbs were demoralized by the Supreme Court decision in April 1971 upholding state laws that give voters of a community the right to block construction of low-rent housing [*James v. Valtierra*]. The National Committee Against Discrimination in Housing and a wide range of other civil rights groups have expressed shock at the ruling. In the absence of administration policy for racial and economic integration of the suburbs, they had looked to the Supreme Court to provide the basis for a continued legal assault on the building of large, predominantly white and exclusive compounds outside the central cities.

What is largely at stake is not so much neighborhood integration or lack of it, as President Nixon has defined the issue, as it is the increasing tendency of large suburban municipalities of 50,000 to 100,000 people to exclude low-income developments through a number of means. This, according to the civil rights people, is now central to America's racial problem and is likely to be the dominant issue throughout the nineteen-seventies.

While the 5-to-3 decision is directly applicable to only a small

Original title: "Housing and Suburbia." From *The New York Times,* April 30, 1971, copyright © 1971 by The New York Times Company.

part of the dispersal effort, the rights leaders predict that it will increase the already strong resistance in communities across the country to housing integration. "It will have all kinds of negative influences," said Jack E. Wood, Jr., of New York, a codirector of the committee. "We are just completely depressed. We think it will increase everywhere the tendency toward local autonomy as a means of perpetuating racial segregation."

The Court upheld the constitutionality of a 1950 California law that has been used by voters to prevent the construction of almost half the low-rent housing proposed in that state in the last twenty years. Eight other states—Colorado, Iowa, Mississippi, Montana, Oklahoma, Texas, Vermont and Virginia—have similar laws providing for referendums on low-income housing.

Mr. Wood noted that "Justice Black implied that it would not be wise for other states to enact referendum laws. But I don't think it is going to work out that way," he said.

The decision is largely applicable, it is believed, to construction of public housing—that which is built, with Federal subsidies, by public housing authorities created by municipalities. It is less applicable, if at all, to construction of Federally subsidized housing built by private and nonprofit developers for low- and moderate-income families.

For example, in Houston, where the city limits untypically incorporate most of the suburbs, officials say the decision will not apply to apartment and single-home construction carrying Federal subsidies, even though there is strong opposition to it in many neighborhoods. But no public housing—that for the poorest families —has been built here in twenty years because proposed projects were rejected by the voters. The authorities said that, if the Houston Housing Authority should now propose more construction and the proposal should raise a controversy, the City Council would undoubtedly submit the matter to referendum.

The effect of public opposition in many other communities across the country has been to confine public housing to the decaying central city, where the projects add to the concentrations of poverty and social problems.

The Supreme Court decision was based on economic rather than racial consideration. Justice Black said there was no evidence that the California law was aimed at racial minorities.

But some lawyers who represented the poor in the case said it was unfortunate that the racial element had not been included. They felt that the decision might have been different if presented on a racial basis, adding that in almost every case of exclusion, race is an important factor. In suburbs across the country, whites have opposed public housing at least partly because the residents believed the projects would open the communities to central city blacks who would bring social problems with them. Thus the lawyers believe that the case for open communities may yet be won in the Supreme Court, on the basis of racial equality. For example, there are a number of challenges in the lower Federal courts to the right of a municipality to use its zoning powers to block low- and moderate-income housing.

ALTERNATIVES TO EXCLUSION

The Dayton Plan

by John Herbers

THE WHITE SUBURBS of Dayton, Ohio, which range from very wealthy to blue-collar, have agreed to provide housing for the poor, despite strong and outspoken opposition by many residents. In what national housing experts regard as a remarkable development, the governing officials involved approved a plan that would disperse federally subsidized low- and moderate-income housing throughout the five-county Dayton area.

Although the plan is said to be unique, the heated public controversy that accompanied its initial implementation and the conditions in Dayton that brought it about are indicative of the urban dilemma across the nation. Further, the development illustrates what is involved in the housing controversy that has been under way in the national government. Plans by the Department of Hous-

Original title: "Suburbs Accept Poor in Ohio Housing Plan." From *The New York Times,* December 21, 1970, copyright © 1970 by The New York Times Company.

ing and Urban Development to make a strong stand for open communities in the administration of Federal grants have been questioned by Attorney General John N. Mitchell and the White House.

In the Dayton plan, each community has been assigned a quota, its share of some 14,000 units, many of them public housing, that are expected to be constructed over the next four years. If carried out, the plan would bring about both neighborhood and school integration, and would reverse a trend of the poor's concentration in deteriorated central-city neighborhoods. Dayton officials say that in the long run a firm Federal policy for open communities is essential to the success of the plan in Dayton. The officials, most of whom are Republicans, are worried about how much support they will receive from Washington. They believe the plan fits the philosophy expressed repeatedly by George Romney, secretary of Housing and Urban Development, but they are disturbed by President Nixon's recent statement that "forced integration of the suburbs is not in the national interest."

The Dayton plan, they say, is voluntary, not forced, but one of the factors that brought its acceptance was the belief that H.U.D. would use Federal grants in a way that would encourage open communities. "If political pressures build up so that the suburbs can continue to flout low and moderate income housing and still get their money from Washington, there is little we can do," said one official.

There already is a sense of amazement in Dayton that the plan has progressed as far as it has. Some city councils approved the plan while crowds of irate citizens fought it vigorously. Dale F. Bertsch, executive director of the Miami Valley Regional Planning Commission, which originated the plan, was subjected to repeated telephone threats and once had a microphone snatched from his hands as he attempted to explain the plan at a community meeting. Acceptance finally came, officials said, because of an extensive educational campaign that alleviated many fears, support by the Dayton "establishment" and the proddings of an irreverent newspaper editor, James E. Fain, who struck out at a "snob zoning" in the "white-on-white suburbs," those lily fields that encircle Dayton and other such urban centers.

Dayton is an industrial city of 250,000, and is the center of a metropolitan area of 842,000. Its growth during the last decade has followed the typical pattern. The city lost population while the suburbs gained. While this occurred, the poor became increasingly concentrated in neighborhoods within the city limits, to a large extent because they could not afford housing elsewhere.

Dayton residents say that a generation ago there was more economic and racial integration within the metropolitan area than there is now. As residents of means moved out of the city, the poor moved in. In addition to the old deteriorated housing that was available, virtually all of the 3,350 units built for low-income persons were constructed within the city limits. As a result, there have been large concentrations of poverty that have led to acute social distress, which is feeding on itself, spreading and causing further alienation of the races. The situation was worsened in recent months as the cost of housing has soared and thousands of families have been shut out of the market.

Thus there is a large demand for subsidized housing of all kinds, from public rental projects to home ownership under which the government pays part of the interest on the loan. Both nonprofit and private builders are looking for sites for subsidized units. But they have been stopped at the city limits.

"If the price is right," the planning commission found, "the utilities are not available. If the price and utilities are right, the zoning is wrong. If all are right, the neighbors do not want it."

Joseph D. Wine, a former city councilman who is now employed by the city in an effort to stabilize transition neighborhoods, emphasized the point by driving a visitor first through the decayed neighborhoods of sagging porches, boarded-up windows, and abandoned automobiles, then outward to the sanitized sprawl of new houses and neat lawns, new factories, and shopping centers. Mr. Wine said he was convinced after years of antipoverty work in the central city that there was an urgent need for neighborhood integration. "The suburbs have got to assume part of the burden," he said. "There is a selfishness that has gotten into people that is very disturbing. But I think we really have something going here in the housing plan. It is essentially moral."

The Miami Valley Commission is made up of elected officials of the five counties and twenty-nine municipalities in the region. In addition to planning the growth of the region, the commission has been delegated authority to coordinate and review Federal grants going into the area.

In July 1969, the commission staff, after a long study, unveiled the housing plan. It divided the area, including the city of Dayton, into fifty-three "planning units," each of which was assigned a quota of subsidized housing under a mathematical formula that took into account the amount of existing housing for low-income families, population density, and other factors.

Kettering, for example, a middle-income, incorporated suburb south of Dayton, with a population close to 70,000, would be required to provide 650 units over the four-year period. Some people say there are seven black families in Kettering, others say there are only four. In any event, the Department of Housing and Urban Development recently rejected Kettering's application for a $65,000 park grant because the city had restrained its human relations commission from seeking housing for black families.

The commission staff took the plan to the communities and sought to convince the residents that no neighborhood would be overrun with the poor, and that public housing was no longer constructed in the large projects that many residents objected to. A twenty-six-unit public housing project in a white, blue-collar neighborhood in Dayton provided a good example. When the project was announced, the residents objected vigorously. But now that it has been completed, the brick townhouses are the most attractive in the area, and black and white families are living there with no trouble.

One of the first suburbs to consider the plan was Oakwood, a community of mansions and middle-income homes. Mr. Fain, editor of the *Dayton Daily News* and a protégé of the late Ralph McGill, the humanist Southern editor, described it as "a compound" and "the local Brigadoon." "The opportunity to live in Oakwood is a burden that should be shared without regard to race, creed, color, religion, national origin or draft status," he wrote.

But residents packed a City Council meeting in opposition to the plan. The audience applauded when Richard Ulbrich, a homeowner, said, "The vast majority of the people can find homes if they're willing to work for a living."

One resident, J. Brooks Walters, who described himself as a member of an old-line Dayton family, invoked the memory of Lincoln in opposition to the plan, quoting him as having said, "You can't strengthen the poor by weakening the rich."

The City Council, nevertheless, endorsed the plan in principle even though it took issue with the quota of 637 units assigned to Oakwood. What was important, the *Daily News* said, was that Oakwood council accepted the principle that "no community has a right to exclude potential residents on the grounds they make too little money."

Trotwood, a suburb west of the city, approved the plan for a different reason. It lies in the path of the expanding black community. "If we don't have this plan, this umbrella," Mayor Edward Rausch told an audience of protesting citizens, "we'll be inundated long before other communities have any."

There was some opposition from Dayton's black community on the ground that the plan would bring a dilution of both political power and antipoverty funds, but this was muted because many blacks did support the plan, and because community leaders said there would be no lessening of assistance to the central city.

Late in September 1970, members of the commission, all representing their respective governments, voted 26 to 0 to implement the plan. Six municipalities, mostly smaller, remote ones, abstained. Since then, commission members have worked to solidify the commitment, which includes changing zoning ordinances to meet the assigned quotas.

The chief test will come when builders move to put up projects in protesting communities. William T. Rogers, a field representative for the National Committee Against Discrimination in Housing, called the plan "exciting and unique" and said, "I think it eventually will be carried out, and pretty much in its present form."

The Madison Township (New Jersey) Decision

by Ronald Sullivan

IN A RULING hailed by organizations striving to open suburban areas to lower-income housing, a State Superior Court judge struck down, on October 29, 1971, the entire local zoning ordinance of a Middlesex County community on the ground that it ignored "the desperate housing needs" of urban New Jersey.

The decision, by Judge David D. Furman, was described by the Suburban Action Institute, a nonprofit organization seeking to gain new suburban jobs and housing for poor persons, "as the breakthrough we have been waiting for." According to Paul Davidoff, the institute's codirector, the ruling may be the first of its kind in the country and is certainly the first in New Jersey to strike down an entire local zoning ordinance that allegedly excludes lower-income families on the ground of regional responsibilities.

The decision involves Madison Township, a community near New Brunswick that has grown from 7,000 people in 1950 to 50,000 in 1971 and which generally reflects the economic and social strata of Middle America. Madison Township, in the explosive growth that shot out from the cities after World War II, provides moderately priced development homes on small lots for thousands of working-class and white-collar families that could not afford the higher prices in more affluent suburbs.

However, in 1970, Madison Township officials apparently concluded that the community could no longer afford the continued influx and adopted a zoning ordinance restricting new housing development to one-acre and two-acre lots. And to ensure that the homes on them would be expensive, Madison Township followed the example of many other New Jersey communities by mandating floor space requirements that the court said would result in housing that would cost at least $45,000. Moreover, apartments that would accommodate families with children were virtually outlawed, while changes were enacted that would inspire new industry to move in.

"It's a classic exclusionary zoning case and an extraordinary court response," Mr. Davidoff said.

An official of the National Committee Against Discrimination in Housing said the decision "sounded like another progressive step in attacking exclusionary zoning in the United States."

Richard F. Plechner, the attorney for the township, said the decision would be appealed. In the meantime, its provisions apply only to Madison Township. Governor William T. Cahill told the Legislature in 1970 that the courts would wipe out New Jersey's restrictive local zoning laws one by one unless the state stepped in with a code that would apply statewide and meet growing demands for a more equitable distribution of housing and jobs.

In his decision, Judge Furman said: "In pursuing the valid zoning purpose of a balanced community, a municipality must not ignore housing needs, that is, its fair proportion of the obligation to meet the housing needs of its own population and of the region.

"Housing needs are encompassed within the general welfare. The general welfare does not stop at each municipal boundary. Large areas of vacant and developable land should not be zoned, as Madison Township has, into such minimum lot sizes and with such other restrictions that regional as well as local housing needs are shunted aside."

In the meantime, the judge said, "population continues to expand rapidly. New housing is in short supply. Congestion is worsening under deplorable living conditions in the central cities, both of the county and nearby.

"The ghetto population to an increasing extent is trapped, unable to find or afford adequate housing in the suburbs because of restrictive zoning.

"In Madison Township's approach to the objective of balance," he continued, "its attempted cure is a worse malady than whatever imbalance existed. About 800 acres of land, apparently prime for low or moderate income housing development, has been taken out of the reach of 90 per cent of the population, prohibitive in land and construction costs.

"The acreage available for multi-family apartment units is minuscule. Families with more than one child are barred from multi-family apartments because of the one- and two-bedroom restrictions, restrictions without any guise of health or safety purposes.

"The exclusionary approach in the ordinance under attack coincides in time with desperate housing needs in the county and region and expanding programs, Federal and state, for subsidized housing for low-income families."

The challenge to Madison Township's ordinance was originally instituted by Nathan Kaplan, a developer who had pledged himself to providing a substantial proportion of two projects he plans for Madison Township for low-income residents.

The suit was widened and made into a class suit representing one white and five black residents of New Jersey cities. They were put forth as representing the 90 per cent of New Jersey's 7 million residents who, according to state housing statistics, cannot afford the housing that is currently being built in the state.

The suit also attacked the 1928 state law that allowed individual municipalities to adopt their own zoning laws. But Judge Furman said the state code was a legislative, not a judicial, problem. In defense of its zoning practices, Madison said it was merely trying to "catch its breath" under the enormous population pressures that have overtaxed municipal services and that have threatened to overwhelm its public schools.

Part **4**

PROBLEMS THAT WON'T GO AWAY

Taxes Take the Bloom Off Suburbia

by Clarence Dean

AUTUMN IS the time of year when, along with the turning leaves, the frost of taxes brings a chill to suburban living. It is the season when the barbecue cart has been rolled to the back of the garage, the swimming pool drained and covered, and, traditionally, the final installment of the year's taxes has become due.

The inevitability is even more sombre now because property taxes in the New York suburban area are higher than they have ever been—a development that residents accept in varying degrees of horror, exasperation or plain resignation. The suburban awareness of taxes at this season is heightened by the general election to be held next month and, in New York, by the state law that requires towns to file preliminary budgets for the year ahead and to hold public hearings on them during October, November, and December.

Taxes are an issue in many of the 175 contests for local offices in Westchester this November. They are the principal issue in the liveliest contest in Nassau, that for presiding supervisor of the town of Hempstead.

In New Jersey, meanwhile, Governor Richard J. Hughes is

stumping the state in behalf of a $750 million borrowing proposal —the only alternative, he says, to a broad-based tax, sales or income, which New Jersey has long resisted.

Yet, despite all the talk of taxes, the discontent and sometimes anguish of individual property owners, the spectacular amount of the increase and the probability that it will continue, there are no discernible signs of a widespread taxpayer revolt in the suburbs. Indeed, except for the individual's acute concern with his own tax bill, there are few signs that suburban residents generally appreciate the extent or the causes of rising taxes.

One finds taxpayers like the elderly woman who stood on the steps of the Yorktown town hall in upper Westchester the other afternoon swinging her cane. "I tell you," she proclaimed, "this is the last tax bill I'll pay here! They raised me $500 in one year. I've put my house up for sale—I'll let it go to the lowest trash that comes along, the lower the better. This town can just go to pot!"

Again, there was the widowed property owner in Babylon in western Suffolk. "Seventeen years ago, when I came here," she said, "my taxes were $7.50 a month. Now they're $45. I've had to take out loans sometimes to keep going. But there's not much you can do about it. I realize everything costs more now."

Yorktown and Babylon are dramatic examples of suburban growth. In each, the population has more than tripled since 1950, and taxes have risen almost correspondingly with the need for new schools and other town services.

Similar, if perhaps less extreme, increases in taxes are the pattern throughout the suburbs. For Nassau County as a whole, Horace Z. Kramer, vice chairman of the Board of Assessors, estimates the rise at two and one-half times since 1950. For the nine-county region of northern New Jersey, the increase has been 9.7 per cent since 1957, according to Dr. Ernest C. Reock, Jr., director of the Rutgers University Bureau of Government Research.

Specific examples reflect the pattern more vividly. Since the ratio of assessment to full market value varies between, and even within, municipalities, the most meaningful comparisons are made in terms of the actual bill the taxpayer incurred. On this basis, it appears that a Lynbrook, Long Island, property owner who paid

$298 in taxes in 1953 paid $767 in 1962. A tax bill in Mount Pleasant, Westchester County, went from $281 in 1954 to $453 in 1963. In Piermont, Rockland County, a $230 tax bill in 1951 had become $688 in 1963.

In Livingston, New Jersey, the rise was from $580 in 1956 to $920 in 1963; in East Orange, from $650 in 1957 to $1,250 in 1963; in Montclair, from $325 in 1953 to $625 in 1963. Even in such areas of limited population growth as Greenwich, Connecticut, the rise has been marked, in this instance largely because of increasing property value. The Greenwich taxpayer who paid $395 in 1950 paid $755 in 1963. The market value of his house had risen from $35,500 to $46,000. In nearby Westport, where property values not only increased but population doubled from 1950 to 1963, a tax bill went from $259 to $806.

By far the largest element in rising suburban taxes has been the cost of schools. In Nassau County, the school levy went from $25,532,251 in 1950 to $170,040,327 in 1963. The Nassau-Suffolk School Boards Association, urging greater state aid for education, recently reported that in Nassau the average local school tax rate had risen from $1.71 for each $100 of assessed valuation in 1949–1950 to $5.76 in 1963–1964.

School costs have been Yorktown's major problem. General municipal taxes have risen only slightly since 1952, when the big housing developments started there, but school taxes have more than tripled. Similarly, Babylon faces the need of a $6.3 million school expansion program, adding an average of $115 annually to the taxpayer's bill.

Yorktown enjoys an advantage not shared by many hard-pressed suburban communities. It has two large International Business Machines installations. They have brought in a great deal of the population growth that underlies the town's school problem, but they have also added some $7 million to the tax ratables, or tax resources.

Yorktown is a composite of many of the aspects of suburban development. Its growth—from 4,800 to 18,900 in ten years—began in 1952. Its attractive, hilly terrain was not only accessible but, in relation to most of Westchester County, inexpensive. It was mostly farm and nursery land then and could be bought at $150 an acre. (The price now is nearer $2,700). Developers ringed its slopes with ranch and Cape Cod types of homes that sold at less than $15,000. Then came I.B.M. and another large employer, General Motors, in nearby Tarrytown. The homes continued, and continue, to rise; now at prices between $20,000 and $25,000.

The town found itself in need of many new municipal services —roads, more police, parks, and, of course, schools. With the help of the industrial ratables from I.B.M. and a townwide revaluation of real estate in 1962, it is meeting most of those needs except for schools without a sharp tax increase.

There is an irony here that is not infrequent in the location of suburban industrial ratables. I.B.M.'s largest installation, while in the town of Yorktown, lies in that part of the town that is within the overlapping Ossining school district. The result is that while children may live in and go to school within the Yorktown school district the school taxes from the large I.B.M. plant are paid to the Ossining district. This typifies the objection that while industry may bring attractive tax revenues to a suburban community, it also may burden adjacent communities where its workers live and send their children to school.

The prime example of an industrial windfall in the New York suburbs is probably Buchanan, also in Westchester. Here, Consolidated Edison has erected a nuclear-powered electrical generating plant. The installation, employing only a handful of persons and imposing no burden on the community for additional services, has added $20 million to the tax ratables, formerly about $3.5 million. Buchanan's tax on real estate is one of the lowest in the county, and it has been able to effect major municipal improvements, such as sewers, roads and street lighting. "We're lit up like a Christmas tree," says Mayor William J. Burke.

Differences in the amount of ratables are responsible for many of the disparities in the burden upon suburban property owners. New Rochelle, for example, one of the oldest cities in Westchester, has taxes in the same high bracket as Yorktown. But only 26 per cent of New Rochelle's land use produces commercial or industrial ratables, while 71 per cent is residential. In White Plains, on the other hand, 50 per cent of the land use is commercial or industrial.

Industrial ratables, however, are not the only element that governs suburban taxes. The nature of the communities also is important. Purchase in Westchester, for example, is an area of large and valuable estates, with a relatively small school population. Statistics compiled by the Westchester Department of Planning show that behind every pupil in Purchase there are ratables of $176,192, while in Yorktown, despite its industry, the figure is $22,785. This results in a school tax five times higher in Yorktown than in Purchase.

The rise in real estate taxes and disparities in the burden on individual property owners are the chief issues in the spirited election contest under way in Hempstead, Long Island. Horace Z. Kramer, forty-five-year-old vice-chairman of the Nassau County Board of Assessors and a Democrat, is trying to unseat Palmer D. Farrington, the Republican incumbent, for presiding supervisor, the town's chief office. Mr. Kramer contends that taxes are unnecessarily high, that they are inequitably levied and that they result from an archaic government structure and inefficient management. He says that there are 308 individual taxing bodies in Nassau—levying separate taxes for schools, fire districts, water supply, parking facilities, and even for escalators at railroad stations.

A man who mentally retains tax figures as another man might retain baseball scores, Mr. Kramer goes from house to house telling property owners what they paid in taxes ten years ago and what they are paying now. He presents examples of disparities, such as: "A taxpayer in the North Merrick fire district pays .462 per $100 of valuation, while his neighbor in the Merrick district pays .273." Or: "The average resident of Inwood pays $404.50 annually for nonschool services, but in Cedarhurst he pays only $245 for the same services."

Mr. Kramer finds the going difficult. "The average taxpayer in Nassau has no idea of what he is really paying in taxes," he says. "If he knew, he would be up in arms."

In Nassau—as in all suburban counties—it is the almost universal custom for property owners to pay their taxes through the mortgage holding bank. Taxes for the year are estimated in advance by the bank and are incorporated in monthly payments.

"The result," says Mr. Kramer, "is that most people have no

realization of their total tax bill. It is paid in monthly fragments and apportioned in a dozen or more separate assessments." A further problem, Mr. Kramer believes, is "invisible government." Because of the multiplicity of taxing and other governmental functions, it is extremely difficult for the individual taxpayer to keep informed on municipal operations.

"And on top of that," Mr. Kramer declares, "the ordinary suburban resident doesn't usually identify himself with the local governmental structure. He commutes to the city, he reads the New York papers and he tends to regard his suburban home as an adjunct, a bedroom. Probably the only exception to that is the question of schools."

School budgets have been almost the only area of suburban taxation where there has been any substantial evidence of taxpayer discontent. This year, eighteen school budgets were rejected on Long Island, four in Westchester, and sixty-four in northern New Jersey.

Some tax authorities, like James A. Arnold Jr., director of research in the New Jersey Division of Taxation, see a significance in this. "Unfavorable school budget votes," in Mr. Arnold's opinion, "are more expressions of discontent with steadily increasing property tax totals than dissatisfaction with school programs."

Others, like S. J. Schulman, Westchester County planner, are not so sure. "It is questionable how much they really mean," he says. "So many local factors, personality questions and emotionalism generally are involved that it is doubtful whether you can draw any general conclusions."

But whatever the significance of the budget rejections, schools usually lie at the heart of the suburban tax problem. They are also commonly the point at which battle is joined between the older residents and the newcomers.

A long-time resident of Babylon was complaining bitterly the other day. "These people from the city who've moved out here don't know what they're doing," she declared. "Every time a school bond issue comes up, they're all for it." She continued, "They want indoor swimming pools and fancy tiled walls in the corridors, carpeted locker rooms, and parking for the kids' cars—the works.

They don't stop to think how it's all going to be paid for. You know why? Because they're not solid, responsible people. They're 'dese' and 'dose' people—the kind that buy a TV set before they pay the dentist. They come from nothing in the city, and now they want everything."

She sighed vigorously and went on. "My taxes have gone from $90 to $500 in the last dozen years. When is it going to end?"

Rising taxes are an especially acute problem for people of fixed income in such a rapidly growing community as Babylon. There are indications that even the newcomers find them burdensome, too.

The mortgage loan officer in one of Babylon's principal banks estimates that the owners of 10 per cent of the properties on which his bank holds mortgages—most of these owners are relatively newcomers—are delinquent in their taxes.

But however steep the continued rise in taxes, it does not seem to overcome the desire to move to the suburbs. Down in Monmouth County, New Jersey, in the level expanse of Matawan, Levitt and Sons is completing a development of 1,910 houses called Strathmore. All but eighty have been sold. They are attractive homes in country Colonial, ranch and Cape Cod types, ranging from $16,990 to $25,990.

On the still unseeded grounds of one home the other day, a man and his wife were setting out chrysanthemum plants. They had moved from Brooklyn three weeks ago.

"Oh, we love it here," said the woman. "It's going to be such a joy here when my husband retires next year. So clean and such wonderful country air!" She hesitated and dusted the soil from her gardening gloves. "Of course," she said, "it's going to be a little hard. It will take all we can do to make the payments. And the taxes—$640 here when they were only $472 in Brooklyn. But I know it will be worth it."

An Alternative to "Slurbs"

by Ada Louise Huxtable

IN THE United States this year, $23 billion worth of suburban houses will go up. In the nineteen years since the war, the suburban development has sprawled across the country, to change the American landscape and the American way of life.

The boom in suburbia has resulted from the romantic pursuit of a dream, and the real need for shelter. The dream of the good life of domestic bliss in a sylvan setting was inherited from the nineteenth-century English planners who had preached a persuasive sermon of everyman's home-of-his-own-in-the-country, a kind of quasi-rural retreat into peace and privacy. The real need was the wartime housing shortages that were never satisfied, and the insatiable peacetime demand for homes as the war generation settled down to family life. But somewhere along the way the suburban dream turned into the subdivision nightmare, the dreary look-alike developments, the slums of the future, the "slurbs."

The sins of suburbia are now familiar to the point of boredom, but ignoring them won't make them disappear. Fortunately, they are no longer being ignored. Improvement may be at hand, with two heartening innovations—the "cluster development" and the

Original title: " 'Clusters' Instead of 'Slurbs.' " From *The New York Times Magazine,* February 19, 1964, copyright © 1964 by The New York Times Company.

New Town, or entirely planned community. Such projects received official encouragement two weeks ago in the president's housing message, which scored "sprawling, space-consuming, unplanned, and uneconomic" expansion, and proposed legislation to promote more orderly suburban growth.

The need for action is clear from coast to coast. Long Island fields and farms have been invaded by regimented hordes of split-levels lined up for miles in close, unlovely rows. Boxes called homes march ruthlessly across the prairies of the Middle West. The orange trees of Orange County, near Los Angeles, have been replaced by houses jammed onto sixty-by-120-foot lots, as a ten-year boom has pushed farmland from $2,000 to $23,000 an acre.

A leading magazine in the field, *House & Home,* refers to the promoters of these mass-marketed houses as "stumblebums" who put together their developments with a few switches on stock floor plans and façades for a transparently superficial kind of variety. Fake hand-hewn shingles, imitation fieldstone, patterned aluminum siding, corny cut-out door and window frames transform the standardized box into what could be called "Dutch Colonial Ranch," "Cape Cod Split Level," or the glory of development glories, complete with scalloped wood eaves, chalet shutters and tacked-on trellises—the "Hansel and Gretel," as it is known to the trade. Regional variations are limited to local preferences for Williamsburg colors or California pastels, New England clapboard or Florida stucco.

Inside, the hack house appeals through gadgets. What is sold is not a house, but double wall ovens and dishwashers, built-in blenders, inlaid vinyl floors over concrete slabs of doubtful thickness, glamorous gold plastic in claustrophobic bathrooms, knotty pine veneer. If the gleaming appliances are enshrined in too-small rooms with too-thin walls, if the layout is bad and the plaster cracks, a girl's best friend is still her washer-dryer, and every builder knows it.

The damage from all this is social, cultural, psychological, and emotional, as well as esthetic. The sociologists tell us of the disasters of the one-class community where mass-produced developers' housing herds one age group, one economic level, and one color into homes as alike as their owners. The psychologists tell us that the bliss of togetherness has turned into the neuroses of development-inspired ennui. The statisticians tell us of the disenchantment that has started a trend back to the cities. The critics point to the devastated countyside and the minimal dwellings of a sameness that promotes stultifying monotony.

Suburban Christmas is a cheap plastic Santa Claus in a shopping-center parking lot surrounded by asphalt and a sea of cars. Suburban spring is not a walk in the awakening woods, but mud in the poorly built roads. Suburban life is no voyage of discovery or private exploration of the world's wonders, natural and man-made; it is cliché conformity as far as the eye can see, with no stimulation of the spirit through quality of environment.

What has gone wrong? Looking at the results of almost two decades of frenetic building, one can see clearly that a basic fault is suburban house design (it would be ludicrous to call it architecture). Virtually none of the vast mass of new housing is conceived as a plan—a plan to utilize the natural features of the land or to provide the unifying services, facilities, and amenities necessary for any attractive and well-functioning community.

Obviously, this is a blueprint that no architect or planner has made. No architect today worthy of his training considers architecture anything less than an environmental art—building design plus land use and site planning, as well as the relationship of each building to its immediate neighbors and to the total group. It is a shocking fact that more than 90 per cent of builders' houses are not designed by architects and that planners are rarely consulted —even when a town-size development is involved. It is an equally shocking fact that too many architects just are not interested in this most critical building field, or are not conversant enough with its problems to do the job well.

Most suburban homes are speculators' houses, without benefit of professional services. They are put up for a quick return and sold as merchandise. They bear absolutely no relationship to any other factors in an increasingly chaotic environment approaching an advanced stage of congestion. What the American house buyer is offered, with distressingly few exceptions, is a poor product of market-tested minimums. The minimum F.H.A. requirements have become the speculative builder's maximums, and once the inadequate formula has been accepted by a defenseless public, it is rubber-stamped on the landscape. The suburban builder has succeeded in carrying off a truly formidable feat—the standardization of America on a surprisingly low level.

The process is aided and abetted by zoning and building codes. The zoning laws of many communities virtually outlaw the possibility of new or different solutions. Most zoning is based on a negative set of restrictions: exact acreage required per house, prohibition of commercial with residential use, specification of distances between houses and of heights, outlawing of flat roofs. This adds up to a rigid mold or stereotype that admits no flagrant residential violations and admits no variety. The status quo is preserved.

Local building codes vary to the point of absurdity, and are generally as up to date as the Model T. And if local codes permit a new design, the unions may not. It is no secret that labor is frequently unsympathetic to processes or materials that can cut building costs or time, and that the building industry is riddled with expensive archaisms.

Financing also discourages innovations. The requirements of the F.H.A. for obtaining Federally insured mortgages are not geared to change; the builder must fit his houses to still another mold. F.H.A. could not be more specific about construction details and materials. The F.H.A. requirements are justifiable attempts to guarantee structural soundness, but that prevents other sometimes more efficient ways of doing the same thing. Private lending institutions are conservative to the point of reaction in their financing attitudes, since the familiar, even if bad, is a preferred risk to the unknown. They lend on the basis of what has already been done, not on what might be done that could be better.

What suburbia needs today ranges from the more imaginative and responsible use of just a few acres of land, to the professional, long-range planning of entire new towns on a community level. There is a discernible movement toward more thoughtful layout of houses and open spaces, and better-planned use of land. This is an urgent necessity as open land shrinks under the population onslaught and the builders' depredations.

The trend toward better land use is being helped by a joint research program of the Urban Land Institute and the National Association of Home Builders. The first visible result is the "cluster development," a way of dividing a suburban tract to eliminate the familiar gridiron pattern of monotonously repeated houses on evenly spaced lots. It groups the houses more closely, and often irregularly in clusters, as part of a carefully and pleasantly related plan, leaving a larger proportion of open land for all of the houses to share.

In cluster developments there is private land, which includes the house plots, and common land, from which all the houses benefit. The common land is often a community "green," in the tradition of the New England village. The green can be park or woods, or a cooperative recreation area like a golf course or swimming pool. (The golf course is usually the first thing built, before a single house goes up.) Common land is maintained by a home owners' association, or deeded to the town or country as parkland.

In many areas, the new developments cannot be built without zoning revision, and the builders have helped bring about the revisions through a more flexible law called "density zoning," which specifies the number of people permitted per acre, without spelling out the arrangement of land and houses. F.H.A. has already come up with a new set of land-use regulations to meet the changing trends.

These new cluster developments can be as small as the sixteen dwellings in three buildings designed as a continuous housing strip on a hillside bordering a golf course in San Rafael, California, known as Peacock Gap Terrace, or as big as a 964-acre project called Hunting Creek, now under construction in Jefferson County, Kentucky. They all avoid the repeated single house pattern by including row or town houses, and even apartment towers. The different accommodations provide visual and social variety.

The result is better-sited, better-looking, more interesting kinds of houses, more open, unspoiled land saved from the bulldozer, and a more "natural" environment. Homes may be grouped around a stream or ravine; a stand of woods may be left untouched. Because there are actually savings for the builder of cluster developments in shared mechanical facilities, party walls, and more salable "choice" sites, the consumer gets a lot more house for the money. For $11,000–$14,000 he finds space and extras now usually available for $15,000–$20,000.

The advantages are obvious, and they have already proved persuasive to the house buyer. The trail-blazing cluster developments have been spectacularly successful. Fifty-six of these projects are being measured in a searching and authoritative report by the American Conservation Association, under the editorship of William H. Whyte, Jr., who was responsible for the landmark *Fortune* study of urban problems, "The Exploding Metropolis." According to the report, "The verdict of the market place is yes."

One cluster, Village Green, in Hillsboro, New Jersey, was completely sold out in six months while conventional houses in the same neighborhood, by the same builders, went begging. Huntington Continental, a fifty-two acre project on former agricultural land at Huntington Beach, California, is a cluster group of connected "town houses in the country" with twenty-two acres of common land. A record sale—685 of 751 dwellings—was made in six months and the local F.H.A. office was so stampeded by builders who had got the message and wanted to change old plans to new ones that reinforcements had to be sent from Washington.

Edward Eichler, the California builder who pioneered with architect-designed modern houses in the San Francisco area, turned to clusters with a town-house scheme built around a common at Santa Clara, which sold out in eighteen months. Georgetown South, in Manassas, Virginia, is an immensely popular East Coast version of the same idea.

There is, of course, the danger that cluster houses will contain some of the same faults as other development homes—poor plans, construction and design—and that some irresponsible builders with a penchant for the cheap copy and a fast buck, will turn them into a set of cut-rate building clichés. But even then there will be some gain from the improved site planning and land use.

The second major breakthrough in the suburban scheme has been the creation of complete communities called New Towns. England and Scandinavia have led the way, with government construction of New Towns. The United States has been extraordinarily slow to follow, relying on private enterprise. All of the obstacles already listed, plus politics, militate against the establishment of New Towns here, but even so, about twenty are now in the design or building stage.

Just what is a New Town? The accepted criteria call for a population of at least 20,000; land under a single ownership or control; a town scheme conforming to a metropolitan or regional plan; provision for a variety of uses, including commercial, industrial and civic as well as residential, and a diversity of residents, including all races, incomes, family sizes and social levels. Often, a New Town may have its own economic base, and industrial and commercial zones are provided. Before a single house plot is allocated in a New Town, there are thorough professional studies of the topography, land use, population trends, transportation patterns, growth potential and relationship to neighboring communities so that the best scientific planning can be brought to bear.

At least half the projects claiming to be New Towns are in California, but one of the best is Reston, 18 miles west of Washington in Fairfax County, Virginia. A 6,800-acre development, it will eventually house 75,000 people. Robert Simon, Reston's promoter, has put together a star team of consultants, ranging from planning to graphics, to establish a superior level of quality and design. A Ford grant has been given to the Washington Center for Metropolitan Studies to record its problems and progress.

Reston's plan, by New York architects Whittlesey and Conklin, focuses on sympathetic and dramatic use of landscape features as the basis of seven coordinated, recreation-oriented villages, and it has the promise of handsome, sophisticated houses in three cluster groups by the New York firm and by Washington architects Charles Goodman and Chloethiel Smith. The rendering of Reston's "first village," now under construction, is an enticing vision.

Inevitably, New Towns may fall short of their objectives, and even share some of suburbia's sins. But only through professional community planning can the chaos of the country's growth be turned into order. Concern with the total community is a heartening sign of sanity, order, rationality and realism in the American approach to the problem of urban expansion. There may still be hope for the suburban dream.

Suburban Auto Glut

by David A. Andelman

TO ARTHUR FREED, Westchester's chief highway engineer, "Christmas is really 25 per cent of the year."

The reason is traffic—mind-rotting, stagnating, frustrating, engine-overheating traffic jams that clog every major artery and scores of two-lane downtown roads, sending elaborate computer-coordinated traffic control systems into total chaos.

"Once upon a time Christmas came on December 25," said Mr. Freed, "Now we get our major traffic escalation in mid-October and it lasts through January, when people are returning things."

But the real reason is the automobile and the suburban mentality of not just one car in every garage, but a car in every garage for each family member older than 16. And it has many of the nation's top planning and highway experts more concerned than ever.

One evening last October, Vic Carney, director of the New Jersey State Safety Council, looked out of the window of his Chicago-to-New York jet liner and knew he was nearing home:

"It was the nightly traffic jam at the Willowbrook shopping center in Wayne at Route 46. I couldn't miss it."

At times in the sprawling 120-store Cross County shopping center in Yonkers, more than 30,000 cars a day roll through the parking fields—when they can roll. Others less fortunate sit in traffic jams that back up on the northbound Major Deegan Expressway as far as 225th Street in the Bronx.

"We've simply got to get them out of their cars and into public transportation," said Lee A. Koppelman, executive director of the Nassau-Suffolk Regional Planning Board, one of the nation's leading experts in suburban planning.

But over the last ten years, the number of cars has been increasing from twice to five times as fast as the growth of the suburban population—a 50 per cent auto increase in Westchester, with a 10 per cent population rise, and a 193 per cent rise in automobiles on Long Island, which saw a 110 per cent population increase.

Mass transportation—buses, railroads, and even the highway construction—has not only failed to keep pace, but in most cases, through disuse and neglect, has fallen hopelessly behind. Even the interim solutions proposed by the planners, striving desperately to encourage mass transportation, have fallen victim to the proliferating automobiles.

Two regional park-and-ride stations in New Brunswick and Iselin, New Jersey, for instance, designed to encourage motorists to leave their cars behind and use trains, have themselves caused new and unanticipated bottlenecks and traffic jams on the narrow streets leading to the park-ride sites.

The problems fall generally into two categories: There are simply not enough highways any longer to contain the number of automobiles on the road, and the alternate modes of transportation are not adequate or sufficiently widespread to encourage drivers to give up their cars for short and medium-length trips.

"The day of building new highways is over," for ecological and financial reasons, said Westchester's Mr. Freed. Now, he said, localities must instead "get the last ounce of safety and capacity out of our existing roads."

Construction of a single mile of highway now costs $2 million or more and complex environmental impact statements are required for each new stretch of roadway.

To compensate for the lack of new highways, traffic departments have initiated a variety of technological innovations—including traffic lights aided by computers and sensors that register traffic flow—improvements in intersection construction and, where pos-sible, widening existing rights-of-way where entire new highways cannot be built.

The recently adopted Nassau County comprehensive plan lists eleven suggested traffic engineering improvements, including com-puter-assisted traffic controls, permitting right turns on red signals, and staggering work hours at major office complexes to smooth out peak-hour traffic loads.

The report notes that Long Island's existing main arteries—the Long Island Expressway, the Southern State Parkway and North-ern State Parkway—are carrying 57 per cent of all traffic on Long Island and are operating at anywhere from 125 to 180 per cent of capacity.

In no portion of the suburban metropolitan region, however, a survey by *The New York Times* revealed, is there a reasonable alternative method of intraregional public transportation.

The Penn Central and Long Island Railroad provide frequent service between the suburbs and New York City, but it is virtually impossible to travel from one portion of Long Island to another by using the train.

Bus systems are so totally fragmented and in such critical finan-cial straits that two months ago, Nassau County was forced to sub-sidize one bus line to keep it from going under.

In New Jersey, where the number of cars registered has in-creased to 3.1 million from 2 million in ten years, the state is in its third year of an interim program that subsidizes bus lines in an effort to keep them operating while a long-range solution is sought, and none has yet been found.

During the Christmas season, some bus lines occasionally add a temporary service on a new route, but generally that service is terminated immediately after the Christmas rush.

Nassau County has been attempting to encourage more bus use by strong marketing campaigns, distributing thousands of red-and-white buttons bearing the slogan, "Try It," referring to riding buses instead of driving cars. But most officials concede it has had little success.

In fact, no major changes for the Christmas season alone have been made in the transportation situation anywhere in the metropolitan area, despite the season's widespread effect on suburban motorists.

Yet Mr. Freed feels that the Christmas traffic could be handled much as rush-hour peaks are now handled—with reversible lanes and changing traffic control signals. "We know what the peak shopping hours are going to be, whether it's in Corpus Christi or Alaska or Westchester," he said—1 to 2 P.M. on Saturdays entering shopping areas and 5 P.M. leaving.

But for the present, in most areas, holiday shoppers will face the same situation they have faced for years this holiday season—situations similar to that in which George E. Borst of Wantagh, L. I., found himself the day after Thanksgiving when he went shopping at Garden City's Roosevelt Field shopping center.

"I sat in my car for fifty minutes just to go from my parking space in the middle of the shopping center out to Stewart Avenue," a distance of less than two-tenths of a mile, he said, "And I was lucky—there were others who sat there for two hours waiting to get in."

The City Crime Wave Spreads to the Suburbs

by David A. Andelman

THE CRIME WAVE of the nineteen-sixties that sent New Yorkers scurrying to the protection of fortified apartments, or the safety of the suburbs, in the nineteen-seventies has begun to follow the moving population, with a new pattern of fear emerging in the suburban areas that used to be called havens.

Narcotics addicts from New York pull off the Garden State Parkway in New Jersey, drive into a prosperous subdivision and loot the nearest empty house.

Weapons arrests have risen more than 40 per cent on Long Island, where for the first time in a decade, two policemen were killed last year in the line of duty.

And more burglar alarms have been installed in Scarsdale than in any other community in the nation.

According to the Uniform Crime Report compiled by the Federal Bureau of Investigation, the total number of crimes in the first nine months of 1971, compared with the same period in 1970, rose nearly three times as fast in the suburban areas as in cities

Original title: "City Crime Wave Spreading to Suburbs." From *The New York Times*, January 30, 1972, copyright © 1972 by The New York Times Company.

with populations over one million—11 per cent, compared with 4 per cent. Overall, crime in the suburbs rose nearly twice as fast as in the nation as a whole.

Of 306 suburban counties in the country, two in New York—Nassau and Suffolk—were outpaced only by Los Angeles County and Dade County (Miami), Florida, in the "total number of offenses known to the police in 1970," according to the same report.

"There is no question there's more stealing going on," said the Suffolk County Police Department's chief of detectives, Patrick Mellon. "But there are new patterns, too, and this makes it more difficult for us. There are also more weapons around, and more people willing to use them. It's fatal to assume otherwise."

One of the most common patterns recently emerging is that of the "commuter burglar," described in this way by one suburban New Jersey police official:

Working in pairs, they drive out from New York City or Newark, drop off the Garden State Parkway into a residential development and cruise until they find a house that appears to be empty. While one drives around the block, the second rings the doorbell.

If the homeowner answers, the thief asks directions to a fictitious address. If no one answers, he finds a rear door or window, smashes it in and quickly goes through the house, picking up small appliances, cameras, money or jewelry, leaving when his confederate returns in the car.

Most are narcotics addicts, and a few minutes' work pays for several days' worth of narcotics. Police officials said it was considerably more difficult to locate this type of burglar, unless a pattern was established, which rarely occurs.

Lately, this new breed of burglar has become even more brazen, frequently driving up in a delivery van to cart away heavy items such as color television sets and expensive high-fidelity equipment, which are abundant in the affluent suburbs. Delivery trucks are so common in suburban areas that they are scarcely noticed.

"I had one case of a television repairman who entered houses, picked up money or occasionally jewelry, then left in his van," said Chief Mellon. "But we could never catch him in a house with the money, and half of the calls were legitimate. We finally just told him strenuously to get lost. That was the only way we could handle it."

In Deal, New Jersey, a plush beach-front resort community in Monmouth County, Police Captain Dominick J. Torchia said the old cat burglar or second-story man who worked while the wealthy occupants of the house slept has been replaced by the daylight hit-and-run thief.

"They just ring the bell and break in," he said.

As a result, forty-five homes in the hamlet have installed burglar alarms connected with police headquarters.

But the greatest number of burglar alarms are in the Westchester County community of Scarsdale, where 623 homes have already connected burglar-alarm systems with police headquarters and, by April, about 2,000 are expected to be installed—nearly one in every three homes.

There were eighty-nine burglaries in Scarsdale in 1971, up from seventy-eight in 1970, but only three of the eighty-nine burglarized homes last year were connected to the alarm system.

Scarsdale Police Chief Donald A. Gray said that there is no real feeling of fear in the community. But, he added, "people are aware of an increase of crime. Because it's an affluent community and the men travel a great deal, the village board and the police got together and decided to see about installing this kind of [burglar alarm] operation in the village."

"When women have a panic button to push in the bedroom, this eases their minds quite a bit," Chief Gray added. The "panic button" automatically dials the Scarsdale police headquarters number and transmits a recording saying that the individual house is being burglarized.

But there are other means that suburbanites are using to ease their minds, with respect to crime. The chief means is the purchase of weapons.

In most areas, the number of licenses issued for weapons has remained fairly constant during the last five years. In New Jersey, for instance, since the 1966 Firearms Control Law went into effect, according to Detective Sgt. Dan Morocco, chief of the firearms investigation section of the state police, the number of new licenses for pistols issued each year has averaged between 25,000 and 40,000.

"But those simply aren't the types of weapons people would buy for defense of their homes," Suffolk's Chief of Detectives Mellon observed. "You just wouldn't go to the trouble of getting a license for a pistol—you'd go out and buy a rifle or a shotgun, and you don't need licenses for those."

And these are the weapons that police officials believe are increasing in number. "They're also the ones that are being used more illegally," Chief Mellon added. The weapon that killed a Nassau County policeman in Farmingdale last month was a sawed-off .22-caliber rifle, purchased legally but turned into a concealed and illegal weapon with the use of a hack saw.

After a burglar recently stole the generator out of his car, parked in the driveway of his Northport, Long Island home, one middle-aged resident started sleeping with a .22-caliber rifle by his bedside, a live bullet in the chamber.

"If they try that again, I'll shoot them next time," said the resident, a quiet, mild-mannered salesman, who asked not to be identified but noted that he had never even thrown a punch at anyone in forty years.

"And I wouldn't hesitate a minute," said Chief Mellon. "Years ago, these robbers would simply turn and run if they were surprised. But lately, they're more liable to stand and hit you over the head if you come on them."

Police officials generally gave two reasons for the great increase in burglaries and robberies in recent years: first, the greater need for cash for narcotics; second, the greater ease of disposal of "hot" items throughout the suburbs.

Narcotics offenses increased up to 25 per cent in the suburban areas of New York last year. Generally, arrests were confined to certain semislum pockets in all counties. But in areas such as the vicinity of the State University of New York at Stony Brook, where large narcotics raids were made several years ago, there have been increases in drug traffic.

And, suburban officials noted, it is no longer necessary for thieves to return to New York City to find "fences" to dispose of items they have stolen. "People will buy things right off the street

—televisions, watches—right here on Long Island, while they never would have considered doing that a few years ago," said one Long Island police officer.

"And television doesn't help any," said another senior police detective. "They get their ideas from television, they see people shooting each other and gun sales keep going up."

But one ingenious thief in Westchester County dreamed up what appeared to be a new idea. Police officers are hoping it won't become the pattern in the next decade.

It was in Briarcliffe, New York, where a young couple went to dinner one evening at a local restaurant, and returned to find their car apparently stolen. After reporting it to the local police, they returned to their home and the next morning were surprised to see the car in the driveway, with an envelope on the windshield.

"There was an emergency and we had to borrow the car," the note read. "Please excuse the inconvenience, but perhaps these two theater tickets will make up for it." The couple, surprised but pleased, told the police that their car had been returned, and the next Saturday used the theater tickets.

When they returned that night, they found that their house had been completely looted.

The School Integration Slowdown

by John Darnton

MANY SCHOOLS in the suburbs of New York have desegregated over the last decade, but an increasing number of parents, students, and educators are despairing that the schools will ever become truly integrated. Behind the despair lies a wide range of persistent problems and inequities: from racial brawls that close down the schools to "special classes" that are predominantly black.

"As far as I'm concerned, desegregation is relatively simple," said Dr. Peter J. Dugan, superintendent of the Englewood, New Jersey schools. "It's just shifting around bodies. But integration is an affair of the heart."

Beyond the immediate problems of desegregation, possible long-range difficulties are appearing. When racial problems arise at high schools which lead in desegregation, they harden the resistance of communities seeking to maintain segregation in their elementary schools. And in districts that have rectified racial imbalance, the troubles are raising doubts among some white parents who originally supported desegregation and among some black parents who are beginning to feel that their children do not fare well in a predominantly white school.

Original title: "Integration Found to Be Lagging in Suburban Area Schools Here." From *The New York Times,* May 30, 1971, copyright © 1971 by The New York Times Company.

As the parents and educators look around for causes of the racial strains, one thing becomes clear: it is not just a matter of the numbers of pupils who are put together through desegregation. In 1970, for example, there was racial discord in Syosset schools, where blacks comprised 0.2 per cent of the population, and in Hempstead, Long Island, where they were 71 per cent.

Among the factors going into the problems of the schools are the following:

• Segregated housing patterns.

• An increasing self-assertion and "militancy" among black students.

• A backlash among white students, especially those with strong ethnic backgrounds.

• New black parental organizations, formed either to achieve desegregation or to press for other reforms.

• A gap of misunderstanding and sometimes suspicion between black students and white teachers and administrators.

• A belief among many blacks that they are being discriminated against, often through institutional machinery.

• Outside influences, such as controversies over busing, which sometimes charge the school atmosphere.

Since 1963, when a Federal court ordered New Rochelle to desegregate, a significant number of other suburban districts with a black population have done so. Some, such as White Plains, desegregated voluntarily. Others, such as Malverne, Long Island, were forced to do so by mandate from the state education commissioner.

There are still a significant number of suburban New York districts—such as Yonkers, Portchester, Ossining, and Mount Vernon—that have segregated elementary schools. But the high schools are usually desegregated out of simple necessity: there is only one. The vast majority of suburban districts are virtually all white. Barring court action, they are likely to remain so because proposals for busing in blacks from other districts are invariably killed by public opposition.

Often a district that has been "integrated" becomes "resegregated," as more blacks come in and whites leave, either by attending private schools or by moving out of the district. The net result is a "checkerboard" pattern with districts like Roosevelt, Long Island, and Wyandanch, Long Island, with black student populations of 81 per cent and 91 per cent, respectively, surrounded by all-white districts.

Many, perhaps most, desegregated districts function in ostensible calm. But few claim to have achieved real integration, in the sense of harmonious social interaction. In many schools, outside of the classroom, blacks and whites have little contact. On the athletic field, some sports, like basketball and football, tend to become "black sports" while others, like tennis and golf, remain almost wholly white. Black students feel a need "to get it together by being together," and white students view this new-found solidarity as something threatening.

"Every day after school they hang out on the steps," said John Zalewski, Jr., a nineteen-year-old senior at West Babylon, Long Island High School, where a racial brawl erupted recently. "It takes guts to walk by them. They get away with murder," he continued, "cutting classes, hiding behind doors, not bringing their trays in. If it was white kids that did that, they'd get in real trouble."

From their side, blacks feel they are being discriminated against educationally, by teachers, by counseling that steers them toward vocational training, by achievement tests that disqualify them from certain courses and by ability groupings they call "tracking." "If you get to the top, they'll say you're in whitey's class," noted a black senior at Englewood's Dwight Morrow School.

More than one disruption appears to have been sparked by jealousy among black girls. In some schools, they have banded together to beat up white girls. In Englewood recently, a white girl had her hair burned by a match tossed by a black girl.

Most school officials blame the problems on segregated residential patterns. When youngsters walk out of school to board buses that carry them to neighborhoods on the opposite ends of town, they argue, you won't find them eating at the same table in the school cafeteria.

"After all, the schools are a reflection of the community," said Dr. Arthur P. Antin, White Plains superintendent. "Any school plan to end racial imbalance becomes artificial if the living plans of the residents are segregated."

"Look out there," said Manson Donaghey, the principal of White Plains High School, pointing toward a spacious lawn where whites clustered in groups of three and four while blacks lounged in a single large contingent. "What you're looking at is neighborhood patterns."

White Plains has had a busing program for racial balance since 1964, and in 1971 its 1,700 black students—20 per cent—were spread among its fourteen schools in a range of from 10 to 30 per cent.

But in March 1971, the high school was struck by the most disturbing racial incident in its history when 50 black students rampaged through the sprawling six-building complex, causing almost $2,000 in damages and shutting down the city's schools for two days. The disturbance grew out of a dispute in the gymnasium in which a black student claimed he had been struck by a tennis ball hit by a white student.

Unlike racial crises in New York City schools, which are often precipitated by grievances that mobilize large numbers to action, those in suburban high schools usually begin with an altercation between two students, one black, one white. Once the spark is ignited, it spreads quickly. The scenario is often the same: the fight carries over to a common meeting ground, usually the school cafeteria; it turns into a general melee, with fists flying and chairs tossed; outside there are angry groupings; the police are called and the school is closed.

After one or two days—and usually some student suspensions and an intense round of "rap" sessions—school is reopened. There is superficial quiet, but the level of potential hostility has been raised to a higher exponent, and the principal waits behind his desk, "knocking on wood," as he tends to phrase it.

At Malverne High School, pitched battles between blacks and whites were set off last March in the school parking lot, known as "the pit," when a snowball crashed through a third-story window and struck a black student in the eye. The school was closed, and when it reopened, uniformed policemen patrolled the corridors and a tough line against demonstrators and disrupters was laid down by the principal.

Of the 1,000 students, half are black. When 3 o'clock comes, the blacks leave by the back doors, toward their homes in Lakeview, and the whites out the front, toward Lynbrook and Malverne. The sections are separated by Ocean Avenue, which has acquired a nickname appropriate to the barrier it represents: "the Ocean."

Malverne has seen considerable racial friction since 1963, when it became the first district in the state ordered by the commissioner to integrate. The order was bitterly contested, until 1965, when a desegregation plan was put into effect. Like many other districts, Malverne chose a "grade reorganization" plan known as "4-4-4." Under it, pupils from kindergarten through the fourth grade go to one or two buildings, pupils in grades five through eight to another, and students in the remaining four grades to the high school.

In 1966, blacks accounted for 44 per cent of the student population. In 1971 they were 50 per cent. The number of pupils going to nonpublic schools—virtually all of them white—has risen from 22 per cent to 36 per cent. The rise in private school attendance has made it harder to pass a public school budget. In 1971, state funds for correcting racial imbalance through busing were eliminated by the State Legislature.

Another district that has been brought to the brink of racial anarchy is Freeport, Long Island. One such clash began when a white student, who had fought with a black student, dashed out of the principal's office and grabbed an Afro comb from another black, smashing it. By noon, a teacher and nine students had been injured—one by a knife wound in the neck requiring twenty-two stitches—in combat involving up to 100 students.

Four days later, the high school was evacuated because of a false bomb threat. As the police were searching the building, the principal, William McElroy, looked out the window to see 250 blacks squared off against an equal number of whites. They were armed with stones, pieces of wood and pipe, baseball bats, and chains. The police intervened, leading to charges of police brutality by black parents who asked the Federal Bureau of Investigation to step in.

Freeport High's 500 blacks and 1,800 whites are split into two racial camps. Some whites belong to racist fraternities. Every school morning, a group of twenty-five to thirty blacks meets outside the school to pledge allegiance to the black liberation flag.

"There seems to be increasing militancy on the part of both whites and blacks, and nothing that has happened here accounts for it," said John Gordon, assistant superintendent. In bafflement, administrators reacted with threats of discipline, enunciated over the school's public address system. Freeport administrators believe that they have tried everything. In response to black demands, they introduced courses in Afro-American history and Swahili, even "soul food" once a week in the cafeteria. None of the programs caught fire.

Many other suburban districts have set up "black heritage" and Afro-American courses, but few seemed to have met with real success. Administrators often take this to mean that their need was not really trenchant in the first place, but others have a different interpretation.

"Some districts institute these courses only after they've had disruptions; some have done so because their neighbors have had disruptions and they don't want to," said Dr. Morton Sobel, acting administrator of the Division of Intercultural Relations in Education in the State Education Department.

"They're fire extinguishers," said Robert Femenell of the same office. "They're not the product of long-range planning meant to produce general institutional or instructional change."

When black students do come together to present grievances, high on the list is a demand for more black teachers and more black guidance counselors. No demand is more keenly felt. In Montclair, an announcement that the high school's only black male counselor was being discharged led to a demonstration that closed down the school. In Huntington, the same thing happened when black students learned that one of the school's two black teachers was not being rehired.

Black students often believe that white teachers are, at best, insensitive to their needs and, at worst, downright prejudiced. Rarely can their stories—that such-and-such a teacher displays a Confederate flag or that so-and-so "said we should all go back to Africa"—be confirmed. The prejudice they speak of appears to be more subtle.

"It's a feeling you get that you don't want to open your mouth in class because you're dumb," was the way Betty Harris, a nine-teen-year-old Huntington senior, put it.

"The expectation of white teachers in dealing with black students is very low," said James Rice of the Nassau County Human Rights Commission. "If you continually say to a child: 'You can't do,' 'You can't do,' 'You can't do,' he won't do!"

Superintendents complain that recruiting black teachers is difficult, that there are few positions open because of budget squeezes and that the ones they have are often raided by other schools or other professions.

The Richmond, Virginia, Decision: Merging City and Suburban Schools

by Ben A. Franklin

SEVEN YEARS AGO, Judge J. Skelly Wright, of the United States Court of Appeals for the District of Columbia, delivered a lecture at New York University that raised the eyebrows of the judicial community.

The Supreme Court, he said, would eventually have to hold that the only way to end de facto segregation in the public schools of many of the nation's ghetto-ized cities would be for the Court to order the merger by judicial decree of black-urban and white-suburban school districts to achieve racial balance in one big, school-bus-riding metropolitan system.

It was "inconceivable," Judge Wright declared, that the Supreme Court would "long sit idly by, watching Negro children crowded into inferior slum schools while whites flee to the suburbs to place their children in vastly superior, predominantly white schools." He

Original title: "A Decision That May Be a Real Blockbuster." From *The New York Times*, January 16, 1972, copyright © 1972 by The New York Times Company.

predicted that the Supreme Court would act "if the problem persists and the states fail to correct the evil."

The states, of course, have not acted. And in the meantime, the black schools of many inner cities—particularly in the North—have become blacker, while those in the suburbs became whiter still.

Last week in Richmond, Virginia, the conservative, monument-strewn former capital of the Confederacy, scene of massive resistance to school desegregation in the 1950's, Judge Robert R. Merhige, Jr., handed down a potentially historic decision. An appeal seems certain, presenting the Supreme Court with the opportunity to vote Judge Wright up or down.

In a massive, scholarly opinion with two main thrusts, Judge Merhige ordered an immediate start on planning for the operational, budgetary racially integrated consolidation by next summer of Richmond's school system (70 per cent black) with the school systems of the city's two well-to-do suburbs (Chesterfield and Henrico Counties, whose schools are 91 per cent white).

He carefully limited his boundary-erasing to the school districts. He held that they are not inviolate and are merely convenience subdivisions of the state, no different from a water or sewer district. His order created a 104,000-student-merged "metro" school system whose pooled student population will be only a third black.

About 68,000 children are currently being bused within the city under a plan the judge previously ordered and which he now says has failed because Richmond has too few whites to dilute its black and "racially identifiable" schools. Under his new ruling, only 10,000 more children will be bused; no school can be more than 40 per cent black.

In Richmond, his opinion said, the "iniquitous" segregationist strategy of the state and county school authorities had amply justified his action, under the Fourteenth, or equal protection, Amendment to the Constitution.

It was Judge Merhige's second theme that gave his ruling powerful potential impact upon the more genteel racism of the North. Almost all previous Federal desegregation opinions have looked upon de facto school segregation as a product of the free choice of residential segregation—the white flight to the suburbs. Judge Merhige held that the school authorities themselves had contributed decisively to the flight and thus to the housing isolation of blacks and whites by building and operating new and better-staffed all-white schools in the suburbs—schools that met the needs created by the initial white exodus and in turn encouraged more whites.

When the Richmond case goes to the Supreme Court on appeal, only eight members of the High Court will hear and decide the issues. Justice Lewis F. Powell, Jr., one of President Nixon's latest appointments to the Court, is almost certain to disqualify himself. Until 1969, he was a member of the Virginia Board of Education, whose actions and inactions Judge Merhige labeled in his opinion as "iniquitous."

But it was a commentary on the large scope of the issues involved that the conservative Mr. Powell in a statement to the state board had warned that "serious imbalances" of the races in the cities and an urban "racial mix which results in serious educational disadvantages" were leading to "disastrous social consequences." A man the president is widely supposed to have put on the Court because of his conservative views, he said then that "there is no longer any debate as to the need for vigorous action to right this educational imbalance."

Vigorous action was Judge Merhige's remedy in Richmond, and the N.A.A.C.P. Legal Defense and Educational Fund, Inc., whose lawyers tried the Richmond case, was quick to point out that similar suits are in less-developed stages of litigation in Detroit and Grand Rapids, Michigan; Indianapolis; Wilmington, Delaware; Dayton, Ohio; and Hartford, Connecticut. "There is no metropolitan area in the country that can escape the implications of this decision," they said—assuming it is upheld.

Among those implications was that school officials could no longer contrive—or allow, however innocently—attendance schemes which merely "reproduce in school facilities the prevalent pattern of housing segregation, be it publicly or privately enforced." For Judge Merhige held that housing segregation in a real sense is a product of unequal schools.

For Judge Merhige, an energetic, fifty-two-year-old native New Yorker, thirty years as a successful Richmond lawyer and jurist have still not earned him full entrée to the city's clubby society (he is a liberal Democrat and a Roman Catholic, besides) his 325-page opinion was hardly calculated to endear him to "the state of mind that is Virginia." Last week he and his Richmond home were guarded by United States marshals. But his action was clearly a landmark—some thought it the most important one since the first school decision of 1954.

The Suburban Poor

by Ralph Blumenthal

A WESTCHESTER HOUSEWIFE sat one evening recently in her sour-smelling, $50-a-month tenement flat where a washline was stretched above the kitchen sink.

"People talk about the rich, rich suburbs," she said. "Let 'em come up here."

For her and her family, living on Ferris Avenue in White Plains, amid a suburban area known for its affluence, and for about 180,000 other families in thirteen counties ringing New York City, life in the suburbs has nothing to do with back yard barbecues, antique shows, sailboat races, or country club socials.

They are the suburban poor, and they number 800,000. They face many of the same problems faced by the urban poor. Indeed, antipoverty officials say, the effort to reduce poverty is more difficult to win in some ways in the suburbs than in the city. "We're fighting not even a holding action because of the limited resources we get," said Adrian Cabral, executive director of Nassau County's antipoverty agency, the Economic Opportunity Commission.

The suburban poor are particularly helpless, he and others note, because the poor lack the population concentration that is the basis of political power. They are victimized by a lack of low-cost housing, isolated by inadequate public transportation, and often scorned by their unsympathetic and more affluent neighbors.

Suburban antipoverty workers and some public officials complain that too many suburbanites still do not acknowledge the poverty that festers among them. "I first ran into this trying to get surplus food for Westchester," said Representative Ogden R. Reid, Republican of Purchase. "People just couldn't believe we needed it."

Similarly, while the suburbs are popularly thought of as affluent, said Mr. Cabral, few realize that the poor have no stake in that prosperity. "It's like," he said, searching for an analogy, "it's like if I say Rocky and I have $2 billion between us. He has $1,999,-999,999 and I have $1. That doesn't help me much. In fact, it often hurts."

In the blighted Nassau County community of Inwood near the Queens line, Mrs. Pat Jones, a mother of two and a welfare recipient, put it this way: "It's hard to be poor around a rich community. My kids are becoming aware of it now. I know it hurts them and I try to explain it won't always be this way and it's not that I don't want them to have nice things like the other children. But," she added, her eyes welling with tears, "the kids still know they get surplus food for supper and wear rummage sale clothes."

Nevertheless, for many of the reasons that middle-class suburbanites also cite, many poor still say they prefer the suburbs to the city. Mrs. Jones, who is separated from her husband, said that she could earn a much larger salary in the city, but the grass and air of the suburbs were better for the children.

Poverty in the suburbs was surveyed recently by *The New York Times,* with interviews concentrated in four key suburban counties —Westchester, Nassau and Suffolk in New York, and Bergen in New Jersey. For the purpose of survey statistics, the suburbs were defined as those four counties plus Rockland, New York, Fairfield, Connecticut, and the New Jersey counties of Hudson, Essex, Passaic, Union, Middlesex, Somerset, and Morris.

The Federal government defines "poverty" according to a sliding scale ranging from incomes of less than $1,600 for an individual to less than $7,800 for a family of 13. The most common indicator is less than $3,200 for a family of four.

A 1968 estimate by the Federal Office of Economic Opportunity put the number of poor families in the thirteen counties surrounding New York City at 179,750, or 6.9 per cent of the total number of families. By comparison, there were 347,420 poor families in the city then, or 12.5 per cent of the total.

Between 1960 and 1966, according to the Office of Economic Opportunity, the number of poor families in the suburbs grew by 35,126, and in the city by 81,075. The percentage of poor, however, dropped slightly, probably because of the large middle-class influx. Based on the 1960 census figures, the number of poor suburban families represents about 800,000 people.

As in the city and elsewhere in the nation, poverty in the suburbs afflicts a far higher percentage of nonwhites than whites. Because of the overwhelming white majority in the suburbs, however, there are many more impoverished whites than Negroes there.

In 1960, when the census provided the latest statistics according to race, there were in the thirteen counties 487,248 poor whites and 144,968 poor nonwhites, almost all Negroes. But on a percentage basis, the picture is different. Westchester, for example, found that while one of every sixteen white families lived in poverty, the percentage for nonwhites was one of every four. Similarly, a 1964 study of Westchester welfare recipients showed that while Negroes made up about 6.2 per cent of the county's population of 875,000, they accounted for about half of the welfare population of 7,891. Since then, throughout the suburbs the influx of Negroes and Puerto Ricans has been increasing and the number of people on welfare rolls has been rising sharply.

Housing remains one of the most critical problems of the suburban poor.

"How many people would you say are living in there?" John Kearse, the director of the Inwood antipoverty office, asked a colleague as they drove past a shabby loft over some stores.

"Oh, I don't know, ten or fifteen," said the other man, deliberately guessing high.

"I didn't ask families, I asked people," Mr. Kearse replied.

All over the suburbs, potential sponsors of low-income housing projects face zoning battles against residents who fear reduced property values and higher taxes to support more school children, if apartments were allowed in.

Meanwhile, deteriorating buildings torn down in renewal programs are not necessarily replaced. In a study last fall, the West-chester Urban League found that fourteen urban renewal projects in the county involved the demolition of 4,217 housing units but at most the construction of only 3,422 new units. Such arithmetic has led some Negro leaders to refer to Urban Renewal as "Negro removal." They charge that the projects are an attempt to drive the poor out of the community.

In Bellport, Suffolk County, where the Long Island Railroad tracks separate an almost all-white, middle-class population on the shore side from a mostly Negro and Spanish-speaking neighborhood of small, rented wooden homes, a white resident stopped polishing his car and squinted into the afternoon sun across the tracks.

"The welfare put them there," he said. "I guess it was the expedient thing to do. We have to live with it. We try to do things for them, but they don't want to help themselves."

On the other side of the tracks, a Negro woman looked back. "They know we're here, but they try to ignore us," she said. "They're too wrapped up in their everyday problems to worry about the poor."

Inadequate public transportation in the suburbs is another common complaint among the poor. In Inwood, Mrs. Charlotte Saunders, an eighty-seven-year-old widow on welfare, who was relocated three weeks ago after twelve years of living in a ramshackle flat without a shower or bathtub, said she did her shopping once a month in a supermarket. She would have preferred to shop at another store, she said, but the one she patronized was only a 50-cent cab ride each way, while the fare to get to the other supermarket was $1. And without adequate bus service, the taxi fare was an important factor in her budget, she said. A special morning and afternoon bus service to major job areas to spur employment was started recently in the Inwood area.

Antipoverty leaders and the poor also complain that social services in the suburbs are often undeveloped and unsophisticated. In Hackensack, Bergen County, Walter Wiggins, a worker in a paper carton factory and the father of eight children, complained that every time he gets a raise, his public housing rent goes up.

"Last year," he said, "I was earning $83 a week and paying $72 a month rent. In January I get a raise to $88 and my rent goes up to $88. I can't afford to get a raise any more. It would just go to raise my rent."

Suburban welfare departments have watched uneasily as their caseloads and budgets have mounted sharply. Between 1962 and 1967, the number of welfare recipients rose 133.6 per cent in Nassau, 130.8 per cent in Suffolk, 133.9 per cent in Rockland, and 88.3 per cent in Westchester, compared with an increase of 96.4 per cent in the city, according to a study released in December 1967, by the International Brotherhood of Teamsters as part of its campaign to have the state take over all welfare programs. The increase, Westchester Welfare Commissioner Louis P. Kurtis told alarmed county officials, was due to "increasing numbers of low-income Negro and Spanish families" and new attitudes and techniques of reaching out to find people in need of help.

Some of those techniques in the suburbs have been successful. In Hackensack, the Bergen County C.A.P. brings "meals on wheels" to fifty-six aged poor once a day. The Westchester Community Opportunity Program, the closest thing the county has to a countywide antipoverty agency, has sent about twenty poor youths to college. Westchester also formed in April 19, 1968, a Westchester Coalition of business, government, and civic groups to attack blight and aid those who have nowhere near the county's average household income of almost $14,000 a year.

But antipoverty efforts in the suburbs, as in the city, are handicapped by a shortage of Federal funds, the antipoverty officials say. And the suburban poor, as a weak-voiced minority, have little of the political leverage of those in the city to demand more aid. Some suburban communities, including Rye in Westchester, have rejected urban renewal and other Federal funds for fear of Federal interference in local affairs.

Meanwhile, the contrast between the suburbia of the popular conception and the other suburbia of the poor remains striking. In the office of the White Plains antipoverty agency, several blocks from the glittering downtown of the increasingly prosperous small city that is Westchester's county seat, a visitor was taken aback recently when an antipoverty official casually flicked from the visitor's shoulder one of the office's large, fearless cockroaches.

The "Invisible"
White Poor of Suburbia

by Thomas A. Johnson

MRS. LINDA NORTH sat in her kitchen—a room empty except for a stove, refrigerator, and a second-hand table with two old chairs—and explained why poverty is so often "quiet," "hidden," or "voiceless."

"People treat you differently if they find you're poor or on welfare," Mrs. North said. "I have friends who never tell. Some landlords will evict you if they find out." Mrs. North, who lives with her three young children on tree-lined Spruce Street [in Plainfield, New Jersey], said she had learned this lesson first-hand when her husband, a welder, abandoned her a year ago.

Mrs. North is white, as are more than two-thirds of the nation's poor. And the poor in the New York, New Jersey, and Connecticut counties sending large work forces into New York City come close to the national average. Poor families—those earning less than $3,968 a year—total between 7 and 10 per cent of the suburban population. The national average is 6.3 per cent.

Many have lived in poverty for years, untouched by the affluence of other parts of the society. But the number of the poor has been growing as the economic recession has cut into employment, forcing families into welfare.

"Many poor people are afraid because most people think if you're on welfare you are lazy," Mrs. North said, as if she could dispel the myth. "They think we're having a good time, rolling in money—living off the cream of the land. I wish I could tell them how I can't get treatments for my son—he's slightly retarded— because I can't travel to the clinic; how we have to do without so many things for my children."

The white poor in the suburbs are quite often "the invisible poor." They often live in neat, working-class communities or along country roads or near waterfronts of old farming and fishing communities, away from well-traveled routes.

The nonwhite poor are much more obvious, because they are most often restricted to segregated housing in areas long defined as black or Puerto Rican districts.

In addition, the commuting suburbs contain some historically impoverished groups like the Poospatuck and Shinnecock Indians of Suffolk County and the hundreds of families of the "triracial"— white, Negro and Indian—community in the Ramapo Mountain area of Ringwood, New Jersey.

The majority of the antipoverty programs are in the obviously poor and nonwhite areas, and the white poor generally are reluctant to participate.

Charles B. Tisdale, the black director of Action for Bridgeport (Connecticut) Community Development, and Miss Carol Harrow, a white field worker for the Bay Area Community Action Program in Center Moriches, Long Island, both said the large numbers of poor whites in their areas feared a loss of "whatever status" they had.

"A lot of whites from Grumman and other places have been laid off and are feeling it bad," Miss Harrow said. "They're finding it's no joy ride to be on welfare, but they are much frightened by the welfare 'image' of people thinking they're drinking, partying, and driving around in Cadillacs."

A white housewife from Levittown, Long Island, who would not allow the use of her name, told of other fears: "You're scared the car will break down and you won't have money to fix it and you're afraid the welfare worker who visits will be known to the neighbors —or be black."

If the welfare worker were black, explained the woman, who works in a department store to supplement the welfare payments, neighbors might also think he or she were looking for a house to buy. Many of the problems of being poor in the suburbs and the city are, of course similar. The housing of the poor is mostly aging and crumbling for example, and suburban leaders generally insist that new public housing be kept within traditionally poor areas. Construction and land costs for moderate private housing in the suburbs run to about $34,000 and require the buyer to earn at least $15,000 a year.

But mobility is a special problem in the suburbs. There is generally little or no public transportation available to reach jobs or get health care. What public transportation there is provides for the daily round trips commuters make to and from jobs in Manhattan, and automobiles are essential travel within suburbs.

Many private physicians and dentists will not treat welfare recipients, complaining that it is too time consuming to process papers for payment from welfare agencies. Welfare clients and others who depend on government agencies to pay medical bills often have to travel to public hospitals or special health centers.

Frank Melendez, a twenty-seven-year-old unemployed punch-press operator in Center Moriches, like many of the poor in the suburbs, has experienced difficulty in each of these areas since losing his job three months ago.

"I had a job for a couple of days last month as a sheet-metal worker trainee but there was a mess up in the welfare check," he said. "The check was for rent and to buy food and the welfare people had me coming to their office for five days straight and I lost the job."

Mr. Melendez, who has seven children, lived in Manhattan as a child until his machinist father moved to Long Island. His wife's family has lived in Islip, Long Island, for generations.

The family moved into the eleven-room frame house that the Suffolk County Welfare Department found for them at 39 Railroad

Avenue in Center Moriches and they used $100 of a $300 check
the department gave them for furniture to buy a 1964 Pontiac
sedan.

"I need the car to look for work," Mr. Melendez said. "I would
need it to report to the welfare and employment office."

Mr. Melendez said that after futile job hunts for many days he
had started caulking the large, frame house's many windows and
doors.

"The man who brought oil for the hot water said he usually
brings 100 gallons of oil every ten days for this house during the
winter," Mr. Melendez said. "That's $80 a month. We have to
cut down on the heat escaping before winter comes."

Mr. Melendez attended college for a couple of semesters while
working full time. "But when you support a family," he said, "you
have to give up school for a while."

The biggest fear of the Melendez family is that one of their
children, ages two to eight, would get sick. "We can't go to the
doctors here with a simple cold," Mrs. Melendez said. "They will
not take welfare people and the nearest hospital that does is in
Bayport," some fifteen miles away.

It was sickness that forced the family of John and Katie O'Neal
of 303 Grant Avenue, Plainfield, New Jersey, onto the relief rolls.

Mr. O'Neal works as a laborer most of the time—"until his
stomach ulcers get so bad he has to stop," Mrs. O'Neal said recently. She had worked in a factory in nearby Edison before the
birth of her eighth child six months ago. She has a bill of $2,300
from Somerset Hospital for the delivery.

"I don't know how we will pay it," she said. Her husband earns
$100 a week "when he works," she said, and the Welfare Depart-
ment sent them a letter saying "we're not eligible because my husband's working." Their oldest child is fifteen years of age.

L. G. McAffee, director of Community Action-Plainfield, assigned a community organizer to appeal for reinstatement of Mr.
O'Neal on the relief rolls because of his low salary. He said that
many of "the poor are proud people who don't want to show
poverty—and they're so often overlooked and uncared for."

Mrs. O'Neal, who had lived in rural Franklin County, Virginia,
until the family "moved north to try to do better," said that "it's

worse here than in Virginia." Like many of the suburban poor, Mrs. O'Neal and her family have never traveled to New York City.

Although the Federal antipoverty and housing programs in the suburbs have not come close to ending poverty there, several have helped to improve the futures of their mostly nonwhite participants.

The "How To," or Housing Operation with Training Opportunity program, seeks to help the "triracial" community of Ringwood build their own six-room ranch homes with Farmers Home Administration mortgages of $12,000. The same Federal agency has provided funds for two housing programs for the mostly black, former migrant farm laborers who have settled permanently in the Riverhead area of Suffolk County.

In Bridgeport, a bustling urban center like several commuting suburban cities, the black and Puerto Rican poor have begun efforts to control their own districts—most frequently, with the aid of antipoverty funds. One of the more dramatic programs there is Project Own, a redevelopment plan for the West End Neighborhood, prepared by the poor residents with the aid of professional planning consultants.

The organization has halted a city plan to bring industry into the district, which is now made up primarily of low-income housing projects, the city dump and a sewage treatment plant. The community plan calls for a shopping center owned by the community people, an industrial park, private housing and parks.

Joseph S. Kelly, chairman of the board of the West End Neighborhood Commission, said the city plan would have "brought factories up to our front door and big parking lots for suburban whites who got the better jobs."

While black community action is common among poor suburbanites, the majority of the poor—the whites—are seldom involved in such efforts in the metropolitan area. And the black and Puerto Rican officials in antipoverty agencies will make but the most cursory of efforts to involve them. "We try," they say officially, but unofficially many contend that whites can pull themselves out of poverty since they do not suffer from racial discrimination. "A white man's got no business being poor in America," is a common black expression.

John Poland, field representative of the Federal Office of Economic Opportunity in Westchester County, who has tried to involve many of the "white farm families left behind when the farms were abandoned," said they were "reluctant to acknowledge poverty problems, since they don't want the poverty stigma."

The stigma is real and while many myths of poverty have been often refuted, they persist in many parts of the suburbs and on many levels.

In Affluent Suburbia, a Problem Parents Only Whisper About

by Irene Backalenick

IT'S A commuters' town, population about 27,000, in southern Fairfield County. But Westport, Connecticut, could be any one of the upper-middle-class suburban communities across the nation. The good life is certainly here in Westport. Family incomes are high. The town has a string of sandy beaches that hug Long Island Sound. It has marinas and tennis courts and swimming pools and golf courses.

It also has narcotics problems.

It has been estimated that as many as three-fourths of the town's young people at one time or another have experimented with some form of narcotics, and that one out of five youths has had drug-related problems. Another estimate indicates there are perhaps as many as 250 heroin addicts in the town.

Only the tip of the iceberg that the narcotics problem represents emerges in the police arrests, the medical examinations, the hospital emergencies. Parents, protecting their children—and the family name—are parties to the secrecy. Money is available—for narcotics, for lawyers, for bonds, for covering bad checks.

From *The New York Times,* August 8, 1971, copyright © by The New York Times Company.

The statistics that do exist must be viewed cautiously. For example, the indication that three out of four Westport youngsters have first-hand knowledge of narcotics is based on a recent random questioning of young people by a Selectman's Committee for Youth and Human Resources that Westport officials set up to help deal with the drug problem. In another survey, conducted in a Fairfield County high school in 1969 by Dr. Nechama Tec, a Westport sociologist, about one in three students said he or she had used marijuana, while about 10 per cent more said they wanted to try it. As to hard drugs, almost 2 per cent said they had used heroin and about 10 per cent had tried such things as LSD and glue-sniffing.

Most people in the area working with the narcotics problem feel that Dr. Tec's figures are much too low and that, furthermore, the picture has changed considerably—and not for the better—in the two years that have elapsed. In short, there are hard drugs here, but no hard facts.

Allen Lewis, Fairfield County probation officer for the last ten years, estimates that narcotics abuse in the county surfaced in 1966, and has increased steadily since that time. Before 1965, for instance, there were few drug-related arrests in Westport. By 1969, the police made forty-eight narcotics arrests, of which four were for heroin or other opiates. In 1970, the total narcotics arrests rose to seventy, with twenty-two for heroin and other opiates.

"Today in Connecticut," Mr. Lewis said, "I would say without hesitation that 80 per cent of the people in prison under twenty-five are there on drug or drug-related charges."

Richard Bradley, director of the Selectman's Committee, said that young people no longer talk about using narcotics, that it no longer seems appropriate or necessary to them to brag about it. Mr. Bradley, who also heads the Drug Action Council, said he feels that the major problem is the indiscriminate experimentation and mixing of narcotics and alcohol, as well as the apparent heavy traffic in heroin.

What is it like to live with a junkie? Does affluence ease the burden or does it create new problems? The story of the Gannons (the name is fictitious) could be the story of any suburban family.

It is certainly the story of many with its mixture of bewilderment, fear, and pain; of ignorance, lies, and evasion; of confrontations and denials; of tearful scenes and promises made and broken.

The Gannons moved to Westport in 1967 from an Upper Westchester County community, attracted by the town and its convenience to Mr. Gannon's work. He is a communications executive in a nearby community. Their oldest son, Douglas, was fifteen and just entering high school. They also have a boy, then fourteen, and a daughter, then five.

"Doug was an average kid, a good football player," his father recalled. "He was a popular kid, had his own band." What Mr. Gannon didn't know was that before the family moved to Westport his son already had been smoking marijuana.

"From what I can see now, being new, he evidently sought out the kids who were the pot smokers," his mother said. Within a year Doug had progressed to hard drugs. "Doug had been going to Boston often with a gang of friends," Mr. Gannon said, "and one day he called us into the living room to talk to us. He said he had taken LSD in Boston and had had a bad trip. It had been recurring for several months and he was worried about flipping out."

Mr. Gannon was sympathetic. He was also uncertain how to proceed, but, at his son's request, he agreed to let Doug see a psychiatrist. Mrs. Gannon didn't want to face the fact at all of her son being an addict. "I sort of turned it over to his father," she said.

"Gradually, I started seeing other paraphernalia that I couldn't understand," Mr. Gannon said. "I found a strange-looking wire clip about two inches long in the bathroom wastebasket. I later learned that the clip was used to hold a bottle cap for melting heroin into liquid. I should have suspected he was on hard drugs, but I lied to myself constantly—that everything was going fine, that he was making progress with the psychiatrist, that he wasn't an addict, that he just had to be straightened out in his head. But all during this time he would be high right here in the house. He would spend long periods in the bathroom, making excuses that I would accept. I didn't really want to face it."

It was Doug's junior year. The telephone began to ring at all hours, often between 1 and 5 A.M. Strange youngsters would appear at the house. Five or six people would stay overnight in Doug's small bedroom.

"I would alibi to myself about that, too," Mr. Gannon said. "I'd tell myself, 'Those kids are homeless waifs on their way to Boston.' "

There were no family arguments then. It was a time of secrecy and evasion on both sides. "Doug conned us," Mr. Gannon said, "and we wanted to believe him."

Ultimately, the psychiatrist told the Gannons that their son was shooting heroin and that he could not help Doug unless he stopped. The time had come for direct confrontation, but the promises Doug made to stop were broken repeatedly. Then the psychiatrist moved to the West Coast and the treatments came to an abrupt end.

Now openly aware of Doug's addiction, the Gannons insisted that he must get help, but he said he could stop by himself. "Again we believed him," Mr. Gannon said. "He would come home with black-and-blue marks on his arm, and we would point to the marks, accusing him of using heroin. He would deny it, saying, 'No, that's an old one.' "

That summer Doug told his parents that he wanted to go to San Francisco, where he could attend a theatrical school and get his high school diploma. They agreed, and Mr. Gannon told him, "Don't come back until you're cured of the heroin." "There were no angry scenes, no arguments when he left," Mr. Gannon continued. "We really wanted to believe he was going out there to get the diploma."

The Gannons later found that Doug started shooting heroin as soon as he arrived in San Francisco, using not only his own money, but a sum he had collected from other addicts who had commissioned him to bring back a large supply of heroin. In the meantime, for the first time in months, there was peace in the Gannon household.

"It was summertime and we were able to go to the beach," Mrs. Gannon recalled. "For the first time in months we smiled. I remember that I would laugh, then catch myself suddenly when I thought of Doug."

For the first few weeks, Doug wrote regularly and then after two weeks of silence, the Gannons had a call from a boy in San Francisco. "He said he wanted to reach Doug right away because two guys were looking for him and wanted to kill him. He was accused of stealing a few bags of heroin and of breaking into an apartment."

Frantically, Mr. Gannon called the San Francisco police and, after a futile two-day wait, Mr. Gannon flew out to the West Coast city and began to search for his son himself. Carrying Doug's picture, Mr. Gannon moved through college campuses, the Haight-Ashbury section, the hospitals, the police stations. He stopped people on the street, showing them the picture of his son. The trail finally ended in a state hospital 200 miles north of San Francisco.

"I wanted to take him home that night, but I stupidly agreed to let him stop at Berkeley first," Mr. Gannon said. "He dashed out of the car, after telling me to wait at a street corner. Even after I had traveled that far I was still stupid. He was trying to swap his jacket for heroin. He came staggering back to the car, his mouth bleeding. They had taken the jacket and beaten him up instead of giving him heroin."

When Doug returned, the Gannons forced him to join Project Renaissance, a narcotics treatment center here. He lasted only a few days before he was thrown out because he would not stop using drugs.

Although the Gannons knew who Doug's friends were, they never contacted other parents. "We were still trying to keep this problem in the family, because we thought it was such a terrible disgrace," Mrs. Gannon explained. "We were so alone."

Doug never slept through a night. Neither did his parents. "He was up and down all night; the bed looked as if it had been slept in by an eggbeater," his mother said. "He would smoke all night, burning things. You would have to check on him."

That fall Doug was a senior in high school, enrolled on the books but rarely attending. By midterm he dropped out completely. During that time the tension mounted steadily.

"We would think he was in a treatment program because we would take him to one," Mr. Gannon said. "Then we would find out he wasn't going. . . . We were running him in and out of hospitals and programs all the time."

During this period, Doug was detoxified in Norwalk Hospital three or four times. He had hepatitis twice. He couldn't keep a job, even a part-time job, more than a few days. He began to steal, finally running into trouble with the police. He would be arrested and his father would bail him out. This, Mr. Gannon recalled, was the family's "yelling, crying, screaming stage."

Doug was fond of his little sister, who in turn adored him. When the shouting and battling began, she would run up the stairs, covering her ears and crying, "Stop yelling at my brother. Stop yelling at my brother."

Unsuccessful treatments followed at two state hospitals. And the thefts continued. "He would steal my checks and forge my name to $25 or $30 checks," Mr. Gannon said. "He stole my $90 watch and pawned it for $4."

Doug's relationship with his brother, which had once been close, deteriorated steadily "because Doug was in another world and nobody could have a conversation with him." Doug stole his brother's birthday money, his camera, and anything else he could pawn or sell. He even broke into his little sister's penny bank and stole $15.

"But I couldn't throw him out, even at this point," Mr. Gannon said, "because I was afraid he would kill himself on dope. I felt I owed him the responsibility of seeing him through this thing. I was frantic and I was doing everything wrong. Every time he was arrested I would go down and bail him out, although by this time my wife disagreed with me strongly."

Eventually the Gannons were carrying a heavy financial burden, with more bond money on their son than equity in their home. If he had run out on the bond, they would have been ruined. Finally, Mr. Gannon faced up to the inevitable. The next time Doug was arrested, he did not provide bail.

"He had to be put away," his father said. "There was no other way to stop him. . . . He never went more than seventy-two hours without shooting heroin." So Douglas Gannon, nineteen, was sentenced to two years in jail and two years on probation.

"He cried and I cried in front of him," Mr. Gannon said. "That experience was more frightening than going to San Francisco to find him. He looked very small and fragile and I knew he was going to jail and there was nothing I could do. I felt it was all lost."

When Doug made one last plea to his father, saying he wouldn't have a chance in jail, Mr. Gannon didn't weaken. "You don't have a chance on the outside," he told his son.

Mrs. Gannon can't forget her visit with Doug while he was in the North Avenue jail in Bridgeport awaiting transfer to Cheshire Reformatory. "It was a long room with a long desk, with the prisoners on one side and the visitors on the other," she said. "I noticed he had an infected finger and I said, 'Let me see it,' and naturally reached for his hand. The guard said, 'No touching,' and I pulled back, startled. It was such a sad and scary feeling. This was the first time somebody had told me that I couldn't touch a child of mine." Mrs. Gannon later learned that the "no touching" rule was because parents had been discovered passing heroin to their own children.

Cheshire was a turning point for Doug. A maximum-security prison for boys sixteen to twenty-one, Cheshire had a newly appointed director, B. J. Leverette, and a modern approach to rehabilitation. Doug spent four months at Cheshire, his attitude changing. He took the high school equivalency test, passing with high marks, and in June was transferred to a live-in drug rehabilitation facility in Massachusetts.

His parents are beginning to express cautious hope, but they agree on one thing: "We love him very much, but we don't want him back in our household with the same things happening all over again."

The Gannons do not hold the community responsible for their son's problem. "I think the drugs are anywhere," Mr. Gannon said. "Today's kids can find drugs in any town they go to. They can make a connection in less than an hour on hitting a town."

The Gannons and other parents like them have come to recognize the need for communication. "If there had been more public openness or awareness at the time we went through it all," Mr. Gannon said, "we would not have tried to handle it ourselves for so long."

One of the major problems is that parents tend, at all costs, to avoid admitting to themselves or to anyone else that their children are involved in drugs. To help counteract this, two strong parents' groups have emerged. Friends and Parents of Renaissance, in existence since Project Renaissance started in 1968, helps parents whose children are in the program, and provides information to anyone concerned about narcotics. HELP, sponsored by the Westport-Weston Ministerial Association, was begun a year ago and is geared specifically to the parents. "Parents come seeking a kind of verification, to determine if their child is involved in drugs and to see if they have a problem," says Edward Turchan, leader of the group. "Then we help them work out specific courses of action."

Part **5**

THE POLITICS
OF SUBURBIA

The Suburbs Are Strangling the Cities

by William Laas

SHORTLY BEFORE the Civil War, when the boundaries of New York City did not extend beyond Manhattan Island, a Democratic member of the park board named Andrew Haswell Green suggested that the time had come to unite "our harbor islands" into a greater city. To his shocked surprise the idea was savagely attacked. People called it "Green's hobby." In Brooklyn local autonomists formed a "League of Loyal Citizens" to defend the town's sovereignty. Politicians snickered as they knifed the repeated one-man campaigns for legislation or a popular referendum.

But Green was a persistent fellow. In 1898, after pragmatically making a political deal with Republican boss Tom Platt, he realized his dream. Manhattan, Brooklyn, Queens, Staten Island, and the part of Westchester known as the Bronx were consolidated into the five-borough City of New York. It was a triumph of social foresight, but by the time it came about it was barely adequate even for the New York of fifty years ago.

Today New York City and its circle of satellite communities stand in urgent need of another Andrew Haswell Green. Since 1900 the metropolis, spurred by the dynamics of the twentieth

From *The New York Times Magazine,* June 18, 1950, copyright © 1950 by The New York Times Company.

century and powered by electricity and the automobile, has exploded over the surrounding landscape. As O. Henry's 4 million swelled into Damon Runyon's 7, they pushed still other millions ahead of them into the open country. New suburbs boomed along rails and highways. Trade and industry followed.

Preliminary figures from the 1950 census make this trend strikingly clear. They show a relatively small rate of growth for New York and other major cities *within* the city limits and a huge growth *outside* the city limits in surrounding suburban areas. The suburban population of most large cities in this country averages about 50 per cent of the population within the municipal boundaries. Director of the Census Roy V. Peel recently took note of the phenomenal suburban growth. He said: "If cities want their population to keep going up, they are going to have to expand their city limits."

His observation goes to the heart of one of New York's biggest problems. During the twentieth century, everything has changed in New York except the city limits. They have remained as they were in the Gay Nineties—a fact which may ultimately spell ruin for the greatest city on earth.

Why, one may ask, is it so essential to expand New York City's limits of authority? What is the danger in our horse-and-buggy political setup? The answers have to do with handicaps placed on the whole of the metropolitan community—not just the core of it— by the myriad of political barriers. These handicaps are strangling the central city and at the same time are preventing any effective planning for development of the suburbs.

Today New York City is the life-giving focus for an area larger than Connecticut and more populous than Canada. Five-borough New York covers 365 square miles of land and has a resident population approaching 8 million. Around it in a fifty-mile circle is a suburban territory comprising nearly 500 separate communities. For Federal Census purposes the New York metropolitan district consists of seventeen counties: the five in the central city, four more in New York State and eight in New Jersey. The more realistic Regional Plan Association's metropolitan "region" consists of twenty-two counties covering about 7,500 square miles and more than 14 million people, of whom at least 6 million live outside the city proper, on 95 per cent of the land. Greater New York is thus in effect a twentieth-century urban empire. In it the central city represents the "motherland" and the 500 suburban cities, towns and other communities represent "colonies"—all with a common stake in the regional welfare. But, unlike some colonies, these have not been "exploited" by the parent city. Quite the contrary.

By the peculiarities of local government, the outer neighborhoods of commuting New Yorkers—comprising 40 per cent of the total population and increasing daily—are living on the life-blood of the central city without contributing the nourishment so necessary to sustain it. The city must provide costly facilities that are used by nearly twice its own population, but it can tax only those persons and properties within its limits. Moreover, it can organize and control only the rather small part of the area's public services which function within the five boroughs, although its life may depend upon what happens outside this area of control. Meanwhile, as outlying communities grow inevitably into urban centers themselves, they find it increasingly difficult to provide urban services out of county taxes. What happens is that the demands upon city and upon suburb become quite impossible to meet as separate undertakings. The disunited metropolis cannot pool its resources, share expenses, streamline operations or coordinate its facilities and land use for the greatest common good.

No modern city is immune to suburbitis, but few can match New York's complication. The basic complication is the split of the metropolitan district among three state sovereignties—New York, New Jersey and Connecticut. The most baffling is the number and variety of the suburbs, comprising 486 separate municipal authorities and additional unincorporated centers.

The confusion has been further compounded by an intricate system of private and public pseudo-governments. These are the so-called ad hoc, or special-purpose authorities, set up in efforts to meet the most pressing needs of the hodge-podge of small communities. Superimposed on the suburban municipal patchwork is a maze of taxing districts; school, library, water, sewage, highway, park, hospital, and welfare districts; parkway and public service commissions; the Port Authority and other technical bodies; police, fire, paving, and sanitation jurisdictions, building codes, zoning laws, and heaven knows what else. The typical suburbanite seldom can say where one boundary ends and the other begins; he is sometimes hard put to it to explain just where he lives.

Such is the nature of the disease. Let us now examine some of its effects.

The political "atomization" of the metropolitan district has steadily piled increasing burdens on New York proper in both fiscal and administrative fields. Taxes are high, especially in Manhattan, in part because of the necessity of providing facilities for suburbanites who pay little or nothing toward their cost. At the same time many of the city's basic facilities are subject to outside control. Albany, not New York City, has the final say on the city's bus franchises and utility rates. The Port Authority has no control over railroads, piers and harbor installations, which are the nucleus of any port. Local transportation to and from New Jersey and Connecticut is subject to the regulations of interstate commerce.

The political disunity is responsible, at least in part, for the fact that New York City's billion-dollar budget—second in size only to the Federal budget—is chronically a deficit operation. Some of the more expensive projects, such as highways, water supply, transit improvements, and public housing, have had to be heavily subsidized by state and Federal funds or by huge borrowings. Thus most of the 6 million nonresident users of the city's facilities pay their way only indirectly, through state and Federal taxation. Bridge tolls, the increased subway fare, the hotel tax, and the city sales tax are efforts—all with grave disadvantages—to shift some of the crushing burden to those who make their living in the city but pay their taxes elsewhere.

The city's resulting high tax is an incentive, in turn, for intensive land use, meaning bigger buildings and more congested industries. While some sections of the city suffer blight and loss of tax values from the exodus of population to the suburbs, other sections are perforce overdeveloped to take care of the daytime nonresident workers. The end products are more traffic, more subway jams, more smoke, more packing in of people—and additional expensive facilities to ease the strain. Manhattan, with a resident population of 2 million, is host every weekday to 3.5 million others whose goings and comings not only create the paralyzing traffic and transit congestion but add immensely to the problems of water and food supply, waste disposal, police protection, and all the rest.

In the outlying areas the effects of political disorganization are somewhat less apparent than in the city, but in the long run they are no less serious. On the surface it may seem that the city dweller who moves to the country is beating the city tax rate (which he has been paying either directly or through rents) while gaining the suburban blessings of space and greenery. But actually he is often in for a lot of unexpected headaches.

Small residential communities, unless populated entirely by the wealthy or balanced by resident industry, can rarely afford the stiff cost of services which become essential when large numbers of people live closely together. The plight of "bedroom" towns that are suddenly called upon to provide paving, lighting, sewers, police, schools, and other services for a horde of cliff dwellers from the city is a grave one. Nor can minor communities reach a hundred miles into the mountains for a good water supply, as a big city can. Some of the postwar mushroom towns have been unable to afford such a commonplace utility as cooking gas.

There are, it is true, a number of lovely oases in Westchester, Essex, Nassau, and elsewhere, but even they have their municipal troubles. Growth affects the most exclusive suburb. Space disappears into subdivisions; the trains fill up; traffic thickens; parking in the village center becomes a nuisance; beaches are polluted; prices rise and taxes soar. Eventually the home owner, who quit the city in the hope of drawing a Wall Street salary while paying a farmer's taxes, may find himself paying Wall Street taxes for Tobacco Road services.

Granting that green lawns and sunshine are better for children than asphalt and exhaust fumes, and that unplanned "urban sprawl" can be as fearsome as a lava flow, the fact remains that the attempt of suburbanites to hold back the normal expansion of the metropolis simply doesn't come off. They may temporarily achieve their private Utopias, but in the long run they cannot escape the overlying public problems of the region. No suburban community can be an island to itself. The lack of regional financing and planning impairs the communal health and progress of outlying towns quite as much as it impairs the city's. Today's pretty suburb, unable to cope with problems larger than itself, can degenerate into the bungaloid slum of tomorrow.

This being so, what are the obstacles that prevent a rational unification of the urban empire for the mutual benefit of its inhabitants? The primary obstacle is a deep-seated suburban distrust of big cities and their mass electorates. The typical suburbanite wants to avoid the crowding and impersonality of city life; he wants a pleasant home in a quiet neighborhood. To protect his investment and way of life he wants a direct voice in local politics. He tries to build a fence against the physical and economic encroachments of the city. This is the psychological basis of "suburbitis."

A result of such thinking is the political device known as "home rule." It is no accident that the Republican party can count on New York's solid suburbs as surely as the Democrats can count on carrying the city. By gerrymandering his districts the suburbanite manages to outvote the city in the state legislature and through home rule to erect his artificial obstacles to normal city growth.

The principle of home rule is a constitutional prohibition of "special acts" by a State legislature aimed at abolishing a particular local office or altering a local charter. Such changes must be initiated and approved by the local electorate, which is often restricted in such cases to property owners. In New York State there is both local home rule and a special kind of county home rule for the benefit of Westchester and Nassau counties. Behind the status quo are various vested interests. One might be termed the Ward Heelers' Mutual Association for the Protection of Paying Jobs. Another is the industrialist who finds local political machines more amenable than city ones. But by far the strongest interest is the determination of the suburbanite to avoid the city's physical conditions while enjoying its economic benefits.

This is an understandable human urge but a negative and short-sighted political theory. Over the long pull the real solution for the suburbs, as for the city, is some form of metropolitan unity based upon geographical facts. Since the New York region is truly one giant community, not 500 little ones, it should be governed by a single political structure. Since its parts are many and various, the structure must be democratic in form. Political unity would not only effect savings by cutting out the senseless duplication and waste, not only permit construction of adequate facilities as populations shift and living habits change. Most important of all, it would make possible a scientific administration, planning, and development of the metropolis as a whole.

If population shifts are planned for and intelligently balanced, the baffling problems we have described need never arise. Urban *sprawl* can be prevented but not urban *growth*. The wise suburbanite seeking to protect his future will accept that growth as inevitable and join in a system of controlling it. This is the positive cure for suburbitis and indeed the only one.

What are the prospects for such a solution? It must be admitted that at present they seem very slight. Attempts to break down the thousand and one spite fences that block unification run into almost insuperable difficulties. So far the efforts made to cope with the headaches fall far short of a comprehensive cure and create new problems almost as troublesome as the old ones. Three lines of attack are currently popular:

(1) The transplanting of stores and industries from the city to outlying areas to lessen congestion and lower costs.

(2) Creation of technical, nonpolitical metropolitan "authorities" to supervise certain bistate or tristate activities.

(3) Unification of municipal enterprises by counties, or by agreement among neighboring towns.

All are open to objections. The first is merely a special form of urban sprawl which spreads congestion and deprives New York City of sources of tax income. The second creates still another layer of overlapping governmental boundaries. The third, although of some benefit to local communities, is at best a stop-gap arrangement that does not strike at the roots of the problem.

Charles R. Merriam, Chicago political scientist, has proposed a more drastic measure as a general cure—the creation of city-states, with the same sovereign powers as the present forty-eight states of the Union, out of the larger metropolitan areas of the nation. Thomas H. Reed, leading municipal consultant, thinks cities should be allowed to grow politically to their proper size by the simple annexation of suburbs, as is permitted in Virginia by state law. But although many campaigns for this privilege have been waged in other states, only two have succeeded—Denver in 1916 and Baton Rouge, Louisiana, in 1949.

It would be unrealistic to assume that New York will in the near future find a way out of its dilemma. There is little likelihood that it will follow the lead of London, which has set up a single authority over all regional problems—a kind of urban T.V.A.— and plans to shift thousands of city dwellers to a belt of self-contained small towns.

New York's one real hope lies in the almost forgotten example of Andrew Haswell Green. Common sense always has its faithful and persistent advocates. In the end even the strongest obstacles established by custom give way to progress when the handicaps become intolerable to a sufficient number of enlightened and influential citizens. The thirteen original states surrendered a measure of their sovereignty to a new Federal government when they found the cost of autonomy too high. In our own time we have seen the same principle evolving on a worldwide scale in the concept of the United Nations.

Perhaps experience as a world capital will eventually prod Greater New York into governing its own huge urban empire. Year by year traffic congestion, smelly rivers, fiscal squeezes, business difficulties, and just plain discomfort produce more glaring evidence of the inability of petty governments to serve a modern people well. Things probably will have to get a good deal worse before they get better. But in a democratic society there is always reason to believe that time and pressures will force a workable compromise between isolationist home rule and metropolitan necessity in this air and atomic age.

Counterattack
by the Cities

by Richard Reeves

RECENTLY ARTHUR NAFTALIN, the former mayor of Minneapolis who is now a professor of public affairs at the University of Minnesota, told the Congress of the National League of Cities that the time had come to give up and admit that "the future belongs to the suburbs." Then he half-seriously told the assembled mayors to "throw themselves upon the mercy of their adversaries . . . claim the entitlement of any vanquished foe, which in their case is to be rescued and rehabilitated by their adversaries."

Two recent developments in the New York area, however, may indicate that the strategy of the cities in the nineteen-seventies will not be to surrender but to counterattack—to try to use commuter taxes and legal actions against suburban zoning to force Scarsdale, New York, or South Orange, New Jersey, for example, to help solve the problems of the city.

Recently Mayor Lindsay began discussing a huge 1971–1972 municipal tax program that would require a commuter with a net income of $30,000 to pay $1,800 to the city in payroll taxes. Moreover, the Suburban Action Institute, a civil rights agency, filed a complaint with the Federal Equal Employment Opportunities Commission against R.C.A. The complaint, which could lead to a

Original title: "Counterattack by Cities." From *The New York Times,* March 8, 1971, copyright © 1971 by The New York Times Company.

suit in Federal court, charged that R.C.A. was discriminating against "brown and black employees" by moving a major part of its operations from the city to New Canaan, Connecticut, a community with zoning laws that prevent the construction of much housing for employees who earn less than executives do.

Those two actions seemed to be part of a developing pattern across the country as big-city mayors and other urban interests, such as the National Committee Against Discrimination in Housing, press for a significant change in the relationships between city and suburb—a relationship that the 1970 Census confirms is essentially rings of white middle-income Americans surrounding deteriorating central cities, where the white suburbanites may work but where poorer blacks and Puerto Ricans are forced to live.

The higher commuter taxes being sought by Mr. Lindsay and others are designed, of course, to tap some of the relative wealth of the suburbs to help pay for coping with welfare, crime, and other problems associated with a lower-income urban population.

The zoning complaints and suits—Mahwah, New Jersey, Blackjack, Missouri, and Concord Township, Pennsylvania, are recent targets—are aimed at such suburban traditions as zoning most of the community for homes on one-acre sites. Such zoning screens out many people who earn less than $30,000 a year—and naturally it screens out the overwhelming majority of minority-group families. The complaint against New Canaan (which has an average annual income household of $24,073) is typical of the new zoning suits. It maintains that if the town changes its zoning laws to let in new business—the 254-acre R.C.A. tract is now a nursery—it must change the regulations prohibiting construction of apartment buildings and cheaper houses on small lots.

The suburbs' reaction to commuter taxes is simple—they are against them. And the Nassau County delegation in the state legislature has already united against the Lindsay plan. An increasingly important part of their argument is that they need their own money as the old problems of the cities—welfare, crime, drugs, and traffic —become the new problems of suburbs.

The reaction to zoning actions is more complex because many suburbs want new industry and business to come in and pay property taxes, but they don't want their way of life changed. Talk of property taxes often dominates suburban conversations, and those conversations tend to go something like this: "We've got to get new industry to help pay the taxes. But we can't let in any more housing because that means more kids, and kids mean new schools, and schools mean higher taxes."

So some of the suburbs come hunting industry in New York City. As John F. McAlevey, supervisor of Ramapo in Rockland County, said: "The property tax occasions urban-growth dislocations because it forces suburban communities to seek industrial ratables, while at the same time trying to discourage the provision of housing for the people who work in the plants. And appeals to the good nature and selflessness of the suburban official or the suburban voter will be pointless if the economic cards are stacked the wrong way."

But there are also suburban voters who prize their way of life so much that they don't want the industrial plants either. "This is a pretty little town, and we want to keep it that way," said Ervin Bickley, Jr., president of the Citizens Committee for Continuing Conservation, a New Canaan group that wants to keep R.C.A. out.

Many people living in pleasant places feel the same way. A resident of Parkway Village in Queens appeared at a City Planning Commission hearing to protest a zoning change that would allow a thirteen-story apartment to be built near his home. "There are not trucks, there are not buses, there are not taxicabs running through here now," he said. "If you bring in a high-rise apartment there to satisfy clients, you overload the facility, endanger the community, you change its whole character."

That speaker was Roy Wilkins, executive director of the National Association for the Advancement of Colored People, which has started zoning suits designed to force suburban communities to accept low-income housing. Mr. Wilkins and Mr. McAlevey would seem to agree that people in the suburbs will not willingly take on the problems of the cities. Mr. Lindsay and other urban leaders are probably convinced of that, too—which makes it even more likely that commuter taxes and zoning suits will grow in the nineteen-seventies as cities try to pull back the resources, if not the hearts, of the suburbanites who have abandoned them by the millions since World War II.

The "Slurbs" Are Ahead of the Cities

by Fred Powledge

IT IS TIME for the cities to get mean and nasty. If the city-dweller's naked eye hasn't told him yet, the current flow of census material and political rhetoric are making it patently clear: The noncities are engaged in a major conflict with the cities, and the cities are losing. Politicians saw it coming a long time ago, and shifted to a suburban strategy, one designed to please the one-third of the population that lives in the suburbs.

Some of the suburbs have so many urban problems that they are in danger of losing their designation as suburbs. As Gail Miller and Donald Canty pointed out in a recent issue of *City,* what used to be called "suburbia" is now really two separate categories of noncity: the older, close-in suburbs, which now look more and more and more like the cities from which they once offered an escape, and the more recent housing developments beyond them— developments which some have tagged with the unpleasant, but apt, name "slurbs."

All this may help a city person rationalize his decision, be it voluntary or involuntary, to remain where he is, but it is not enough. It is time for cities to recognize that nobody's going to

From *The New York Times,* May 22, 1971, copyright © 1971 by The New York Times Company.

help them but themselves. They have got to become aggressive.

Cities that want it should press for immediate statehood. In New York, the idea has been in the talking stages for some years; now is the time for action.

Cities should set up special departments of legal redress that would attack legislation and governmental practices that deprive them of their equal rights. Such a department would not act passively, but rather would strike for the jugular vein of discrimination.

Cities should levy extra taxes against the outsiders who work in, befoul, and use their space. The taxes would be sufficiently fair that the slurbanites would call them discriminatory and confiscatory. Mayor John Lindsay's payroll tax, which would hit residents and commuters about equally, is a good step in this direction.

In anticipation of massive retaliation from the slurbs, which probably would take the form of blockades, cities should set up municipal air forces to bring food and other supplies in. New York would swap housecoats from the garment district, for example, for steaks from Kansas City.

While it would be unfair, and probably unconstitutional, to require municipal workers to live in the city, as some have demanded, it would be appropriate to reward those who do. Policemen, firemen, and sanitation workers, especially, who demonstrated their faith in the city by living there would be paid extra.

Cities should issue passports for their residents. The certificates could be styled after military medals—depicting, perhaps, an abandoned car rampant on a vacant lot of garbage. Motorists entering the city via expressways, bridges, and tunnels would be stopped by border guards; those without passports would be required to pay a fee. A driver traveling alone in a standard-size automobile would pay double.

The passports, far from being a form of repressive control on their holders, would entitle them to special privileges. Residents with passports could enter free of charge or for a small admission price city parks, libraries, museums, and concerts—all forms of recreation, entertainment, and cultural enlightenment partly or wholly financed by the city. Persons without passports would pay. This is not a revolutionary idea. The slurbs do it now with their restricted parks and beaches.

A passport would allow a resident to ride the subways and other forms of public transportation free. As the city achieved financial stability, the passports could be rigged to provide other benefits. They would be good for free air and tire repairs at city-run bicycle shops; magnetic strips embedded in them would unlock pay toilets and ring up free half-hours on parking meters.

In time, the passports would become extremely valuable possessions, and their misuse would have to be strictly forbidden. Any slurbanite convicted of forging or stealing a passport, for example, would be placed by the city authorities under a form of house arrest. He would be allowed to remain free in the city, but he would be required to live there for a specified length of time—say, six months or two temperature inversions, whichever came first.

Toward
a Suburban Coalition

by David A. Andelman

A NATIONAL SUBURBAN coalition designed to attract more attention to the problems of the suburbs was proposed to the executives of many of the nation's urban and suburban counties. Nassau County Executive Ralph G. Caso presented his proposal, a twenty-five-page document prepared over the last two months, to county executives gathered in Milwaukee for the annual convention of the National Association of Counties in July 1971.

Mr. Caso said that a projected major shift of national Congressional strength away from the rural and urban areas to the suburbs, on the basis of the 1970 Census, compelled the county leaders to band together as a counterweight to the Legislative Action Committee of the United States Conference of Mayors, headed by New York Mayor John Lindsay. The Congressional projection, apparently the first of its kind in the nation based on 1970 Census data, was compiled by the members of Mr. Caso's staff in Mineola, Long Island. It projected that in the 1972 Congressional elections, suburban areas will account for 165 seats in the House of Representatives, a gain of twenty-one over the present total, with the cities' representation dropping from 148 to 136 seats and rural areas' from 143 to 134.

"The balance of political power and influence should continue to shift to those political leaders who articulate and strive to maintain the suburban way of life an increasing number of national voters have chosen," Mr. Caso's report stated. "Unfortunately, from a suburban point of view, many pieces of Federal legislation still appear to concentrate on resolving problems which affect the suburbs by exclusively directing Federal attention and aid to either those rural or urban parts of the problem area."

The solution, Mr. Caso concluded, is the formation of a "suburban action team," representing the elected county executives of many of the major suburban areas. "I think it high time that the counties of this country get together on a united front to press for our own needs in Washington," Mr. Caso said. "We just can't sit back and let the cities walk all over us."

Among the major areas in which Mr. Caso said a suburban action team might take immediate action and make suggestions were the following: the national order of domestic priorities, the comparative advantages of revenue-sharing versus the Federal assumption of welfare costs, the effect of foreign-made supersonic transport planes in terms of noise pollution in major suburban areas and the "wetport" concept of building offshore airports in oceans and lakes. He said that new legislative proposals benefiting the suburbs might also be made in the fields of health maintenance, housing and development assistance, public transportation, federalization of welfare, education, pollution control, and law enforcement. He did not spell out any specific pieces of legislation he envisioned.

The proposals themselves point up a major shift within the National Association of Counties, an organization that for years has represented the rural areas that have formed the bulk of its membership. Now, however, the organization is "redistricting"— instituting a voting procedure based on the population of the county, rather than a one-county, one-vote system, which in the past has meant rural domination of the organization. Officials hope that this will make the body more responsive to the needs of the larger urban and suburban counties, enabling a suburban coalition such as that proposed by Mr. Caso to continue to work through the counties' group in its lobbying efforts.

1970: The Year of the Suburbs

by Jack Rosenthal

ONE DAY this year—it may already have gone unnoticed—the United States passes a major social and political turning point. On that day, according to census estimates, the nation's suburbs, with more than 71 million residents, become the largest sector of the population, exceeding for the first time both central cities (59 million), and all the rest of the country outside metropolitan areas (about 71 million).

In short order, this turning point will be translated into political power, with reapportionment of Congress and state legislatures based on the census. The changes are awaited gloomily by the nation's big-city mayors, already disillusioned with reapportionment ordered by courts. Legislators represent people, not trees or acres, the Supreme Court said in its historic decision of the nineteen-sixties, and joyful urbanists proclaimed the imminent salvation of the cities. At last, they believed, the iron grip of rural minorities on state legislatures had been broken. At last, city residents could command their rightful share of state power, concern, and funds.

They were only half right. The rural grip has been loosened.

Original title: "The Year of the Suburbs: More People, More Power." From *The New York Times*, June 21, 1970, copyright © 1970 by The New York Times Company.

The principal beneficiaries, however, have not been the cities but suburbs. They were both the most badly underrepresented in state legislatures and the fastest growing segment of the population.

The problem for cities has been that the swelling new crops of suburban legislators have generally been indifferent, even antagonistic, to the calls for help from tormented big-city mayors. "Reapportionment has suburbanized the legislatures," says Mayor Wes Uhlman of Seattle, "and the suburbanites are as hostile to the city as the farmers ever were."

That view, repeated in Denver this week by many mayors at their annual conference, is strongly supported by a survey made by correspondents for *The New York Times* in every state capital. At the same time, the survey disclosed, there may yet be an urban center swirling in the heretofore nonmagic lamp of reapportionment. Once-new suburbs are growing older, more susceptible to urban sympathy and support for urban remedies.

Even before reapportionment based on the 1970 census, suburban legislative power had mushroomed dramatically in every part of the country. *The Times* survey, which defined suburbs as metropolitan areas outside cities larger than 100,000 population, showed the following:

• In the forty-member California Senate, suburban representation rose from 18 per cent in 1960 to 47 per cent now.

• In the Minnesota legislature in the same period, suburban representation rose from 4 per cent to 21 per cent.

• In New Jersey's legislature, suburban representation was 25 per cent in 1950 and 32 per cent in 1960, and it is estimated to be 46 per cent now.

For the most part, these gains have been at the expense of overrepresented small towns and rural areas. In New York, however, it is the cities that appear to be overrepresented, an imbalance likely to be corrected as a result of the new census. Suburban Suffolk County, for example, is still represented in the state legislature on the basis of its 1960 population of about 600,000. The present population is estimated at 1.5 million.

In state after state, rising suburban strength has meant rising opposition to legislation benefiting cities. The most common victims have been measures to provide new tax revenues, educational support, and assistance for city-operated services like zoos and museums, which benefit an entire metropolitan area.

"The suburbs are where you are finding so much of the opposition to urban legislation," says Haven J. Barlow, president of the Utah Senate. He cited a legislative proposal last year for an optional sales tax increase, needed by Salt Lake City for increased fire and police protection. The bill died in committee, largely because of opposition from suburban and rural legislators. Cities suffered a parallel tax defeat in Minnesota in the 1969 legislative session. Suburban and rural legislators combined to stop a tax proposal, arguing that the cities should raise property taxes instead.

Urban observers regard this not so much as hostility as apathy and ignorance. Nonurban legislators, they argue, simply will not recognize that central-city populations are aging and that older people are less able to pay property taxes. In Minneapolis, they observe, about a third of all homeowners are at retirement age.

The setbacks cities have suffered in their efforts to obtain increased state aid for their hard-pressed schools are typified by California's 1969 legislative action. The Legislature appropriated about $45 million in extra funds for "low wealth" suburban school districts, but virtually nothing extra for big-city districts. An all-white Sacramento suburb gained twice as much in increased funds as the city, where 25 per cent of the school children are from minority groups.

Cities in different parts of the country have sought state assistance for facilities used by many noncity residents. For example, a bill was proposed in 1970 in the Missouri legislature to establish a metropolitan area cultural district to support the city zoo and art museum and the suburban science museum. The city facilities are paid for by city property owners, the county museum by private funds. Last month, the bill was defeated with fifteen of the twenty-six suburban legislators opposed or absent.

The larger subject of state aid to cities has been the subject of a two-year dispute between Governor Warren E. Hearnes of Missouri and Mayor A. J. Cervantes of St. Louis. "I just don't believe in revenue sharing," Governor Hearnes has said. "I don't feel we should tax McDonald County to pay for the problems of St. Louis."

Mayor Cervantes recently retorted that a state tourism booklet portrayed Missouri as "a kind of wildlife preserve peopled by hunters, woodsmen and fishermen. Clearly, someone is getting robbed and I think you will agree with me that it is the people of Missouri, who, in large part, are not forest rustics but city dwellers."

Dollars are only one of the reasons evident for suburban opposition to urban aid. "What seems destined to become increasingly the gut issue is black versus white. The core cities increasingly are turning black," says Walter de Vries, Michigan professor and former state official. "There is latent hostility and resentment," he believes, "merely because the cities have the problems—drugs, crime, housing—and make many of the suburbs' headaches."

Urban supporters make precisely the same point in arguing that suburbs should be allies, not enemies, of the city. They cite aging suburban municipalities bordering major cities—in some cases now indistinguishable from the cities. Such areas, they say, demonstrate that city problems cannot be quarantined within city limits. There are in different parts of the country signs that suburban legislators are moving toward cooperation with the cities—moving fast enough to make some authorities believe that suburban hostility is not a final result, but only a transitional stage, of the reapportionment revolution. These are some examples:

In Colorado, suburban and rural legislators have combined on several measures sought by Denver. But, says Allen Dines, a Democratic State Senator from the city, "we seem to be a lot less at each others' throats than we were even five years ago."

In Indiana, suburban-rural alliances have defeated revenue measures favoring cities, but in 1969, rural and some suburban legislators supported the successful creation of unified government for Indianapolis and suburban Marion County.

In Georgia, until two years ago, suburban legislators were regarded as enemies of urban legislation. But then city and suburban members joined in an Urban Caucus. The move was motivated at least in part because areas around Atlanta, including Cobb County, began experiencing many of the same traffic, pollution, health, and housing problems as the city. On one occasion the Urban Caucus secured the critical vote of a single rural legislator for an urban measure by giving him all of its eighty votes against a tobacco tax.

In Ohio, the "crabgrass brigade" of suburban legislators is regarded as just as conservative as the "cornstalk brigade" from rural areas concerning social issues like urban blight and welfare. But as elsewhere the "crabgrass brigade" evidences considerable concern about problems shared by cities and suburbs, notably police protection, housing and mass transit.

Such changes are a result not only of shifts in problems, but also of shifts in the type of legislators elected. In Ohio, older, conservative members have been supplanted by legislators who "are younger, brighter, and more aware," says Charles F. Kurfess, Republican Speaker of the House. They may not be more liberal, but "they are of a higher caliber and have a more progressive outlook," he says.

The combination of contagious problems and progressive suburban legislators may yet, in the view of urban authorities, vindicate the hopes expressed when the Supreme Court first ordered reapportionment. "Suburban legislators," says Herbert Fineman of Philadelphia, Democratic Speaker of the Pennsylvania House, "are for the most part still identifying with rural areas. They should be aligning themselves with the cities. They will eventually have to."

The Political Role
of the Elderly

by Linda Greenhouse

A HIGH SCHOOL bond issue defeated in Rye. A swimming pool referendum turned down in Bronxville. A petition for reduced bus fares that is signed by 10,000 people. Local candidates who show up at senior citizens' centers prepared for undemanding pleasantries and find themselves the targets of tough political questions. These are examples of the growing impact that the elderly are exerting on life in the suburbs. The examples are not always clearcut—vote tallies, of course, do not include the age of the voters.

But many people who work with the elderly, as well as many retired persons themselves, believe they see a definite trend toward an increased involvement of the elderly in issues that affect them. Some observers are even convinced that the elderly are about to emerge on the local level as the next major voting bloc. Among the factors that appear to be contributing to this trend are the following:

• Suburban residents have the chance to vote on school budgets and many other major appropriations. The financing of education by the local property tax means that the burden of rapidly rising school costs falls especially heavily on the people living on fixed

Original title: "Elderly Exerting Power in Elections in Suburbs." From *The New York Times,* February 21, 1971, copyright © 1971 by The New York Times Company.

incomes, trying to keep up their homes in the face of rising property taxes. Taxes of $1,500 a year on modest homes are not uncommon.

• Many people who might once have considered selling their homes and moving back to New York City when their children were grown are now deterred by the lack of housing there and by what they hear about city life, and so feel more or less trapped in the present circumstances.

• People are living longer and retiring earlier from careers that prepared them to take a more active interest in community affairs.

• Faced with the need to increase their tax base, a growing number of towns are opting for special zoning laws that permit the construction of apartments for the elderly while continuing to bar general apartment construction. The idea is that housing for the elderly will not bring more schoolchildren to the district. So substantial numbers of the suburban elderly will be living near each other for the first time.

• While the older members of this age grew up at a time when self-reliance was an exalted virtue and political protest was considered unseemly, those who are about to enter the retired group came from an era of quite different attitudes. They can be expected to accept the problems of old age with considerably less resignation.

It is, to be sure, a mixed picture. Perhaps largely for this last reason and because the suburban elderly are often isolated by long distances and the lack of public transportation, there has not been a rush to organize.

Groups of old people wearing buttons printed with "senior power" or some other slogan were probably just handed the buttons by an eager young social worker and will probably just as quickly lay the buttons aside when they get home. Also, many elderly people, especially as their health deteriorates, remain preoccupied with their own pressing problems and have little energy left over for community issues.

In a survey conducted two years ago for the Westchester County Planning Department, 48 per cent of those over the age of sixty-five, as contrasted with 28 per cent under sixty-five, answered "none" to the question of what additional facilities they wanted in their communities. Roy Gerard, the consultant who conducted the survey, interprets this response as indicating a high degree of alienation among the elderly, and an apparent belief that it is not within their power to solve their problems. And Daniel Sambol, associate executive director of the Westchester Council of Social Agencies, points out that "People who never cared about community issues in their lives don't suddenly start caring at age sixty-five, and, after all, they have the right not to care."

But on the other hand, the attitude of the newly aware elderly person is typified by Mrs. Julia Davis of Eastchester. A few months ago, Mrs. Davis, who is widowed, decided that it was time to do something about the price of public transportation. It cost her 45 cents to go by bus to White Plains, and 40 cents to go to New Rochelle. Using her local senior citizens center as a base of operations, Mrs. Davis drew up a petition asking for half-fare bus rides for senior citizens between the hours of 10 A.M and 4 P.M. She circulated copies of the petition to more than sixty senior citizen centers throughout the county. To date the petitions have collected about 10,000 signatures, with more still coming in. Mrs. Davis plans to present her petitions to the county government, which this year for the first time has a department of transportation with the power to regulate bus service in Westchester.

"A few years ago I wouldn't have done this," Mrs. Davis said. "A few years ago we all would have just sat back. But we're just being pushed to the limit, and it's awfully hard. When it's hitting the pocketbook, everyone starts to wake up. We're not demanding much. Just something to make us feel as if we're getting something after all these years of building Westchester up. We just like to let them know we're still around."

If widespread organization is lacking, one indicator of the growing impact of senior citizens is their unwillingness as individuals to leave the decision-making to someone else. Last December, voters in the town of Rye turned down an $8.4 million bond issue for a new junior/senior high school. What was surprising was the turnout—more than 95 per cent of those eligible voted, in a town which in the past has seen turnouts of ninety voters for school budget elections. There were not many elderly people in School District 5, which takes in about half of Rye town. But the referendum vote was close, 1,167 to 1,074, and it was widely believed on both sides that the elderly voters made the difference.

"We played to our strength," said Bernard Abel, a local newspaper publisher who organized the opposition campaign. He said that his committee's mailing went to all 1,400 homes in the district, but that the phone calls and other special attentions were for those voters who no longer had children in school. In several cases members of his group drove nursing home residents to the polls to register them and again for the actual election.

"It was a case of people feeding on the problems of the elderly," said Dr. Jack Kabcenell, the school board president. "I'm sure if this had not been the case, the referendum would have passed."

In general, school administrators are reluctant to talk about the role of the elderly in budget defeats, not wishing to alienate this segment of their constituency any more than necessary. But all expressed sympathy with the elderly voters' plight. "Frankly, if I were of retirement age, I wouldn't have voted for the budget either," one superintendent said. "It's a question of survival."

It is not a question of elderly voters suddenly becoming anti-education. Rather, those who might once have stayed home and not expressed themselves at all are now going to the polls. This is not the case everywhere, however; at the Osborn Memorial Home, a residence for 175 women in Rye, it is a "house rule" that the residents do not participate in school elections. "It's understood that since they do not pay property taxes, they should not vote," said R. Eugene Curry, the home's former executive director. However, most of the elderly voters in District 5 are home owners.

Joseph Conway, Westchester County's supervisor of senior citizen activities, says flatly that "senior citizens are responsible for most of the school bond issue defeats as well as for rejecting many other superfluous expenditures." Louis J. Belserene, Jr., outgoing president of the Westchester County School Boards Association, says that "it's reached the point where you can expect the resistance on any vote."

"What you have to try to do is to get the elderly to participate before the vote," Mr. Belserene said. "But that's difficult. It's very hard to get them to relate to the type of kid and to the laissez-faire structure in our schools today."

There is apparently a distinction between the older residents of a community who have lived there for many years and newer residents who have moved into suburban communities to retire. The latter, without strong links in the area, are less likely to participate. For example, the northern Westchester town of Cortlandt had an increase of more than 40 per cent during the last decade in its population over age sixty. But almost all of the increase was attributable to the construction of the Springvale Apartment complex, which has 1,000 retired residents. Town officials report that aside from the lifting of the town's tax base Cortlandt has felt little impact from the projects.

"We feel part of Springvale, but not really part of Cortlandt," said Mrs. May Burfiend, president of the Springvale Senior Citizens Clubs. "I guess we're sort of snobbish about it."

On the other hand, the 1,200 homeowners at Rossmoor, a retirement development in Monroe Township, New Jersey, had a decided say in the way the town is run because they do choose to participate. In a recent school board election, 40 per cent of the Rossmoor residents voted, as compared with a 5 per cent turnout for the rest of the town. Now two Rossmoor residents serve on the nine-member school board and another Rossmoor resident, George E. Maxwell, is the town's mayor. The town's total population is about 9,000. The Rossmoor vote is credited with defeating the township's $6 million school budget last month.

Many people believe that as the elderly become aware that they can have an influence they will look toward broader issues. Overcoming apathy is in some respects a matter of gaining confidence in their own abilities.

"I thought they should be more politically involved," said Mrs. Jeanne Blum, coordinator of the Senior Citizens Center in Eastchester, which serves 120 members from a tiny storefront. "At first, I found a very negative attitude of 'Well, what can we do about anything anyway?' But, then, we started badgering the housing authority for space in a new community room, and they listened to us. I called the mayor and said 'How about a paint job?' and we're being painted, and everyone's shocked."

Now, Mrs. Blum said, public officials appear at the center once or twice a month to answer questions. "They don't come here to make speeches; they come to listen," she said. "Of course, senior citizens are the next pressure group. It's a mental attitude. They no longer want to be relegated to playing checkers."

Senior citizens are also increasingly directing their frustration at nonlocal targets, such as the provision of the Social Security law that restricts Social Security benefits after $1,680 of earned income in a year.

"If we treated any other group of citizens this way, we couldn't get away with it," said Mrs. Selene Rosenberg, who fifteen years ago founded the Senior Personnel Employment Committee to help retired workers find jobs. She reports that a growing number of people are seeking work with the remark, "I thought I could make it on my Social Security and my savings, but I can't."

However, qualified workers occasionally have to turn down jobs that offer salaries high enough to jeopardize their Social Security benefits. "These people were brought up to believe that nice people don't march around waving banners," Mrs. Rosenberg said. "But they are getting desperate. They don't want assistance. They just want to be able to work and survive old age without indignity."

Dr. Kabcenell, the Rye School Board president, specializes in prosphodontics and sees many elderly patients in his practice. He believes that, especially with the retirement age dropping, the elderly are going to demand a reexamination of the quality of their lives, as well as their financial situation.

"Giving them more money to do nothing is not the answer," he said. "They're going to start saying no, we want something more. Needs change with age, but the need for self-respect never changes. We must make a concentrated effort to maintain their productivity rather than penalizing them for surviving past the age of retirement. People are going to start demanding their right to decide when they want to be called old." Dr. Kabcenell said that he detected in conversation with his patients a "definitely rising class consciousness" among the elderly. "What's lacking is some kind of leadership," he said. "All they need is a Martin Luther King and it could be a revolution."

"I wouldn't call it militancy yet," said Joseph Conway, who helps coordinate senior citizen activities through more than 90 clubs and centers in Westchester. "It's more of an educated involvement. We are still dealing with the generation 1900 to 1910. But the nineteen-twenties are coming up. They're going to be swingers."

The Changing Political Pattern

by Clarence Dean

THE NATURE OF political organization and leadership in the suburbs has changed, as have other elements of the suburban power structure. Fragmentation and dilution of power characterize the change. Omnipotent political bosses are disappearing. The Republican monopoly on suburban votes is declining. Being a Democrat is now respectable. New sources of power have come into being. The bedroom communities of yesteryear now house, or have nearby, large industrial organizations and vast highway shopping centers. The power of the banking industry has been altered by widespread mergers and by the multiplication of branches, some of them from New York City. The single local bank no longer is the financial pillar of the community.

All these aspects of the evolving suburbs are reflected in the change in the nature of political leadership. The era has passed when the late William L. Ward could rule Westchester as a benevolent Republican despot from his roll-top desk in Port Chester, or when J. Russel Sprague, now seventy-seven years old and ailing, was the unquestioned leader in Nassau. Mr. Ward, a wealthy manu-

Original title: "The Changing Political Pattern in the Suburbs." From *The New York Times*, June 1, 1964, copyright © 1964 by The New York Times Company.

facturer of nuts and bolts, a Quaker and a man of unquestioned probity, had no aversion to being identified as the boss of Westchester. For thirty-seven years he was. He filled county offices without hesitation, sometimes quite informally as he sat on the spacious porch of his home on a Sunday morning. He built the county's parks and its parkways and ruled out the proposed extension of the city's subways to Westchester. The county, he decreed, was to be "class instead of mass"—and so it has remained.

The present Republican chairman of Westchester is no such patriarch. A quiet-mannered apple grower from Yorktown, Theodore Hill, Jr., accepted the position with some reluctance; he felt, he says, he was needed there. One of the attributes that led to Mr. Hill's appointment was his talent, demonstrated as a member of the State Assembly for twenty-three years, in diplomacy and conciliation. "In politics today," he says, "you have to kiss your way along." As chairman, Mr. Hill succeeded Edwin G. Michaelian, who was also the County Executive. Dissension had arisen within the party over Mr. Michaelian and his dual office.

Another political power in Westchester today is the Democratic county chairman. A liberal, urbane in mien, William F. Luddy commutes to New York, where he operates a news service for retailers. He personifies the social acceptability that Democrats now enjoy in the suburbs.

In Nassau County, where Mr. Sprague, a lawyer and a master of political strategy, held the reins for twenty-four years, the change is visible, too. The Republican leader now is Joseph F. Carlino, a handsome, immaculately groomed forty-six-year-old lawyer from Long Beach. Nassau is not Mr. Carlino's only political interest. In Albany he serves as Speaker of the Assembly, and some of his critics say his heart is in the capital. But even at home Mr. Carlino does not enjoy the unchallenged authority that belonged to Mr. Sprague. Nassau now has its first Democratic County Executive, Eugene F. Nickerson. Mr. Nickerson reflects the change not only in being a Democrat, but also in his person. Ivy League, forty-five years old, Mr. Nickerson is a former corporation lawyer. Since his election in 1961, he has established a record of improved county government. His prospects for reelection this fall are considered bright. Allied with Mr. Nickerson is John F. English, the county

Democratic chairman. Mr. English is thirty-eight, a lawyer, and a tough in-fighter whose Irish blood boils readily.

Elsewhere in the suburbs, the political titans of the old era have passed without leaving counterparts—Supreme Court Justice Arthur S. Tompkins in Rockland, R. Ford Hughes and W. Kingsland Macy in Suffolk. Even in Jersey's staunchly Republican Bergen County, Walter H. Jones, the county chairman, does not approach the power held by his predecessors, John Dickerson and Walter Winne, whose regime collapsed in the gambling scandal of the early nineteen-fifties.

As strong political control has diminished in the suburbs, new sources of power have arisen through the development of industry and commerce. Long Island has the aircraft industry, Westchester has industrial giants like I.B.M. and General Foods, Bergen has Ford and Curtiss-Wright. Huge highway shopping centers have come to the suburbs. In Paramus, Bergen Mall and Garden State Plaza represent a total assessed valuation of $41.5 million. All of these, in some degree, exercise power and influence, but it is diffused and fragmented—in part because of absentee ownership of the enterprises. There is a parallel in banking. The movement toward merger of banks and the rapid development of branches—Nassau has more banks per capita than New York City—has made the locally owned suburban bank a rarity. Competition is sharp, and the mortgage seeker who once had no choice in banks now can shop around.

In all this change, a few vestiges of the old order remain, especially in the New Jersey suburbs. In Hudson County there is the taciturn, remote John V. Kenny, who broke the back of the notorious Frank Hague machine in 1949 and who has remained the Democratic helmsman ever since. And in Essex County there is Dennis F. Carey, described by friends and foes alike as a throwback to another era. He was elected in 1964 to his eleventh term as Democratic chairman of the county, which includes not only Newark, New Jersey's largest city, but also such well-heeled suburbs as Short Hills, Montclair, and West Orange. Now sixty, Mr. Carey has been politically active for forty years. The suggestion that his influence is very considerable he modestly disclaims, but *The Newark News* and others have been assailing him for years—

unavailingly—as the county's boss. Mr. Carey prefers to describe himself as "a business type of politician." He spends full time in his modest office on the sixteenth floor of the National State Bank building in Newark. Aspiring postmasters and others can be found waiting in the anteroom. Ruddy, white-haired, and dapper, Mr. Carey can be imperious and ingratiating in turn. He is given to aphorisms: "If you don't tell a lie, you don't have to remember so much." "It's better to say 'no' and have a ten-minute argument than to say 'yes' and have six months of grief."

In Mr. Carey's domain, the party organization turns out the vote with block-by-block precision. A problem is developing, however, with the rapid growth of Newark's Negro population, now estimated at 36 to 50 per cent of the city. An all-Negro slate was entered in the last election under the label "New Frontiers" and polled 10,000 votes. While Mr. Carey's strength is preeminently in Newark, he and the Democratic party have been helped in such areas as Montclair by a development common to all the suburbs, the increasing respectability of being a Democrat. "I remember the time when corporations wouldn't be found dead with a Democrat," Mr. Carey says. "Now they're in my office."

Nassau provides the conspicuous example in its election of a Democratic County Executive. A dozen years ago, Republican control in the county was so tight that new residents moving out from the city, many of them Democrats, were told pointedly they would be well advised to register as Republicans. Many did. Democratic respectability has grown in status-conscious Westchester, too. Mr. Luddy, the county chairman, believes it was forwarded greatly here by the eminent acceptability of the late President Kennedy and his wife. Local elections reflect the trend. The city of Rye in Westchester elected two Democratic councilmen in 1964 for the first time. Yorktown named a Democratic supervisor and two Democratic councilmen for the first time in sixty years. In state and national elections, Republican pluralities of 85,000 were once commonplace in the county; in recent years, they have been closer to 40,000.

The drift away from a monopoly Republican power structure in the suburbs is illustrated, although perhaps enigmatically, in Fairfield County, Connecticut. The home of many well-to-do commuters, Fairfield has long been a Republican bastion of Connecticut. But the voter registration figures now indicate 111,000 Republicans, 84,000 Democrats and 130,000 listed as "independent." The growth in the number of unaffiliated voters, which seems to have accompanied the decline in Republican allegiance and the increasing Democratic respectability, has engaged the attention of many political professionals in the suburbs.

John Regan, secretary of the Board of Elections in Bergen County and former Mayor of Edgewater, describes the change this way: "People tend not to commit themselves to parties any more. The electorate is more sophisticated, and people realize that there is no clearcut delineation of either major party. There are liberal and conservative elements in both." Other professionals, like Robert L. Bliss of New Canaan, Fairfield County Republican chairman, believe that the transiency that characterizes much of the suburbs is a factor. "People are transferred here by their companies for a while and then move on," he says. "They don't bother to affiliate with a political party."

Another element in the weakening of one-party power appears to be the decline in patronage opportunities. The era of tremendous development in the suburbs is past, most of the roads are built and the sewers laid. Municipal jobs are increasingly on a civil service basis, and the general prosperity has diminished the lure of moderately paid elective offices.

The diffusion and the dilution of power, politically and economically, that has come into the suburbs—the evolution of a predominantly rural and residential society into one increasingly urban—has led such students of the suburban power structure as Dr. Marvin A. Rapp, vice-president and executive dean of the Nassau Community College, to conclude that the structure no longer has clearly visible dimensions. "We are in a transitional period," Dr. Rapp feels. "The old power structure is passing and a new one is developing." If there is a dominant power in the suburbs today, it is probably government. And because of an increasingly sophisticated, independent electorate, suburban government today is more democratically based than ever before.

Part **6**

SUBURBIA
REVISITED

THE OUTER CITY: AN OVERVIEW

Suburban Turmoil in the United States

by Jack Rosenthal

RAPIDLY, RELENTLESSLY, almost unconsciously, America has created a new form of urban settlement. It is higher, bolder, and richer than anything man has yet called city.

Transfixed by the image of bedroom towns in the orbit of true cities, most Americans still speak of suburbs. But a city's suburbs are no longer just bedrooms. They are no longer mere orbital satellites. They are no longer sub. They are broad, ballooning bands, interlinked as cities in their own right. In population, jobs, investment, construction, stores, political power—all the measurements that add up to "urban"—the old inner city is now rivaled, often surpassed, by the new.

This is the Outer City.

And from its massive, centerless development, repeated again and again across the country, spring the most serious implications for the quality of urban life. In 1940, suburbs contained 27 million people, two out of every ten Americans; 19 million fewer than the cities. In 1971, they contained 76 million, almost four of every ten; 12 milion more than the cities that spawned them.

Once-rustic fringe villages now have their own zip codes, area codes, big league stadiums. They are the sites of luxury hotels and industrial plants, fine stores, and corporate offices.

In New York the population remains about equally divided between urban and suburban. But elsewhere the suburbs are already two, three, four times more populous than the inner cities they surround. Commonly, 40, 50 or even 60 per cent of those who live in a city's suburbs also work in them. Half or more of every retail dollar is spent in the suburbs. More than $8 of every $12 spent on housing construction is spent in the suburbs. About two-thirds of all industrial construction is in the suburbs, in the outer cities of the nation.

The suburbs are individual, diverse communities with a diversity of problems. In the distant exurban greenery, planners worry about how to channel new growth. In closer suburbs, officials struggle to show that age need not bring decay. In the closest, decay has already begun.

But taken together, the suburbs have, like New York's, become informally federated in many areas. Their residents use the suburbs collectively: as a city, a centerless city.

Mrs. Ada Mae Hardeman is a Californian who says she doesn't really know where she is from: "I live in Garden Grove, work in Irvine, shop in Santa Ana, go to the dentist in Anaheim, my husband works in Long Beach, and I used to be president of the League of Women Voters in Fullerton." She doesn't much mind. "I don't miss central-city pleasures out here in spread city. Honestly, I have to say I love it."

Now such independence of the city is being massively fortified with concrete. Broad highways already encircle ten large cities and will soon rim seventy more—the accidental new main streets of the outer cities. And the residents of the outer cities have become so independent of the inner cities that it is common to hear people brag that they haven't been downtown in months, even years.

Still, like many inner-city residents who think that the urban world revolves around downtown, they do not concede that the suburban rings constitute an alternate city. They prize the array of urban facilities of their outer city. But many, as in parts of New York's Westchester County and Northern New Jersey, still identify with the image of the pastoral town.

They are alarmed by the consequences of their own growth, like increasing density and pollution. But they still cling to the governmental forms of isolated villages. They are increasingly willing— even, surprisingly, in the most conservative communities—to endorse Federal action to assuage the poverty and blight left behind in the inner cities. But otherwise they shrink from these problems, often with indifference, sometimes with anger.

Tormented city officials, like Larry Reich, the Baltimore city planner, may denounce what they regard as unfairness: "The city of Baltimore makes the suburbs possible because we carry the burdens of the old, poor, black, and deviants. Why should we keep carrying the burdens?"

But in the suburbs, many people quote with unabashed candor the old troopship cry: "Pull up the ladder, Jack, I'm on board."

And the new outer cities continue—rapidly, centerlessly—to grow.

• For all the vitality of downtown Houston, the fashion center is not downtown. Tiffany's in Houston now is a block from the Loop beltway, one small segment of a $300 million retail, commercial, and hotel development called City Post Oak. Even in the twilight, the rows of plaza light globes, like luminous pearls, only soften the staggered concrete shapes behind them that stretch outward for eight blocks and upward for twenty-two stories.

• It was once second-rate farmland out amid the slash pine and red clay fifteen miles from Atlanta's old warehouse district. Now H. C. Pattillo, who calls himself merely a medium-size local builder, has developed an industrial park, serving local and national concerns alike. It contains long, low, attractive plants, 103 of them, on a 2,000-acre tract.

• Roosevelt Field, the lonely litle Long Island airport from which

Charles Lindbergh took off for Paris in 1927, is now the Roosevelt Shopping Center, one of the East's largest. In place of the tiny crowd that watched the Spirit of St. Louis disappear into the morning fog are the crowds of housewives shuttling from Macy's to Gimbel's.

• In Orange County, California, Newport Center, once a sprawling bedroom for Los Angeles, a vast alabaster oasis, gleams against the tan foothills near the Pacific. The floor space in the fashion stores and eighteen-story office towers already nearly equals that of Manhattan's Pan Am Building, and they are forty-nine miles from downtown Los Angeles.

"Everybody thinks a city needs to have a center," says Richard Baisden, a political scientist at the new University of California at Irvine. "Well, why does it? Downtown has ceased to have any real relevance. Its functions have dissipated and decentralized out to where the people are."

This decentralization is nearly complete. The barges, boxcars and industries that once gave the inner city its preeminence and jobs have not disappeared. But now they are rivaled by tractor-trailer rigs, beltways, and fork-lift trucks that make desirable such low-rent industrial plants as the Pattillo development in Atlanta.

The central cities, their variety of apartments, flats, and homes growing old, are no longer the sole or even the most desirable location of housing. For milions the automobile and Federal insurance for new housing in outlying areas have crystallized the American dream.

"The suburban house," says Edgardo Contini, a noted Los Angeles urbanist, "is the idealization of every immigrant's dream— the vassal's dream of his own castle. Europeans who come here are delighted by our suburbs, even by the worst sprawl. Not to live in an apartment! It is a universal aspiration to own your own home."

The movement of people in turn has sped the outward spiral of shopping, a movement so rapid that in some cities total suburban retail sales now far exceed those in the inner city. And now have come the circumferential highways, what Baltimore calls the Beltway, Houston the Loop, Atlanta the Perimeter—and what one developer calls "the ribbon of gold."

Pasadena, Texas, near the Houston Loop, expects to double and redouble its population. This growth will come, says Mayor Clyde Doyal, despite the fact that "we have no bus station, no railroad, no airport; what we've got is a freeway."

In Atlanta, people call the Perimeter the lifeline to development of the outer city. "People are learning to use it, learning to drive faster by driving farther," says Harold Brockey, president of Rich's. "No one says it took me ten miles to get here; they say it took me fifteen minutes."

The beltways are generating yet another level of growth. Suburban development once meant tract homes, schools, and flat shopping centers. Now it is typified by monumental complexes like Mario Doccolo's $22 million Hampton Plaza in suburban Towson, Maryland. Why did he build this gleaming, round, twenty-nine-story tower of tan stone—with offices, fine shops, and condominium apartments—in the suburbs? Because, Mr. Doccolo says, "This is the city. They're getting out of Baltimore. People go there to do what they have to do and then—zoom!—back out to the suburbs. I could see Mohammed wasn't going to the mountain any more, so I said, 'Let's build the mountain out here.' That's what I bet on."

Thus the outer city: people, houses, plants, jobs, stores, space, greenery, independence.

But it is not, at least not yet, the complete city. Some functions are still left to the inner city. Rapid high-rise office development in many cities testifies to one. White-collar professionals—lawyers, brokers, bankers, government workers—still require frequent face-to-face contact, a central verbal marketplace.

Inner cities also remain culture centers. But many suburban residents are willing to do without downtown museums, theaters, and symphonies, satisfying their cultural needs at outlying universities or amateur performances.

Most notably, the inner cities, despite the erosion of their economic strength, are still called on to perform a major social function: caring for the needy and bringing the poor fully into society. The inner city remains the haven where the rural migrant, the poor black, the struggling widow can find cheap housing, health care, welfare, and orientation to the complexities of urban life. The burden of this function, clear from the straining budgets of every major city, prompts officials everywhere to talk of the swelling new outer cities as parasites.

"The middle class has entirely abandoned the city," says Norman Krumholtz, Cleveland's lean, intense planning director. "Twenty years down the road, it's perfectly conceivable that the city will be just one great big poorhouse."

Where, asks Baltimore's Larry Reich, are the blacks in the suburbs? It is a rhetorical question. He knows the suburbs are less than 7 per cent black, compared with the city's 47 per cent. Where, he asks, do hippies, many of them children of the suburbs, congregate? Where is the suburban skid row? Where is the fairness?

In Orange County, California, the black population is less than 1 per cent. Yet nearly 7,000 of the county's 10,000 blacks are concentrated in beleaguered Santa Ana.

In Cleveland, a suburban-dominated regional council, overriding city protests, voted a new freeway that would chew up more of the city's eroding tax base.

The speaker is a suburban city manager in California, but his words convey the sentiments of outer-city residents across the country: "Social problems in the city? People here would say, 'Sympathy, yes. But willingness to help? That's their tough luck. That's their problem.' "

There Is No Firm Stereotype

by Douglas Kneeland

AFTER WORLD WAR II, when the trickle to the outer cities became a tide, a myth was built. It was called suburbia. The myth—the easy stereotype—was nourished by television and the movies, by newspapers and magazines and novelists, even by Dick and Jane and Alice and Jerry, those monosyllabic suburban tots who ran, jumped, looked, saw from the pages of most of the nation's first-grade readers.

Somehow the suburbs, despite their diversity, became one, frozen in the American mind as solidly as the Main Street of Sinclair Lewis—all green velvet lawns and swimming pools and two-car garages viewed through picture windows by practicing Republicans. Main Streets there were and are, hundreds, perhaps thousands, almost interchangeable. But the myth is unreal. The homogenized, split-level dream is only a fragment of the new America of 78 million people that has taken root around the nation's inner cities.

Visits in the outer urban areas around five major cities across the country produced ample evidence of problems and life styles as diverse as those found in the New York area's Bayonne and Levittown and Scarsdale.

"Campaigning in the new suburbia drives you crazy," complained a politician from DeKalb County, which takes in a corner of Atlanta and grew more than 150,000 to 416,000 in the decade of the sixties. "It's different from one neighborhood to the next."

And that is the pitfall for politicians or planners or economists or sociologists who view the new America of the outer cities as monolithic, predictable, and single-minded.

Pasadena, just south of Houston, is a clutch of what once was suburbia. It is pushing 100,000 in population and is plagued by pollution and the reluctance of its people to let loose of small-town concepts.

Lakewood, Ohio, on Cleveland's west side, did its growing in the early part of the century. Despite a scattering of new luxury apartments along the shore of Lake Erie, its population is relatively stable at 71,000. Lakewood worries most about preserving its property values, its sense of quality. It has adopted strict building codes and last year conducted a door-to-door campaign to check on enforcement.

Newport Beach in Southern California's Orange County is a wealthy playground turned bedroom, where sailboats are as ubiquitous as automobiles. And while its residents fight high-rise apartments and small-home developments, a tract of 6,500 homes in the $250,000 class is being built.

Decatur, Georgia, a small and gracious, but aging, island, one-third black, is awash in the surge of migration into metropolitan Atlanta's DeKalb County. As one of the few refuges for blacks in the county, it is shunned by whites and fears the fate of such overwhelmingly black suburbs as East Cleveland, Ohio, and Compton, California. Turner's Station in Maryland's Baltimore County, crowded onto a bleak point on the outskirts of the steelworkers' town of Dundalk, has never had that worry. It was built for blacks and suffers from most of the problems of the inner-city ghettos.

And so it goes, across the land. Suburbs all. Or what were suburbs. Now caught like hundreds of others in the web of the new outer cities—with problems as varied as their landscapes.

The Nixon administration has been pressing hard for decentralization and local solutions to the nation's troubles. But from Baltimore County to Cleveland's inner and outer cities, from Orange

County to Houston and the Atlanta suburbs, mayors, county officials, planners, poverty workers, and urbanologists all sounded the same note: Without strong Federal leadership and financial assistance, no dent can be made in a multitude of problems, ranging from poverty, housing, and integration to sewers, pollution control, and population dispersal. In every case, the pleaders were not talking about revenue sharing; they were asking for moral leadership and a national policy, as well as aid.

Even Santa Ana, the seat of conservative Orange County, is seeking help through a number of Federal programs to deal with its woes. "Until four years ago I was never permitted to take any Federal money, even for civil defense," City Manager Carl Thornton said.

And in nearby Anaheim, City Manager Keith Murdoch declared that, in all probability, only the Federal government could deal with the problems of poverty. "It will take something with a much broader economic base than a single city, even maybe than a single state," he said.

In Pasadena, hard against the so-called navigation district along the Houston ship channel, where miles of petrochemical plants and other industries spew smoke and gases, Mayor Clyde Doyal was also looking for Federal help. "Pollution is our biggest problem," said the mayor, tall and tan, as he relaxed behind his desk. "Up to this point we've been unable to do anything. We're close to them, but we derive little revenue from there. And we can't go outside the city limits to enforce pollution laws."

Noting that even if Pasadena had control, local laws might frighten away, rather than clean up, the industries on which its growth have been based, he added: "I think it's going to cost a lot of money to clean up pollution. That's why I think the Federal government should set the standards. If the Federal government set national standards, it wouldn't cause any loss of jobs."

Under the shadow of a new freeway that has yet to feel the rush of cars, the Vernon Collins Motel and trucks and the old Wright Grain Company Store languish as grimy reminders of another Pasadena, another Texas. The contrasts in Pasadena, with its half-vacated old downtown and the new steel-and-concrete center springing up around its modern City Hall, in some ways mirror the contrasts in the suddenly emerged outer cities. In Pasadena, $16,000 will still buy a three-bedroom house with airconditioning, but there are growing neighborhoods of $60,000 homes.

While Mayor Doyal is concerned about pollution, he is not especially worried about the population growth troubling many of the outer cities. With workers flocking to the area for jobs along the ship channel and whites fleeing a black southward push in Houston, Pasadena, which has "one or two black families," went from a population of 58,000 in 1960 to 89,000 in 1970. A recent annexation and continued in-migration, the mayor said, have put the total at about 100,000. He believes it will reach 400,000.

This poses some difficulties for the Pasadena that grew up with the Vernon Collins Motel and the Wright Grain Store. For one thing, the city has had to stop serving free coffee in its municipal offices. Last year the bill was $4,500. And there are other problems.

"You're starting like a new city and yet you had all these people already here, used to doing things the old way," Mayor Doyal said a little plaintively. "We had this small-town atmosphere. We went to one-way streets and that kicked up a hell of a furor. We went to paper sacks for garbage collection and that caused a flap. But they like it now."

The citizenry may be lagging, but Pasadena is catching up with itself. Already filling the open stretches around City Hall are a gleaming, twelve-story bank, a low-built but luxuriantly landscaped post office, a department store, a new telephone building.

"And we've got another little development coming," Mayor Doyal said casually, gesturing toward a big field on the north side of the building, "out there behind City Hall. It ought to run, oh, about $100 million." With that, he pulled out a brochure for the planned forty-acre Triton Center, a complex including a hotel, office high-rises, shopping and parking structures, and a labor-sponsored Robert F. Kennedy Memorial Hospital. That is the Pasadena, Texas, twentieth century—part of the new America, the Outer City.

Can it be stereotyped with Santa Ana, California, an aging city caught up in Orange County's voracious growth? Twenty years ago, when Carl Thornton went to Santa Ana as city manager, it had 42,000 people. Now it has about 160,000 and harbors 66 per cent of Orange County's 10,000 blacks and many of its Mexican-Americans. Ghettos and barrios, some shabby and forlorn, some middle-class and well-kept, freckle the city.

While Pasadena, Texas, dreams of 400,000 citizens, Carl Thornton shudders at what would happen if unchecked apartment construction, which is threatening as banks make more money available for that than for single-family homes, should drop 50,000 more people into some sections of his city. He also fears the pull of the new city of Irvine that is planned on the outskirts of Santa Ana—a city that some day would have 430,000 people. If whites should abandon Santa Ana for Irvine, he said, his city could follow the path of Pomona in Los Angeles County.

"Pomona has racial problems till hell wouldn't have it," Mr. Thornton said, his wrinkled brow tightening. "What has happened is welfare cases have moved in. As the housing developed, the new towns, their people moved, some of them in flight, some to upgrade. Vacancies became available. Welfare didn't put them in, but the vacancies were there. This could happen to my town— over my dead body. I'm going to fight."

But while he's battling to force Irvine to include enough low-income housing in its new city to ease some of the flow of poor and blacks and Mexican-Americans into Santa Ana, he can already see the signs of blight that cause him to characterize the western part of Orange County as much like an old inner city. "You have a tendency to get old fast under such circumstances," he said, shaking his head wearily. "This is a pressure cooker."

Or can you equate Turner's Station, Maryland, a black enclave of dreary apartments across an estuary from the red smoke and flame of Bethlehem Steel's Sparrows Point Works, with Newport Beach, a paradise of yachts and sailboats and sandy beaches where narrow but elegant waterfront homes command $100,000 to $250,000? They are both on the waterfront. They are both by definition suburbs.

At Turner's Station, where the shabby brick apartments were built primarily for black workers at the steel mill, a small beach on the muddy water is littered with cans and glistening shards of glass. A power line right-of-way, grown to weeds under the humming wires, slices through the community. The streets are pot-holed, and only a few struggling flowers brighten the yards outside the buildings. Most of the small frame stores have been boarded up.

Standing on her plot of grass behind a wire fence, an elderly black woman, who refused to give her name, summed up life at Turner's Station. "It's terrible," she said, "but it's better than Cherry Hill." Cherry Hill is a festering ghetto in the city of Baltimore. She lives in the suburbs, too.

Negroes Find
Few Tangible Gains

by Paul Delaney

A SMALL, growing number of black families is increasingly able to penetrate the new outer cities of America, the swelling bands of suburbs that ring the stagnating inner cities. But for most of the 800,000 blacks who fled, technically, to "the suburbs" in the last decade, the move has been to municipalities like East Cleveland, just a political dividing line away from Cleveland's ghetto.

It has meant little more than exchanging one hand-me-down neighborhood for another. If there is improvement over the inner-city ghetto, it is more in the state of mind than in the quality of life. "They feel that at least they are not living in the inner city," says Gladstone L. Chandler, Jr., the stocky black city manager of this town of 39,600—which went from all-white fifteen years ago to 60 per cent black now.

Even the total number of Negroes who moved to second-hand suburbs on the inner rim of the outer city has been relatively slight. In the Cleveland area, as in other inner and outer cities visited for an assessment of suburban growth, the figures appear dramatic compared with 1960. The black population of Cleveland's suburbs increased almost 500 per cent in the decade. In raw numbers, the black "suburban" population increased from 8,000 to 45,000—but that 45,000 is out of a total outer-city population of 1.3 million. Meanwhile, the outer city has meant nothing to the far larger number of Cleveland blacks, 300,000, still in the inner city.

Actually, the suburbs may have had an effect that is worse than nothing to inner-city blacks, considering the deep hostility of middle-income whites, and Negroes, toward making any room for those with low or moderate incomes.

There has been one kind of change, however slight, that a black with a good income can now often penetrate the white suburban noose. "You have to earn at least $10,000 or $12,000 a year to move to the Cleveland suburbs," remarked Gerta Friedheim, young, petite Cleveland Heights housewife who heads the Suburban Citizens for Open Housing, an organization pushing for integration of the outer city.

In the upper-income areas of the outer city, there is salt-and-pepper integration, a sprinkling of Negroes here and there, but it is insignificant. For example, of 71,000 residents of predominantly Republican and ethnically proud Lakewood, made up of neatly kept neighborhoods and high-rise luxury apartments on Lake Erie west of downtown Cleveland, twenty-one are Negroes. In the predominantly Jewish, upper-income bedroom community of University Heights east of the city, there are eighty-eight Negroes out of 17,055 residents. Anaheim, California, has 170 blacks in a population of 166,701, In nearby Newport Beach, a resort town on the Pacific, there are forty-one blacks in 49,422.

Even these handfuls have not found the move to better suburbs easy. Judson Robinson, Jr., a tall handsome black realtor and defeated candidate for the Houston City Council four years ago, explained that blacks literally had to have money in hand if they were interested in a house in a white section. "If blacks attempt to dicker a little, like even wanting to sleep on a price, the house is gone the next day," Mr. Robinson said. "It is very strange, but somehow the houses seem to sell overnight if blacks express an interest."

Upper-income blacks are also victims of the "Ralph Bunche syndrome," according to a white Baltimore County developer. "Few whites would complain if a Ralph Bunche moved next door," the developer said as he drove visitors through exclusive sections of Dulaney Valley. "Maybe they would if two moved in. They wouldn't complain about a Ralph Bunche, but these same whites would oppose low-income housing in their area, and low-income housing certainly does more for blacks than allowing one Ralph Bunche in."

Thus, most outer-city integration has been restricted to areas contiguous to black sections of the inner city, leaving heavier concentrations of poorer blacks at inner-city lines, and a few in middle-income and upper-income suburbs farther away from the city. Black blue-collar workers replaced white blue-collar residents in East Cleveland, which is a good example of the pattern of black movement from the inner city.

It is repeated in Compton, California, with its winding, tree-shaded streets of small houses, populated by blacks who left Watts and East Los Angeles. It is repeated in the outer city of New York, in Yonkers, New Rochelle, and Mount Vernon, as blacks have worked out from the Bronx and Harlem.

The move to East Cleveland has merely meant stepping across the boundary lines from the black Glenville section in northeast Cleveland. The homes look exactly alike on either side of the line —two-story and three-story frame homes, most painted white, with detached two-car garages in back and side entrances off the driveway, sitting twenty to thirty feet from the curb, small lawns in front.

The process by which blacks got to East Cleveland was typical and went like this:

Prior to World War II, blacks were relegated to the deteriorating Central section on the near east side around downtown Cleveland, in big two-story and three-story frame houses situated very close to each other on the side streets of Cedar, Central, and Woodland Avenues.

During and right after the war, the Hough area, farther eastward, with its bigger and better homes and many apartment buildings, opened to blacks through a combination of block busting and white flight. It immediately felt the tremendous impact of larger families as blacks from the South poured into the city to work in its steel mills and heavy industry. The larger dwelling units were split into smaller units to accommodate the overflow of people.

In the early fifties, Glenville, even farther eastward, became "the" section for middle-class blacks, with its mixture of smaller homes, fewer apartments, and grand old homes along East Boulevard, where black lawyers and doctors resided. However, by the late fifties, Glenville had followed the fate of the Central and Hough areas as the poor flooded in. And then, in 1961, poorer blacks began spilling over into East Cleveland, and middle-class blacks moved to the Mount Pleasant and Shaker Heights areas.

The migration to the East Cleveland bedroom community, one of the oldest in the area, has improved the self-esteem of blacks more than it has their condition. They still work at the same jobs, whether at the Ford plant in the western part of Cuyahoga County or the Fisher Body factory nearby. The deterioration still follows them.

The move to the outer city has mainly meant transferring the inner city. "We are an inner-city suburb with all the problems of the central city," remarked Mr. Chandler, the articulate East Cleveland city manager. He said that larger and poorer families were moving in, taxing the city's services and schools and reducing its revenue, and thereby causing fast deterioration. A few blacks whose incomes grow move on to other outer cities, such as Shaker Heights and Cleveland Heights, he said.

The same complaint was registered by the Compton, California, city manager, James Johnson, thirty-seven years old, quiet and, like Mr. Chandler, black. Mr. Johnson said that Compton was a town of middle-class Negro professionals—blacks are 70 per cent of the city's 78,611 residents—but that they were moving farther out in the outer city, most to bordering Carson, leaving as replacements low-income families with more children and more problems.

Although middle-class and upper-income white outer cities grudgingly accept a few blacks of similar income levels, the resistance to most blacks, as well as to other minorities and whites who are poor, is probably greater than ever before. The resistance is couched in new terminology and techniques that still mean "keep out," such as being against "high-density" developments, "low-income" housing, and "forced integration" of the outer city.

The fear of blacks moving to the outer city influences many actions of whites living there and attempting to protect themselves from integration. Dan Colasino, administrative assistant to the Baltimore County executive, noted that the all-white, lower-income, working-class section of Dundalk, in the eastern part of Baltimore County, was quite self-contained. "Yes, it is its own community," commented Mr. Colasino, a conservative Democrat who wears a key ring with twenty-six keys on it. "The only thing we need is a swimming pool. But as soon as we do that, the colored'll come in from the city to swim."

This fear of migration by lower-income persons does not mean that there are no poor in the outer city, as believed by many residents. New census data show that 53 per cent of the increase in the number of poor families in the country between 1969 and 1970 was in the outer city. Poverty in the outer city is often invisible. Much of it is camouflaged by greenery. It is harder to see the poor blacks and other minorities in even Santa Ana, California, than it is on Chicago's South Side or Atlanta's Vine City.

What is the future for poor blacks in the city and suburban resistance? "I really do believe this thing can work," Mrs. Friedheim said at lunch in a Shaker Heights restaurant. "I'm not about to bat my head against the wall unless I think it could work." She believes that race is disappearing as a factor and that people are at least willing to accept well-to-do Negroes into their neighborhoods.

"The big question, then, is about the poor," she said. Mrs. Friedheim paused, then sighed, and added: "There is no political force for them at all, other than Mayor Carl B. Stokes of Cleveland. If it's going to come at all, it has to come from Federal leverage."

A Deep Uneasiness About the Future

by John Herbers

WHILE AMERICA has been creating a dominant, vibrant new form of urban settlement that the residents point to with pride—the outer city—the proliferating communities themselves have become filled with anxieties, frustration, defensiveness, and a deep sense of uneasiness about the future. Out along the beltways, where high rises, factories, educational parks, and superhotels are springing up out of the farmlands and suburban sprawl of the nineteen-fifties and sixties and where 76 million people now live, there are diverse, warring jurisdictions, ranging from emerging slums to encampments for millionaires.

Yet a common trait stands out in virtually all of them: a turning inward, a determination to shut out the decay and social upheavals of the central city, a lack of concern about the spreading agony and distress only a few miles away. There is a lack of concern because the new urban development is based so much on the individual pursuit of a better life and escape from the central city.

There are 121 separate and diverse municipalities around Cleveland, and Harry Bolk, an editor who knows them well, says each "represents some sort of escape from the city."

In Atlanta, a legislator says, "The suburbanite says to himself, 'The reason I worked for so many years was to get away from pollution, bad schools and crime, and I'll be damned if I'll see it all follow me.' "

But in many instances, all these things are following him, and when they do the tendency is to look individually for further escape. In Orange County, California, where restless migrants are pushing against the Pacific Ocean, there is even talk of escaping to Australia. Richard Baisden, a professor at the University of California at Irvine, said, "We offered an extension course in doing business in Australia, expecting maybe two people to show up. Well, about forty-five showed up. For the most part they were quite serious."

Almost nowhere in this teeming complex of people, cars, grass and concrete, the outer city, is there an awareness that this now, is the city. The political and business leaders still view their settlements as Norman Rockwell villages where one goes to escape the torments of urbanization even while skyscrapers are going up all around.

The residents, whether rich or poor, often live in compartments or compounds. Most are rather well-off and seldom, if ever, see or come to understand the decay and social trauma in the central city. Unlike their ancestors, who had some first-hand knowledge of "the other side of the tracks," the people of the outer city tend to exaggerate unseen threats—just as the people on the back roads of Mississippi fear the streets of New York and the people on the streets of New York distrust the back roads of Mississippi. Overall, there is a Balkanization of government and authority, a feeling of fragmentation and centerlessness and a sense that no one is in charge of this growing, pulsating thing.

Against this backdrop, it is not surprising that the people of the outer city feel threatened in a number of ways—by poor blacks from the inner city, by crime and drugs, by pollution, by high density and zoning change, and by declining values. Out of this has come a fervid, participatory brand of politics that is fundamentally negative. Proposed zoning changes, a decline in garbage pickup, suggestions of new apartments on Federal projects that might import blacks—all bring citizens by the thousands out to the overburdened city halls and courthouses.

An observer of the American scene expects to find a degree of this. It is apparent in both national and local debate, in zoning battles, court bases, and the mere appearance of the urban scene. But interviews with scores of community leaders showed the protectiveness and insularity to be surprisingly pervasive and widespread. Here are some of the signs:

• In Garfield Heights, Ohio, the residents refer to their scrubbed city of 41,000, nestled against decaying Cleveland, as a last place of refuge for second- and third-generation Europeans, an enclave to be protected at all costs.

• Along the Beltway around Baltimore are vast settlements of what one leader there called "the nouveau white collar," refugees from the central city who he says feel so insecure that they have injected a "paranoid mentality" into the body politic of Baltimore County.

• In East Cleveland, a close-in suburb where blacks have spilled over from the central city until they make up a majority, the cry of both Negroes and whites is, "We don't want that mess from Cleveland coming out here," according to the black city manager, Gladstone L. Chandler, Jr.

• In Orange County, California, the beautiful city of Newport Beach is rich and removed from central city decay. Yet the people there feel no less embattled than those in Garfield Heights—by pollution, freeways, airports, and the suburban sprawl from Los Angeles.

• Garden Grove, California, a municipality of more than 100,000, is a segment of the sprawl around Los Angeles. "We call it the phantom city," said an Orange County planning official. "You can't tell when you enter it, and you can't tell when you're leaving it."

• In De Kalb County, Georgia, a white-collar, upper-middle-class satellite of Atlanta, the residents are constantly up in arms about such things as taxes and new apartments. "They raise hell twenty-four hours a day out there," said Howard Atherton, a state legislator from nearby Marietta. "It's enough to drive a normal person insane."

All of this has not yet been without divisive effect. Highly emotional politics has split some liberals who ordinarily would be working together. Carl B. Stokes, the mayor of Cleveland, and

Irvin W. Konigsberg, the mayor of University Heights, a pre-dominantly Jewish suburb with a median income of $14,000, are both liberal Democrats, but they have been fighting one another bitterly, each reflecting the views of his constituency.

Because Cleveland is left with the poor, most of the blacks and the old, and a declining tax base, Mr. Stokes has insisted that the only logical position he can take is that of advocacy for the poor and a refusal to submit Cleveland affairs to the mercies of the white majority outside the city. But this is little understood by the liberals of University Heights.

"Cleveland still wants full control," said Mr. Konigsberg. "Well, the day of the suburbs' being appendages of the city is over. The city is not going to dominate any more. The power is shifting to the suburbs."

The suburbs are the city now, but they are fighting each other as each twirls in its own orbit. Newport Beach seems at war with almost everyone. Once a village of summer homes, it is now a bed-room and pleasure city of 53,000 where there are more boat docks than auto parking places. A new development of 6,500 homes in the $250,000 class has scarcely caused a ripple.

"Newport Beach people don't want to identify with anything else," said Philip Bettencourt, twenty-eight-year-old acting mana-ger, who, in white bell-bottom slacks and green blazer, looked as if he had just stepped off a yacht. "They came here because they don't like any other places. They like Newport Beach the way it is and they don't want it changed." So the residents are fiercely fight-ing the proposed Pacific Freeway, which would cut through the city, a planned extension of the Orange County Airport and the encroachment of other cities.

When the neighboring city of Cosa Mesa, which has some pov-erty and social problems, grew close, Newport Beach annexed a strip, one foot wide and several miles long, around a large section of unincorporated land to keep Cosa Mesa from annexing it.

Consolidation, when it is proposed, is usually a defensive move. East Point, Georgia, is willing to give up its identity and govern-ment and merge with five rival cities to stop the southward en-croachment of blacks from Atlanta. Mayor R. E. Brown is asking the Georgia Legislature to form the city of South Fulton, which would have a population of 120,000 and might eventually rival Atlanta. Under state law a city can locate public housing ten miles outside its boundaries, and Mr. Brown says Atlanta has a deliberate policy of herding public housing projects in the direction of East Point and other blue-collar communities.

"If we incorporate all our own land into our own city," said Mr. Brown, "we would be immune from this public housing requirement."

The defensiveness seems to be more than a desire to avoid minorities, lowered property values, and social problems. Perhaps a substantial portion of it stems from a real threat to the single-family home, which brought many to the suburbs in the first place.

Soaring construction costs and the high cost of land many miles from the central city are pricing the single-family home out of the reach of many who a decade ago would have considered nothing else. Developers across the country say the banks will readily extend loans for apartments but are increasingly reluctant to lend for single homes.

But the desire of families to have a private home, yard and swimming pool, if possible, runs deep, even as many people are turning to apartment living out of a desire to get away from mowing the lawn and repairing the faucets.

"The big issue in De Kalb County," said Georgia Representative Elliott Levitas, "is not whether blacks will come in. It is whether apartments will come in." And apartments *are* coming in, in increasing numbers.

The people of the outer city are disturbed, too, that they are running out of places to move to. Many have moved from a farm or another country to the central city, then to a close-in suburb, then to a farther-out suburb, and they are tired of moving.

In the small city hall of Garfield Heights, Ohio, there was a smell of lemon wax as Mayor Raymond A. Stachweicz, a short, stout man meticulously dressed in sport coat and wide tie, looked out on the manicured lawns and neat shops and said: "We are a community of land-lovers. We are mostly Polish and Italians, all mixed. Sixty-five per cent of our people moved out from Cleveland and they consider this the last place for them. They are determined to stay here and keep their houses as they are now."

The words and tone left the impression that no rational man would bring high density and low-income families to Garfield Heights. In the outer city, each resident has pursued his own dream and each community its own goals. Now in the babble and confusion, there are only the first gropings for order and community.

Growth Crying Out for Guidance

by Linda Greenhouse

GROWTH, THE snow-balling, leap-frogging, growth that for so long held out to the suburbs the promise of an endlessly prosperous future, has suddenly developed into a shadow across that future. Everywhere in the new outer cities, politicians, planners, and residents of subdivisions that were strawberry patches or orange groves less than a generation ago are taking increasingly worried looks at the growth rates they once welcomed and pointed to with pride.

In Orange County, California, the population doubled in the last ten years, from 700,000 to more than 1.4 million. But public opinion has turned so decisively against keeping up that pace that the new chairman of the County Board of Supervisors can make a statement nearly unthinkable a few years ago. "The Chamber of Commerce tells us that growth is wonderful," Robert Battin says. "I see it as a cancer."

In the last decade, the number of people living in the nation's suburbs climbed from 55 million to 76 million. The 1970 Census figures, still uncompiled, will show that the suburbs contain more high-rise construction than ever before. A twenty-nine-story office tower in Towson, Maryland, a 103-warehouse industrial park outside Decatur, Georgia, a planned city for 430,000 in Orange County tell only a fraction of the story.

Thirty years ago, only two out of every ten Americans lived in the suburbs. Now the suburbs claim four of every ten. Only recently have these people come to realize that the city they now live in—the new outer city—is becoming the city they thought they had left behind, with many of the same problems and responsibilities. They know they cannot turn Santa Ana back into an orange grove, and for the most part they would not want to. People are seeking not to reverse the tide but to hold it—or at least to channel and direct it, to soften the impact.

But for all the numbers and potential power, the outer cities remain largely masses of little islands, unable to work together to harness the forces shaping the future.

So development continues to accelerate beyond the grasp of a Santa Ana, in Orange County, which fears that apartment construction may soon bring in 50,000 new people, more than it can provide services for. Despite Mr. Battin's fighting words, the outer city is not yet in control of its future.

The turn against growth was gaining momentum even before the emergence of ecology as an issue in the last year or two. Suburban residents, like those in New Jersey's Bergen County, as well as California's Orange County, had already begun to worry about the traffic jams, the rising taxes to pay for more schools and public services, the spillover of racial problems, the first signs of what one suburban planner calls "the spreading great central crud."

Now the ecology movement has given these worries a new focus and momentum and, even among conservatives, a new respectability. "Many politically conservative people want the natural assets of the county preserved for their own use, and don't want other people to come in and glop it up," says Forest Dickason, director of the Orange County Department of Planning.

Even in Houston, Texas, which its boosters delight in calling a boomtown, one of the city's wealthiest men can muse: "Houston is still not prepared to say no to growth, despite the traffic and pollution. But I personally would like to see the streets rendered passable and the air cleared before I'd invite anyone else to come here."

And in Baltimore County, Maryland, Dan Colasino, administrative assistant to the county executive, mentioned a proposal to build 25,000 units of low-income housing for blacks and commented: "We don't have enough for whites. This county is growing very fast—too damn fast."

The rising public wariness toward growth has brought subtle shifts in the balance of power between the private market and the public planners, long the flabby step-children of the local government. When 1,700 people crowd into a junior high school auditorium in White Plains, New York, on a Saturday morning to hear the Regional Plan Association's presentation of "The Future of Westchester County," there is no doubt that suburban residents care about what planners have to tell them.

When the public outcry on behalf of the Baltimore County Planning Department, which last fall removed large sections of the county's vacant land from potential commercial development, is so great that the County Council has to withdraw the changes it tried to make on behalf of the developers, there is no doubt that the planners have acquired new muscle.

But visits and interviews around the country produced clear evidence that, despite the planners' new leverage, the private market remains by far the most powerful engine of growth, shaping the future of the new outer city as it once gave form to the old. The new suburban landscape itself—with its growing concentration of high-rise office buildings, sprawling industrial parks, luxury housing in planned unit developments—offers dramatic evidence.

To support "high-density" development is still bad politics in most suburban areas, arousing such negative feelings that most planners are reluctant to squander their credibility by advocating more apartments. But the private sector is not only building apartments at an astonishing rate; it is both creating and satisfying a rapidly growing public demand for them.

While many families still live in apartments because they cannot afford to buy houses, an increasing number of suburban middle-class families welcome the imaginative design, convenience and recreation facilities that the new developments offer.

"A child who has grown up in a typical suburb has had his fill of cutting all that grass," said Clark Harrison, chairman of the board of commissioners of De Kalb County in suburban Atlanta. Mr. Harrison offers De Kalb as an illustration of the paradox reflected around the country—that suburban residents denounce apartments and seem to rush into apartments at the same time. "It's the strangest thing," he said. "People around here complain when they can see a high-rise building through the trees." Yet apartment construction in De Kalb is now outpacing single family homes by two to one, and the ratio is certain to increase.

Just as residents of the outer cities are turning to these new forms of social organization, they are looking to new governmental structures to ease the impact of the growth. Everywhere people talk as if the forms themselves matter. In Cuyahoga County, for example, civic leaders complain that countrywide cooperation on planning issues is impossible with Cleveland and fifty-nine other towns and cities to contend with. But liberals in Baltimore County, 600 square miles without a single incorporated city, make the opposite complaint. They insist that the lack of community governments makes it harder for individual views to be heard.

Meanwhile, many city leaders say that if only they had metropolitan government—to offset the flight of their tax base and middle class to the suburbs—they would have the resources to solve their problems.

But Houston's experience indicates that structure alone can never be the panacea people seek. Houston, in effect, does have metropolitan government. A strong Texas law allows it to annex the areas which in other states would become suburban rings.

But instead of using its resources to attack its poverty problems or improve its housing and schools, it chooses to tax itself at the lowest rate of the twenty-five largest cities. Its school district, for example, spends $511 a pupil annually, $300 below the national average and less than half of New York's expenditure.

The new public concern about unlimited development has challenged both local governments and the private market. Government's attempts to channel growth have been largely ineffective. For its part, the private market has responded to the challenge with new attention to quality in planning and design. It does not matter whether that change is born of conviction or is merely a concession to the mood of a public no longer willing to pay for the unimaginative urban sprawl. The final product is the same, and it is often stunning.

Builders who admit that they might once have been content to put up rows of identical little houses say now that they are willing to spend the extra money that quality design requires. "Good architecture pays off fast—and it doesn't necessarily cost that much more," said Gerald D. Hines, whose $50 million Galleria has become a new urban center six miles southwest of downtown Houston. "People now will pay that little extra for quality."

Nevertheless, the very scale and quality of the new growth, itself a response to problems of the past, is creating a problem that may eventually make the victories over poor design and unmanaged growth look pyrrhic indeed.

In Santa Ana, the seat of Orange County, that challenge is already dramatically apparent. While its population is only a tenth of the county's 1.4 million, Santa Ana already has two-thirds of the black population, a third of the welfare caseload, and at least a third of the poor Mexican-American barrios.

Even its better areas, like those in much of the older portions of the county, are vulnerable to change. Eighty-five per cent of the housing in Orange County has been built since 1950. "Like the one horse shay, it will all wear out at once," says Alfred Bell, principal planner for the County Planning Department. "Within the decade, our rehabilitation needs will be massive." And now change stares Santa Ana hard in the face. The city lies adjacent to the 80,000-acre Irvine Ranch, said to be the single most valuable parcel of undeveloped urban land in the world, which already is being developed into a handsome, planned city for 430,000.

The city fears that the Irvine development will be a magnet, drawing people and resources away from Santa Ana. Unless the Irvine developers can be persuaded to include substantial amounts of low-income housing in their plans, says Carl Thornton, the Santa Ana city manager, "our city will look like downtown Kansas City, downtown Detroit."

And so the cycle begins anew. It appears to be a new natural law that even areas that grew up as satellites to inner cities must, as they themselves grow, create their own poor cores, their own repositories for the infirm, the incapable, the unwanted.

Whether through lack of resources or lack of will, if local government remains powerless to guide the form or pace of growth—to make sure there is room for the poor as well as the rich, for people as well as cars—what is the future for the new outer cities?

Will the private market, motivated by the new public desire for quality, be free to create still newer forms, more daring and imaginative than anything we have yet seen—as different from the present as the glass towers of New York's Lexington Avenue are from the four-story, red-brick tenements that preceded them a generation ago?

Or, operating without consistent guidelines for balancing public and private needs, are the developers of the new cities bound to repeat the mistakes of the old? Or will local communities themselves, with or without coherent government, somehow be able to compel virtue from the private sector through zoning or new government forms?

Edgardo Contini, a noted Los Angeles urbanist, is convinced that to rely on local government to save the new cities from the fate of the old is to insure failure. "Solutions have to come from a level higher than the problem," he said. "Don't ask for virtue retail. Don't ask local communities to martyr themselves. You are asking them to be noble, and people are not like that. The leadership has to come from the top, from the Federal government."

The pace of growth this time around is quicker. The scale is bigger, and the stakes, in the outer city, are vastly higher.

As Professor Richard Baisden, dean of the extension division of the University of California at Irvine, said during dinner at the resort enclave of Corona del Mar:

"I came here in flight from smog and congestion and I've found relief from both, temporarily. But after this, I don't know where people will go. I don't know where we can go from here."

SUBURBAN LAND DEVELOPMENT

Toward Suburban Independence

by Jack Rosenthal

THE LARGEST CITY in America is now the suburbs of New York. They contain 8.9 million people, a million more even than New York City. They cover 2,100 square miles, 600 more even than Los Angeles and its suburbs combined. They represent the fullest flowering of the historic migration of Americans out of their cities. For even here, in the orbit of New York—the Big Apple—the suburbs are strikingly, fiercely independent.

Huge numbers of suburbanites neither live, work, play, shop, nor go out to eat in New York City. And they fight, with passionate hostility, against the feared intrusion of change, of the inner city and of the people left behind. As dramatically evident from official studies and five weeks of interviews by a team of *New York Times* reporters, the most critical commodity in this struggle against the city is land. It is the land—and especially the emotional issue of how it will be used—that shapes politics and power in the suburbs, that governs the suburban economy, that determines where people work and where they live and how they travel.

New York's suburbs created a national image of bedroom towns for city workers. Yet how many of the counties around the five boroughs now send even half their workers to jobs in the city? None. Nassau County has net commutation to New York of less than 38 per cent. Westchester has less than 32 per cent. In Suffolk County, 80 per cent of the workers who live there work either in Suffolk or Nassau. In Passaic County, 79 per cent work in Passaic or Bergen Counties.

The suburbs now have about half the area's manufacturing jobs, retail jobs, and restaurants. And they have a full range of "urban" facilities. Gleaming new office towers contrast sharply with the rolling greenery of pastoral Piscataway, New Jersey. Every morning crowds of businessmen with briefcases at McArthur Airport in Islip, Long Island, board nonstop flights to Chicago or Washington. Downtown for Wayne, New Jersey, is now a carpeted and airconditioned area, framed by shrubbery and fountains, in an immense covered shopping mall.

The impact of such decentralization of urban functions can be quickly seen in other merely regional cities, where the business districts become ghost towns each nightfall. Here decentralization is masked by two factors. One is size.

"There are three things one must always remember about New York City," says Edward J. Logue, president of the State Urban Development Corporation. "They are scale, scale, and scale." Two million whites may have fled the city in the last twenty years, he acknowledges. But still, "There is no other city with anything approaching New York's proportion of the metropolitan population."

The second factor is New York's enduring role as a national city—a financial hub, cultural capital, media center, and mecca for young adults. And, for the most part, that is the city that the residents of New York's suburbs relate to, in the same way that residents of the suburbs of other cities do—the national city, a place to visit and enjoy, not as residents but as tourists.

Ask suburbanites the last time they went to New York. Again and again, they give answers like "for the last antique show" or "last December, to show the kids the Christmas lights," or "in the fall, for a play." And after the show, with a wince at the $30 or $40 tab for tickets and parking, they speed back to the spacious, centerless world they have created in the suburbs.

Like suburbanites everywhere, they strive to protect that world against change with a ferocity that has become a national political fact. The hostility was typified, says a Suffolk County official, at a recent town zoning hearing on the construction of luxury apartments.

A New York City fireman leaped onto a chair, waved a newspaper full of city crime and welfare news, and shouted: "We don't want this kind of trash in our neighborhood." Yet for all the ferocity, even irrationality, signs of change are now emerging in the mushrooming, maturing New York suburbs, signs that could well foretell the next cycle in the life of suburbs across the country.

The dikes of hostility appear slowly, but with gathering speed, to be leaking, eroded not by an ominous outside urban tide, but by feared Federal pressure for housing integration, but by enemies within. In town after town, residents find they are excluding not only outsiders but their own grown children, older adults, and civil servants. These are often unable or unwilling to maintain the expensive single-family homes so frequently required by tight exclusionary zoning.

Increasingly suburbanites find that their exclusionary strategies no longer work and may even promote the very sprawl, scrambled land use and urban chaos that these strategies were intended to prevent. At this point the hostility remains intense; the forces for change are far from decisive. But, in the opinion of some authorities, the trend—for the complex array of suburbs here, as well as for the more easily definable rings of suburbs elsewhere—is inevitable.

In smaller, newer cities, "suburbs" more clearly mean communities that have developed since the start of the automobile era on urban land around the urban core. Here, prior to the automobile, there was no such clean slate. The metropolitan area already included railroad suburbs dating to the eighteen-seventies; independent cities like Newark, White Plains, or Bridgeport; and resorts like Long Beach or the Jersey shore.

But it is the automobile—and the freeways it has generated—that has turned the land between and beyond the old towns and the old rail lines into a vast urban complex. Its primary characteristic is centerless independence of the city. In place of an urban center, mobile suburbanites use the varying facilities of their separate communities collectively, as an interlinked outer city.

Elsewhere sweeping circumferential freeways have made development of a unitary outer city literally possible. Here the population, diversity and distance of the suburbs are too great to be overcome by an eight-lane concrete loop. Yet even here, the signs of expanding centerlessness, of the collective suburban "city," are clear.

In Nassau County, Leona Baum, a petite mother of two teenage boys, describes how her family lives in almost exactly the terms people use in the outskirts of Los Angeles:

"We live in East Meadow. I work in Garden City. My husband works in Syosset. We shop for clothes in Hempstead. My husband's Pythias Lodge meets in Great Neck. Our temple is in Merrick. The children's doctor is in Westbury. And we pay our parking tickets in Mineola."

And the centerless growth continues. On the moon, the terminator is the moving line between light and dark. In many suburbs, a similar line marks the contrast between development and farmland. In Westchester the line moves out a mile a year, says Peter O. Eschweiler, the planning commissioner. "If you want to see what your town will look like ten years from now," he says, "drive ten miles back." On Long Island the urbanization line is instantly visible from the air. That line, planners say, moves even faster—two miles a year. In Middlesex County, New Jersey, the line is not so easily visible, says George M. Ververides, a planner. "There's no front. It's like Vietnam. It's happening all over."

The suburbs have, however, sought to protect their development from unwanted change by controlling their most valuable resource: land.

Each small community exercises its local zoning power zealously. Repeatedly, town boards engage in what is called, variously, up-zoning, exclusionary zoning, or lace-lot zoning. Whatever the name, the purpose is identical: If the only housing permitted is single-family homes, and if these must be sited on half, full, or even four-acre lots at a minimum, only the middle-income and upper-income can afford to move in.

In Suffolk the typical new house cost $14,500 in 1960. Now the cheapest new house is $30,000, according to a study made for the National Council Against Discrimination in Housing.

The council estimates that at least 80 per cent of New York area families are now priced out of the new housing market entirely. Some of the reasons for such vigilant exclusivity are straightforward. Municipal costs, particularly for schools, are soaring and more people can easily mean more deficit. Many suburbanites moonlight or put their wives to work to save enough to escape from the city. They are quick to block the intrusion of any urban problems into their refuge "in the country."

But other explanations for suburban hostility are not so candid or rational. "New York has a lower proportion of blacks than many cities," says a suburban planner, asking anonymity. "But even so, the sheer raw numbers are great. So people out here perceive a great tide of black and Puerto Ricans they could be engulfed by."

Other suburbanites disguise their hostility behind code words. They talk of the need to protect "the country image" or to preserve "our environment." One county, says Jack Wood of the National Council Against Discrimination in Housing, defends itself by saying it supplies an "airshed" for the metropolitan region. Still other suburban residents concede fears of the outward movement of city crime, welfare costs, and other burdens of the poverty population. But almost none admits openly to a desire to keep out minorities. Again and again, suburbanites insist that they have welcomed black families to their neighborhoods.

And yet: "There's a tremendous upsurge in the Conservative party vote from people who were Democrats in the city. Like Jews who envision being surrounded by the blacks," says a Long Island official, himself a Jew. "Surrounded! Just like the Arabs are surrounded by the Israelis."

The effects of suburban exclusion are clear. New York's black population in the nineteen-sixties went from 14 to 21 per cent. The suburban proportion, meanwhile, went from 5 to 6 per cent. In town after town, population figures show that one-tenth—or one-hundredth—of 1 per cent is black.

"We are very fortunate in our welfare situation," says Newton Miller, the mayor of Wayne, New Jersey, where the population doubled, to 50,000, in the sixties.

What is the welfare proportion, he was asked. "Under ten." Under 10 per cent? "No, under ten families."

The issue now is not whether exclusion has succeeded, but whether it may, in fact, have succeeded too well. Some urbanists press the moral argument of unfairness. The suburbs, they say, cannot in good conscience continue to pirate from the city only its desirable functions and people.

Suburbs must, the argument goes, take their share of the social welfare task now being left almost entirely to impoverished central cities. They must also provide lower-income housing near suburban jobs. In recent months this argument appears to have become a centerpiece of liberal thought about urban problems. There are, however, some strikingly contrary views.

George Sternlieb, an authority on inner-city housing, believes that "the only thing that's holding our central cities together is the suburban housing shortage." If the suburban barriers were lowered, he contends, it would not be the poor or black city residents who would move outward. It would be the city's remaining middle-class and lower-middle-class residents, now deterred from moving by high costs that are made still higher by exclusionary zoning.

The result could be to diminish even further the tax base from which cities now try to finance costly social services for the needy.

Others agree with this assessment. If suburban zoning were relaxed, "it would be the middle class that would move first," says Alfred B. Del Bello, the energetic young mayor of Yonkers. "They would continue to vacate the cities, leaving an increasing proportion of poor black and Spanish population."

In the suburbs, meanwhile, there are growing signs that people now wonder whether exclusion is so wise after all. The doubts have nothing to do with morality, fairness or concern for the urban poor. They arise from practical reasons of self-interest.

Some towns, says David Bogdanoff, Westchester's largest developer, are coming to realize that not every community can assure its finances and its image by emulating Scarsdale. "Setting yourself up as a prestige town, with large lot zoning, won't work any more," he says. "There just aren't that many people who can afford upper-middle-class housing to fill all those towns."

Another practical reason for rising doubts about the tactics of exclusion is that those tactics may hurt as much as they help. On Long Island, planners say, oil spillage is a hazard because it is shipped to twelve harbors, and oil truck traffic is a nuisance. But the solution—a pipeline—has been blocked because the Town Board of Babylon refused in early July to permit construction of an essential storage terminal. "It's a classic case of not-on-my-block-itis," says Lee E. Koppelman, Nassau-Suffolk Planning Board director.

In Westchester, recalls Robert Weinberg, a developer, officials in every town insisted on specifying where bus routes could go. "The result was such a zig-zag that it made express routes impossible."

Still another reason for doubts is evidence that present exclusionary tactics are not exclusionary enough. "The suburbs develop elaborate master plans and tight zoning which they are eager to corrupt whenever a big company, a good 'ratable' that would pay lots of taxes, comes along," says one developer, asking anonymity. "To find anything that's considered a bad land use but a good ratable," says another developer, "look at the village line. That's where the gas stations are. 'Let them bother the people in the next village,' the town official thinks. 'They don't vote for me.'"

This is exactly what happened, Harry Butler says, with the enormous Willowbrook Center in Wayne Township, New Jersey, where the wares include a marquise-cut diamond ring ($2,215), a Lhasa Apso puppy ($279), and a potted stag horn fern ($75). "Willowbrook doesn't bother anyone here," Mr. Butler says, "because it's way on the south border, next to Little Falls Township. It bothers them; they get all the traffic and harassment. We get all the taxes."

People like Harry Butler around the suburbs wonder out loud about the long-range result of such narrowness and hostility. Stretches of Nassau County, where booming development of the fifties has now matured, may provide strong clues.

Drive north from Garden City, Long Island, and in a few minutes, one passes an elegant country club . . . and an intersection where narcotics are said to be sold at night; the miracle mile of elegant stores in Manhasset . . . and a roadside beauty shop whose name may betoken both the race and occupation of its patrons: "Ebony Maid." "The whole county's like that," says Dominic Badolato, a youth program director. "It's all a jigsaw, scrambled eggs."

Will the suburbs remain an exclusive sprawl, closed to those who can't afford the cost?

"It's going to break," says Herbert J. Gans, a noted Columbia urbanist, "because of middle-class demand. So many young families are already starting to form that change has to come."

Wayne's mayor knows the dilemma firsthand.

"There are very few places in Wayne he can afford to live," Mr. Miller says of his twenty-three-year-old son. And his parents, in their seventies, live in a retirement village in South Jersey.

"We'd welcome lower-cost housing for our youth and elderly," he says warmly. "But there's no guarantee we could keep it for them. And given the choice, we just won't do it."

The Battle over Land

by Richard Reeves

LAND IS the coin and the treasure of the suburbs around New York City, and that land—some of which has risen in value in twenty years from $700 to $90,000 an acre—is the prize in a continuing battle for control of the 775 municipalities that make up the world's largest suburban area.

The struggle over the land within 100 miles of Times Square, in its simplest terms, is between the people who already have some —whether a seventy-foot-wide lot in Massapequa, Long Island, or a 1,000-acre estate in Far Hills, New Jersey—and those who want new residents and more intensive development in the suburbs for their own personal profit or social goals.

In town after town there are fights over land use with large numbers of people sharing a single goal—to keep other people, new people, out of their community. The people who live in the towns, who have their own property, appear to be winning the struggle.

But this is not the whole story of the New York suburbs. The people there often watch, helpless and frustrated, as their lives and towns are changed by decisions of Federal and state governments or by profit-minded combines of developers and politicians. But, in general, the people who now live in the suburbs have one super-

Original title: "Land Is Prize in Battle for Control of Suburbs." From *The New York Times,* August 17, 1971, copyright © 1971 by The New York Times Company.

weapon—zoning—and they have used it to become the dominant force in the struggle over land use.

The other side of the struggle, the forces of change, involves an uneasy coalition between the men who will make money if the land is intensely developed and men who seek social change, civil rights activists and professional planners who want to move low-income and moderate-income people out of the city. The builders, land-owners and politicians, some of them vulnerable to the corruption that comes with the profits of land development, win a few battles. Many suburbanites interviewed, in fact, thought the builders were always winning—they complained about new gas stations along their highways and new homes or apartments rising.

Westchester County, for example, has moved steadily toward more and more restrictive zoning and its population capacity (if every vacant lot were built on as densely as possible) has dropped from 3.2 million in 1952 to 2.3 million in 1957 and 1.8 million today.

The Rockland County *News-Leader-Independent* commented editorially on the trend two months ago in the following way:

"At a recent meeting of the Nanuet Rotary, a fellow said half-jokingly, 'You know who runs Rockland County? Fifty women with baby carriages who turn out to protest everything and anything.' . . . He's right. They seem to wield more power than a bevy of legislators, supervisors, mayors, and councilmen all put together. They are indeed the new power elite—a force that sets officials trembling at their very approach."

John F. English, the former Nassau County Democratic chairman who is now a key figure in the presidential campaign of Senator Edmund S. Muskie, noted: "Suburban government is much more responsive to the people than other American government. It's the politics of the territorial imperative, the protection of their property. That means opposing new housing and new people, anything that might change the status quo."

"The power is really with the people," said Paul Davidoff, co-director of the Suburban Action Institute, which has filed several suits in an attempt to force suburban communities to drop restrictive zoning and accept low-income housing. "They act perfectly rationally to protect their interests by keeping everybody else out," he said. "And you can see their success by looking at the number of development projects turned down by any suburban government. They only change zoning if they desperately need industry to help pay the tax bills."

Three miles away from the institute's small office in White Plains, Robert Weinberg, founder of Westchester County's largest developer, Robert Martin Associates, unhappily agreed. "I'm one of the largest landholders in Westchester," he said. "Within a half-hour of here, I've got 500 to 600 acres I can't do anything with because of zoning. It's all zoned for one house an acre to keep out anyone earning less than $25,000.

"All they want here is the status quo—a guy wants to walk his dog in my woods, he thinks they're his woods. Citizens have an absolute right over zoning. We just can't run with local little home-town rule. Every idiot can come down to the town hall and have his say and the guys up front tremble because they're afraid they won't be reelected."

However, the metropolitan area's population keeps expanding and now people want to live in the suburbs, especially as more and more companies move there. The pressure of that expansion, basically involving the white middle class, is becoming so great that some observers believe that Federal and state governments will soon have break down local zoning restrictions—as the Urban Development Corporation already has the power to do in the State of New York.

A good illustration of the impact of zoning can be found in Wayne, New Jersey, 20 miles west of the Lincoln Tunnel. There, the value of an acre of land has risen from about $700 to as much as $90,000 as the township's population grew from 12,000 in 1950 to 49,000 in 1970. But the top value of that acre depends on zoning—an acre worth $90,000 today for high-density use like office buildings or garden apartments is worth only $10,000 if it's zoned for one single-family home.

"The power to zone is the power to make millionaires," said Lee Edward Koppelman, the director of the Nassau-Suffolk Regional Planning Board. And millions were made as the population exploded into Wayne and a hundred other towns around New York.

Who made the money? "The land speculators and real estate operators made most of it," said Harry J. Butler, a former Mayor of Wayne. "The farmers who originally owned the land here never realized its value."

Mr. Butler, a Democrat, spent a stormy term in office publicly denouncing the profitable relationship between politics, land speculation, and zoning in his town. It happened that the township officials he was denouncing were Republicans. In one case, for example, he pointed out that three municipal officials involved in the rezoning of two residential acres to allow construction of a private medical center were the principals of the corporation owning the land.

The value of that little tract increased by $80,000 with the rezoning. Without a variance, he said, the same medical center could have been built in a "business-professional" zone only 1,000 feet down the same road, but there would have been no $80,000 rezoning windfall. But in Wayne, as in most suburban municipalities, the people opposed to further change have had at least their share of victories. Petitions signed by 7,500 Wayne residents and clamorous opposition at public meetings that sometimes lasted into early morning hours have just killed a proposed high-rise apartment development.

The key to citizen participation in suburban governments, according to some political scientists, is the newness of those governments and the fact that many local politicians are amateurs who allow an unusually large proportion of public business to be conducted as open meetings. The number of people who attend such meetings or who come out to vote is usually low, but apathetic citizens are often aroused and organized instantaneously around public issues, such as zoning variances.

These issues might be considered and decided in private within city governments, which have had centuries to perfect the art of decision-making within a shielded bureaucracy rather than at town council meetings. In a study of Levittown, New Jersey, which has since changed its name to Willingboro, Herbert J. Gans, a noted sociologist, offered polls showing that governmental decisions were "remarkably responsive" to the wishes of the majority of citizens, even when those decisions were primarily influenced by small private-interest groups.

"The people generally win if they find out what's going on, but most of the money changing goes on before the people get there," said Mr. Gans, the author of *The Levittowners* and one of the nation's suburban scholars. "When it's still farms, everyone who lives out there shares in a bonanza before the new voters get there. After that, if Mr. X wants to subdivide his land to increase its value, he can bribe every town official $50,000 and see those officials voted out fifteen minutes later when the people get angry. Then new guys are elected and they stop the building."

The land action has now moved out from places like Wayne. It is in locales like eastern Suffolk County, where Mr. Koppelman estimated that 40 per cent of the vacant land might be held by speculators; in Putnam County and in western New Jersey—even as far out as the Sussex County farm country that will soon be linked to the city and inner suburbs by Interstate Route 80.

Somerset County is made up of 198,000 people living in an area about the size of New York City—in lovely little places named Peapack-Gladstone and Bedminster, 35 miles from the Hudson River—and it is one of the next battlegrounds. In fact, the battle is already well under way as Western Electric learned when it tried to move its national headquarters to Bedminster and withdrew the plans after facing 400 unhappy residents at a town meeting in the local high school's gymnasium.

There are, of course, already growing clusters of development and industry in Somerset. But, mainly there are miles of gently rolling hills where Mrs. Jacqueline Onassis and friends sometimes fox-hunt, where Doris Duke, C. Douglas Dillon and the Englehard family own huge estates.

There is also a master plan in Somerset County and some of the most restrictive zoning in the country. The Somerset County Planning Board projects a maximum population of 400,000 by the year 2000 and its planning director, William Roach, Jr., talks hopefully of holding out and letting most of the population growth leapfrog to rural Hunterdon County to the west—where Western Electric is now trying to situate. That would leave much of Somerset as a kind of giant country club, the place where the best-paid executives live and commute to jobs, most of them in other suburban areas.

Somerset has the zoning to do just that—63 per cent of the county is zoned to restrict building to one-family homes on lots of one to ten acres. Only two of the twenty-one towns have multi-family (apartment) zoning and 95.3 per cent of Far Hills Township is zoned for ten-acre building. It's possible that with such zoning, and with the personal power of some of its residents, Somerset is immune from the kind of growth that overwhelmed much of Nassau County. But even in protected communities—Mr. Gans calls them "vest-pocket principalities"—some people are beginning to have second thoughts about what kind of future they are making for their towns.

Police Lieutenant George D'Amicao of Northvale—a north Bergen County town of 5,200 people where 1,600 residents signed petitions that helped block a garden-apartment development—put it this way:

"My daughter will be getting married in a few years and I'd like to see her remain here. A nice little development wouldn't hurt anyone. Give our kids a chance. It's unfair. We had our chance to move out here."

Mr. D'Amicao's way of expressing a thought came up in almost every interview about government and power in the suburbs: Does democracy and home rule mean that the people who already live within the arbitrary boundaries of a comunity have the right to keep everybody else out?

Mr. Weinberg, the Westchester builder, and civil rights activists like Mr. Davidoff and Mr. Gold all favor the same solution to their different problems—they want state or Federal action to allow zoning at higher levels of government. "The housing mix should be mandated at a higher level where it's more difficult to get at the public official," said Mr. Weinberg. "How long can the cities stay in misery while everybody out here sits, enjoying the American dream? What right does a person living on a quarter-acre lot have to make the next guy live on a half-acre? If you want to live in a park, buy it."

"The Federal government will eventually have to step in," Mr.

Gans predicted, "because the people who want to live there will be middle-class people, people who can make their demands felt. Zoning and other safeguards will fall."

If he is right, the power of the people will be tempered by direct intervention of higher government. It is already tempered, of course, by many other factors, such as the pressure to reduce home-owners' tax bills by bringing in industry, especially along highways and the borders of neighboring municipalities, which must then deal with traffic problems.

When you ask Mr. Koppelman, the planner, and Mr. English, the politician, about the most powerful visible forces on Long Island, both men immediately answer: "the Republican organizations and *Newsday*."

And in each town, residents agree on an answer, generally naming a man or an institution with heavy local economic interests who becomes involved publicly or privately in a wide range of issues, winning more often than losing. In Islip, the names that came up in interviews were Anthony Pace, a lawyer and town Republican leader, and Edward McGowan, a former Republican leader and one of the town's largest landholders.

The name of *Newsday,* the 458,000-circulation daily newspaper published in Garden City, is also mentioned again and again, not surprisingly, since the newspaper began the investigations of land dealings that sent greedy local officials to jail.

"Planning has a chance on Long Island," said Mr. Koppelman, "because *Newsday* supports it. And *Newsday* is the only thing that's kept Long Island from going all the way down the drain of dishonesty."

In other suburbs, the pattern of power is the same but the names change: *The Record,* with its circulation of 148,000 in Bergen County; the League of Women Voters in Westchester, reflecting the fact that the most active citizens of the suburbs are often well-educated but nonworking housewives; taxpayers' associations in many towns which regularly fight to reduce school and municipal budgets; Spyros Lynos, known as "The Golden Greek" in Wayne because of his land and construction dealings, and similar financial-political operators in other towns; International Business Machines, Inc., in Dutchess County and Johnson & Johnson, Inc., in Somerset

County, both with thousands of local employees, including many in elected offices, but both reluctant to become so visibly involved in local affairs that they become issues, or targets in local elections. And, in town after town, the Republican party.

The suburbs are not the Republican monolith often portrayed in the past. In fact, half the eighteen United States Representatives from New York's suburbs are Democrats. But Republicans do tend to dominate suburban politics for several reasons, especially because they are permanently organized in many small communities along lines reminiscent of big-city Democratic politics of the nineteen-forties.

The home as the center of politics, of course, is still a major part of the story of suburban power. "People came here to get away from it all, from the problems of the city, of the country," said Mr. Butler, the former mayor of Wayne. "The only thing that arouses them is a zoning change near them or higher taxes. They don't think they have any responsibility for things like low-income housing and the officials they elect understand that their responsibility is to keep the community the way the people here want it."

Jobs and Housing

by Linda Greenhouse

TEN YEARS AGO much of Bridgewater Township, New Jersey, still looked much as it did when George Washington camped his troops in the safety of the first range of the Watchung Mountains. The township's population was 15,000 in 1960 and it contained industrial and commercial property valued at $30 million. Its mountains were wooded and untouched, corn grew on its plains and apple trees in its valleys.

Today, Bridgewater has 30,000 people. Houses are silhouetted on the crests of the hills and office buildings dot the flat plain. The town's industrial value has climbed to $161 million.

To a greater or lesser degree, the Bridgewaters are everywhere. The physical monuments to the economic success story of the New York suburbs cover the landscape: office towers rising at every highway intersection; shopping centers providing new definitions of the word with their sculpture gardens and community rooms; the sprawling campus-style headquarters of the corporate refugees from Manhattan. But that success story has another side.

Land is more than wealth and power. It gives much more than merely physical shape to the suburbs. The economics of land use is the prime factor in the growth of two closely related, vital components of the suburbs' economic health: jobs and housing.

Original title: "Rise in Jobs Poses Problems in Suburbs." From *The New York Times,* August 18, 1971, coyright © 1971 by the New York Times Company.

Because local government must pay for itself by the property tax, land can mean either profit or peril to a town. If, because of the tax structure, some kinds of development—housing—cost the town much more than other kinds—industry—the town will inevitably avoid one and seek the other. Severe imbalances are the inevitable results.

Job opportunities in the suburbs have been increasing, but the availability of housing there lags so far behind that a majority of the region's labor force must endure long and expensive commuting to reach the jobs.

And while industrial development has meant huge tax advantages for some suburban communities, some neighboring areas that are not equally blessed with shopping centers or industrial parks stagger under huge tax burdens.

Although no one is yet suggesting that the boom is about to end or that the suburban monuments are crumbling, the growing imbalances have raised the question: How long can the suburbs sustain their record of economic accomplishment when the benefits fall so unevenly on the region's population?

According to the Regional Plan Association, 2.4 million additional jobs will be created in the metropolitan area by 1985. Two million will be in the suburbs. In 1910, according to the Regional Plan Association, New York City contained 80 per cent of the region's office jobs. The proportion was 70 per cent in 1940 and by 1960 it had dropped to 60 per cent. Today the figure is 56 per cent. The figures are adjusted for the R.P.A.'s current definition of the thirty-one-county metropolitan region.

New York City's proportion of total manufacturing employment dropped from 54 to 51 per cent from 1959 to 1965 and is expected to fall to 42 per cent in 15 years.

Fourteen suburban municipalities in New Jersey have a combined population of 380,000, almost equal to the population of the state's largest city, Newark. They contain industrial property worth $2.1 billion, according to figures compiled by the Suburban Action Institute, a foundation-supported research and civil rights organization in White Plains. The value of industrial property in Newark is less than a third of that figure, $665 million.

If there is one factor held in common by suburban communities surrounding New York City, it is a growing economic independence from the city. In many cases, the perception of independence may not yet have caught up with reality. Suburban residents, after a lifetime of hearing their communities described as bedrooms for the city, often persist in believing that to be true even if no one on their block commutes.

In fact, the city is moving toward becoming the bedroom as the suburbs approach the point of being net importers rather than exporters of labor. Brooklyn, the Bronx, and Queens, with their vast supply of apartments and aging single-family houses, are becoming dormitories for those who work beyond the city limits.

The new suburban jobs are not only jobs for executives and office workers. As the suburban economy continues to diversify, wholesaling and manufacturing become more important. According to an unpublished study by the National Committee Against Discrimination in Housing, 150,000 of the 750,000 new suburban jobs created in the nineteen-sixties were blue-collar jobs, but during the same period the number of blue-collar workers living in the suburbs increased by only 50,000. By 1985, the study predicts, the suburbs will have 65 per cent of the region's blue-collar jobs but a much smaller share of the workers.

With apartment development blocked by zoning regulations and with the minimum price for new houses ranging from $30,000 in Suffolk County to as high as $50,000 in Westchester, the vast majority of people taking new blue-collar jobs in the suburbs will continue to find themselves priced out of housing near their places of employment.

Figures compiled but not yet released by the Tri-State Transportation Commission show that in Nassau County there are 139,000 more low-income and middle-income jobs than there are comparably priced housing units. In Bergen County, New Jersey, the deficit is 77,700 units.

The deficit is 82,200 units in Westchester County where, according to the County Planning Department, the number of jobs will exceed the number of employed residents for the first time in history within ten years—an astounding milestone for an area that is virtually synonymous in the minds of a nation with the stereotyped commuter suburb.

These figures illustrate the change: In 1950, 76,000 people were regular commuters to New York City and elsewhere, and fewer than 10,000 people commuted to jobs in Westchester. Now, 116,-000 commute from Westchester and 81,000 travel to the county, with the ratio getting smaller all the time.

The cost of the imbalance between jobs and housing is high, requiring expensive and time-consuming traveling. The cost is also high for the suburban employers, who have to depend on an outside labor force and who are concerned over the possibility of labor shortages.

One such company is the Mem Company in Northvale, New Jersey, manufacturers of the English Leather line of men's toiletries. With 350 employees, the company is Northvale's largest employer. Its clerical positions are filled by housewives from the surrounding Bergen County communities. But half its employees are blacks and Puerto Ricans, most of whom commute from New York to their jobs on the assembly line and in the packing rooms.

Every morning the company runs a bus from the George Washington Bridge terminal to its plant in an attractive industrial park, but a new employee may spend as long as two years on the job before he gains enough seniority for one of the fifty-four seats. "Even though most of them can't get on the bus and have to use carpools, it gives us a psychological edge in recruiting," said Danz, the company's personnel director. The bus costs the company $13,000 a year.

At least some employers have started to worry about the situation. A survey in 1970 by the Somerset County (New Jersey) Planning Department showed that 59 per cent of the county's major employers felt that the cost and availability of housing would restrict their plans for expansion. More than half said that they would not be able to meet their labor needs under the current residential zoning restrictions, and half answered yes to the question: "Do you feel that some of your employees live so far away as to affect their efficiency and present an economic burden?"

Eugene J. Schneider, executive director of the New Jersey County and Municipal Government Study Commission in Trenton, said, "Unless the imbalance between jobs and housing is corrected all our natural advantages for industry will disappear." But there have been few signs so far that companies are willing to exert pressure on local governments to change the zoning restrictions that underlie the housing shortage. Such restrictions rule out apartments and modest houses on small lots that workers with low incomes could afford.

The corporate giants that have the power to influence housing patterns are, because of their size, the least likely to feel the impact of any labor shortage. "They know for a few dollars extra they can always get someone," said one Manhattan-based company executive who has been a close student of the corporate moves to the suburbs. "If you ask them why they don't use their leverage to change things, they say, 'Well, we just want to be a good citizen.' But, after all, they used their leverage to get in and get their zone changes in the first place."

The argument that suburban towns offer against residential development is nearly always financial. As long as the property tax is the chief source of revenue for local government, a town stands to lose money on every but the most expensive house.

In Princeton township, for example, a $60,000 house barely pays enough in taxes to offset the services—such as schools, sanitation, and the like—made necessary by its presence. North Castle, in Westchester County, breaks even on a $52,000 house. In New Canaan, Connecticut, the break-even point is $70,000.

The tax burden in the metropolitan area is not only heavy— property taxes in the Northeast have historically been the highest in the country—but it is distorted as well by the patchwork nature of development in the suburbs. An example can be seen in Bergen County, where the two boroughs of Rockleigh and Northvale, each a mile square, sit side by side. Rockleigh has 200 people and a 126-acre industrial park that pays 90 per cent of all local taxes, and as a result the property tax rate is 72 cents for every $100 of assessed valuation.

Northvale, with 5,200 people, depends on residential property for more than two-thirds of its tax revenue. The owner of a $40,-000 house, who would pay $288 a year to Rockleigh, would get a tax bill in Northvale, where the rate is $3.87 per $100, for $1,362.

George Kershaw, an Eastern Airlines pilot who serves as councilman, fire chief, and tax assessor of Rockleigh, discussed the matter recently as he drove slowly through the industrial park. "The trend may be to try to stop this kind of town," he said, "but we're not simply a tax haven. We did this through good, judicious planning."

Equally dramatic inequalities exist within towns. Buttonwood Avenue, a hilly dead-end street in the Town of Cortlandt in northern Westchester County, cuts across a school district which has 8,500 students and a base of taxable property worth $178 million. The other end of the street lies in Central School District 3, which has 3,150 students and property worth $273 million, in-cluding two $100 million Consolidated Edison power plants. The owner of a $25,000 house in District 3 pays $868 in school and town taxes. Halfway up Buttonwood Avenue, the tax on the same house would be $1,216.

As William Hitt, the Cortlandt town supervisor, explains it, the situation has become a vicious cycle. Industry does not want to move into the high-tax area, which has high taxes for the very reason that there is not enough industry on the tax rolls.

The inequities, as well as the actual weight of the tax burden, are what fuel voter resentment and the growing demand for reform, and both New Jersey and New York State have special commis-sions studying the property tax. According to Thomas A. Dorsey, staff director of the New York State Joint Legislative Committee on Metropolitan and Regional Area Study, the basic question is "whether the property tax is still at all relevant."

If it is not, the problem is how to replace it. According to Mr. Dorsey, municipalities in New York State raise $3.8 billion a year through the local property tax, and "you'd have to go a long way to find another tax that can give you that kind of money."

There have been numerous suggestions for reform, although most are still at the discussion stage. Most focus on the financing of education, such as the assumption by the state of all local education costs. Other proposals include sharing tax burdens, or tax ratables, on a county level or among groups of towns, and consolidating school districts.

Some planners and tax experts are skeptical about what impact reform, however needed, would have on zoning patterns. The economic argument is a valid one, they say, but it is not the only reason the towns resist additional residential development.

"You get rid of the economic argument and then, if you are opposed to certain people moving into your neighborhood, you have to say it," said Arthur Kunz, assistant director of the Nassau-Suffolk Regional Planning Board. "You can't hide behind another argument. It would pull the bigots out of the woodwork."

Dick Netzer, dean of New York University's School of Public Administration, said, "Everyone knows that, strictly speaking, you're not supposed to spot-zone on the basis of how it will affect taxes. But short of openly stating that purpose, you can be pretty damn overt about it. But you can't be overt at all about other reasons. There's some question as to how much the fiscal thing is a screen for others."

If suburban towns no longer needed tax ratables, Dr. Netzer suggests, they might quickly become disenchanted with the non-residential development they are now so actively seeking. "You might find that nobody wants any factories any more," he said. "If it's not going to do them any good, they'll say, put it in the next town."

There are those who think that even without such a policy change, the flow of the glamor companies to the suburbs may be reaching its peak before slowing down.

"If a few things were different, I could argue as a businessman as strongly in favor of staying in the city," said D. Bruce Wiesley, a senior vice-president of the American Can Company who was in charge of the company's move to Greenwich, Connecticut in 1970. "After all," he said, "in the city you have modern, beautifully convenient offices. When you pull down the blinds you don't even know you're in New York. And when you close these blinds, you don't know where you are either."

Others disagree, pointing out that the suburbs have natural advantages that seem to assure their continued economic success.

The Regional Plan Association estimates that a campus-style office building can be built for about 60 per cent of the cost of a skyscraper with the same number of square feet. And the availability of land is important to manufacturing operations that function most efficiently spread horizontally through a one-story or two-story plant.

And there are such intangibles in the suburbs as the prestige of the suburban address and commuting over tree-lined parkways instead of tenement-lined railroad tracks. And no matter how high a price the suburban housing shortage may exact in the future, the executives who make the decision to move are not themselves much affected by the cost of housing.

The Highways Shape the Suburban Future

by David K. Shipler

THE SLEEK new highways begun under the Eisenhower administration are nearing completion at the edges of the metropolitan region, and they may have already set the basic course of suburban growth for the rest of this century. Every graceful multi-lane ribbon of asphalt that skirts a small town and winds through farmland is like the touch of Midas, transforming old pastures and woods into precious real estate ripe for the developer who wants land for an office building, a shopping mall or a tract of houses.

The New York metropolitan area is now laced with 575 miles of Interstate highways, almost all of them in the suburbs, paid for with 90 per cent Federal funds, 10 per cent state money.

As the region grows—adding a predicted eight million people and enough office space to fill 300 new Empire State Buildings by the year 2000—the highway network virtually guarantees that the growth will lead away from urban areas into new land, perpetuating the centerless sprawl that has characterized the suburbs built since the end of World War II.

The evidence is visible now in a huge, lopsided ring around the metropolitan area, the new line where, in effect, country meets

Original title: "New Highways Shaping Future of City's Suburbs." From *The New York Times,* August 19, 1971, copyright © 1971 by The New York Times Company.

city, where the suburbs thin out, where most land is still vacant. The ring passes through Middlesex County and northern Morris County in New Jersey; Dutchess, Putnam, and northern Westchester Counties in New York; eastern Suffolk County on Long Island; and parts of Fairfield County in Connecticut. Here is where the twentieth century will leave its final mark.

The power of the highways is surer to determine how land develops, and thus how millions of people will live and where they will work, than all the careful reasoning of government planners or the defensive rhetoric of small-town politicians.

Every day in the outer counties, planners who try to fight sprawl and revive mass transportation by encouraging new development in downtown centers are being defeated by the growth that spreads along the highways, that clusters around the new interchanges. The highways' influence has been enhanced by the resistance of many suburbanites to growth in their own towns.

Strict zoning that limits development is defended with the greatest passion in residential parts of town. Along highways, especially at the town lines, offices and shopping centers with their badly needed tax payments are often tolerated because they appear to leave the rural nature of the countryside undisturbed. And yet the highway planners who draw the new routes and thus map the future for the suburbs say they never consider the advantages or the liabilities of rapid growth in one place or another. They never weigh the impact of their highways on the older suburban towns that must compete with the glittering shopping centers.

"We've never been able to be that luxurious," said Nicholas Sinacori, regional chief of the New York State Transportation Department in the Hudson River Valley. He said development patterns were not his responsibility, but rested completely on the shoulders of the towns that controlled zoning.

Highway authorities say they simply try to meet transportation needs, and that in doing so they search for routes where the land is cheapest and the political resistance weakest. This technique brings real estate booms to out-of-the-way places.

"It's gone crazy—it's wild!" exclaimed Robert J. Eckstein, a real estate man in Parsippany–Troy Hills, New Jersey, which is fast becoming one of the region's major crossroads. Eventually, five highways—three of them new interstates—will cross in what was once a small town in Morris County. Even before their completion, the roads have begun to stimulate rapid growth.

In 1950, the population of Parsippany–Troy Hills was 15,290. Now it is 55,112. Since 1961, the total value of commercial and industrial buildings and land in the town has jumped from $14 million to $86 million. The value of all property has risen from $107 million to $483 million in ten years.

Nine years ago, Mr. Eckstein and a partner bought an old Victorian-style house on an acre of ground for $30,000. Now he estimates the value of the land alone at $85,000.

The reason is simple: Only yards from Mr. Eckstein's property, in swirls of dust, steamrollers rumble along a swath of brown-red earth, packing it into a roadbed for Interstate 80. On an overpass above, a little local traffic makes use of the short strip of Interstate 287 that has been completed.

"We all knew where Route 80 would go," Mr. Eckstein said. "When 80 is complete, it's just going to be the ultimate hub."

Route 80 will connect the George Washington Bridge with the Delaware Water Gap, and Route 287 will run from the New York Thruway to the New Jersey Turnpike.

Mr. Eckstein realized the potential of this spot, and five years ago he had the Victorian house demolished. And now, near the intersection of these two incomplete highways, he already has a three-story office building under construction.

Elsewhere, development usually occurs several years after the highway is completed, either because local towns along the roads use zoning to restrain the growth for a time or because the highways probe more deeply into the countryside than people need to go to escape the spreading congestion of the inner suburbs.

Acres and acres of brush and scrub oak and pine along the extended Long Island Expressway in Suffolk County, for example, have recently been opened to industrial development by a rezoning decision in the town of Islip. Local real estate men say the rezoning pushed land values from $7,500 to $40,000 an acre.

Development has proceeded further along Smithtown Bypass,

which runs for ten miles from Hauppauge to Port Jefferson, and, with its many intersections, is anything but a modern superhighway. But, stimulated in part by proposals that a bridge be built someday across Long Island Sound from Port Jefferson to Bridgeport, Connecticut, developers have made the Smithtown Bypass a strip of new car showrooms, Carvel stands, treeless tracts of single-family houses, gasoline stations, movie theaters, and even a Holiday Inn. All of this is mixed in with a few remaining potato fields.

In Piscataway, New Jersey, small one-story and two-story offices and factories already have been erected along a newly completed stretch of Interstate 287. And in nearby East Brunswick, so many shopping centers now line Route 18 that planners have come to call the divided highway "the main street of East Brunswick."

Continuing growth of this sort is viewed as ominous for the cities, not only the core of Manhattan but also such smaller centers as Jamaica, Queens; downtown Brooklyn; Newark, Paterson, and New Brunswick in New Jersey; White Plains; Stamford, Connecticut, and Hempstead, Long Island.

The Regional Plan Association has long been campaigning for an end to what it calls "spread city" and a concentration of future development in subcenters around Manhattan. The planners note that otherwise, the region's residents will continue to be slaves to the automobile, since bus and train service need estimated densities of five to ten families an acre to be practical. But virtually every force seems to be pushing hard away from the downtowns. Relentlessly, developers are driving out, not up, seeking vacant land, pressuring towns to relax zoning, trying to appeal to what they believe is an insatiable American appetite for open space, even if it is merely the open space of a shopping center's parking lot versus the curbside of a downtown street.

Trenton, for example, found itself the victim of this aversion to downtown, according to Eugene J. Schneider, director of the New Jersey County and Municipal Government Study Commission. Having spent years condemning property and clearing land for a downtown shopping mall, Trenton was able to obtain tentative commitments from four large department stores to build branches on the site, Mr. Schneider said.

Then, eight miles away on Route 1, a developer announced plans for a vast regional shopping center with four department stores. In the face of that prospective competition, the stores bound for downtown Trenton backed out.

Regional Plan officials are afraid of the same thing happening to Newburgh, New York, where the State Urban Development Corporation is trying to renew and revive the decaying downtown.

Macy's has made plans for a major shopping center at Fishkill across the Hudson River from Newburgh, attracted by new Interstate 84, recently opened to traffic, and by state plans to convert intersecting Route 9 into a four-lane highway.

The location of a major shopping center at that intersection, planners reason, threatens to sap downtown Newburgh of what vitality it has retained.

Even government facilities are attracted to the highways. Suffolk County built a complex of county offices not in a downtown, but on rural land near the Long Island Expressway, Veterans Memorial Highway and the Smithtown Bypass. The state is planning an office building nearby, also shunning a downtown site.

Despite the enormous power of highways to determine the pattern of suburban growth, highway planners interviewed in the metropolitan region said they determined routes and located interchanges not with regard to their impact on future development, but instead to catch up with growth and meet what they judge as transportation needs. "Our planning has been one to date of reaction," said Keith Rosser, planning director of the New Jersey State Department of Transportation. "The money is not there to plan intelligently."

Mr. Rosser and others said they picked highway routes where land was cheapest, where the fewest structures had to be demolished and where local opposition was the least vocal. They do not locate highways to influence development in one place or another, they said. "We construct highways, very frankly, where we're permitted to construct highways," Mr. Rosser said.

The view of the highway network as simply a transportation device that responds to existing development was characteristic of the arguments surrounding the proposal of the Interstate highway system by President Eisenhower. In the fifty-three-page message from the president to Congress on February 22, 1955, recommending such a road network, there is not a single word about the impact of the highways on the cities or on the future development of the suburbs.

Mr. Eisenhower gave four reasons for advocating the 42,500-mile system, of which 31,899 miles now have been completed.

He said that present highways were unsafe, that people were experiencing enormous traffic jams, that poor roads saddled business with high cost for transportation, and that modern highways were needed because "in case of an atomic attack on our key cities, the road net must permit quick evacuation of target areas."

In a report, the President's Advisory Committee on a National Highway Program, headed by General Lucius D. Clay, hailed the dispersal that planners are now cursing. The nation's highways, the committee wrote, "have been able to disperse our factories, our stores, our people; in short, to create a revolution in living habits. Our cities have spread into suburbs, dependent on the automobile for their existence.

"The automobile has restored a way of life in which the individual may live in a friendly neighborhood, it has brought city and country closer together, it has made us one country and a united people."

After the House of Representatives approved the program with a voice vote and the Senate voted for it 89 to 1, Lewis Mumford wrote gloomily in his book, *The Highway and the City:*

> When the American people, through their Congress, voted a little while ago for a $26 billion highway program, the most charitable thing to assume about this action is that they hadn't the faintest notion of what they were doing. Within the next 15 years they will doubtless find out but by that time it will be too late to correct all the damage to our cities and our countryside, not least to the efficient organization of industry and transportation, that this ill-conceived and preposterously unbalanced program will have wrought.

The fifteen years have elapsed. The search in those years for an alternative to the city "has provided residents with the worst of both worlds," wrote William B. Shore, a vice president of the Regional Plan Association, in a recent issue of *City* magazine.

"In some ways," Mr. Shore declared, "they have little more variety and choice and opportunity than the small-city resident. Yet they are imbedded in a huge urban region—everywhere there are people. Houses march over hilltops, cut into forests, fragment stream valleys, 'Downtown' is the highway strip."

But "spread city," as Mr. Shore terms it, is cheaper for developers to build, and the expense of new construction has become the major source of fear for builders.

"Everyone is catering to the few who can afford our product," said Robert Weinberg, a partner in Robert Martin Corporation, one of Westchester County's largest builders. "But that customer can be a super shopper. One misstep is fatal for a builder."

Peter Taylor, a vice-president in charge of Levitt & Sons' Long Island region, agrees. "We're a mass builder," he said. "But our market is rapidly decreasing. We've tried to drive the cost down, but we still can't sell to a guy who makes under seventeen grand a year."

When the original Levittown was built on Long Island in 1947, Mr. Taylor said, the houses were about 750 square feet in area with one bathroom, and the capacity to have bedrooms added to them later. For years after that, he said, "our houses had two bathrooms and could not be added to."

"They were larger," he said. "Now high construction costs have thinned out the market so much, we've almost come full circle. We're selling expandable houses, and now two bathrooms are a luxury. We're going back to one-bathroom houses."

In the midst of this economic squeeze, land has become the most precious commodity in the suburbs. Wall Street investment houses and large corporations have begun investing large sums in vast tracts in Putnam County in New York and Morris County in New Jersey, according to planners. And while most people still try to keep highways out, a growing number of landowners—many of them farmers—are asking for highways and interchanges near their property to enhance its value, according to Mr. Sinacori.

Someday, the land will surely be exhausted, gobbled up by campus-style offices, one-story factories, concrete and asphalt. Housing will then have to go up, Mr. Taylor said.

He foresees a megalopolis of high-rise apartments on Long Island. "I tell my kids that they can tell their kids that Grandpa Taylor lived in a single-family house on two acres, and they'll say 'Yeah?' "

Suggested Reading

Bennett M. Berger, *Working Class Suburb: A Study of Auto-Workers in Suburbia,* Berkeley, University of California Press, 1960.

David L. Birch, *The Economic Future of City and Suburb,* New York, Committee for Economic Development, 1970.

Samuel D. Clark, *The Suburban Society,* Toronto, University of Toronto Press, 1966.

Marion Clawson, *Suburban Land Conversion in the United States,* Baltimore, Johns Hopkins Press, 1971.

William M. Dobriner, ed., *The Suburban Community,* New York, Putnam's, 1958.

Scott Donaldson, *The Suburban Myth,* New York, Columbia University Press, 1969.

Harlan P. Douglass, *The Suburban Trend,* New York, Century, 1925.

Bryan T. Downs, ed., *Cities and Suburbs,* Belmont, California, Wadsworth Publishing Co., 1971.

Herbert J. Gans, *The Levittowners,* New York, Pantheon Books, 1959.

Herbert J. Gans, *People and Plans,* New York, Basic Books, 1968.

Charles E. Gilbert, *Governing the Suburbs,* Bloomington, Indiana, Indiana University Press, 1967.

John Kramer, ed., *North American Suburbs: Politics, Diversity and Change,* Berkeley, California, Glendessary Press, 1972.

328 • *Suggested Reading*

Max Neutze, *The Suburban Apartment Boom: Case Study of a Land Use Problem,* Baltimore, Johns Hopkins Press, 1971.

John B. Orr and F. Patrick Nichelson, *The Radical Suburb,* Philadelphia, Westminster Press, 1970.

John R. Seeley, et al., *Crestwood Heights: The Culture of Suburban Life,* New York, Basic Books, 1956.

Frederick Wirt, et al., eds., *On the City's Rim: Suburban Politics and Policy,* Boston, Heath, 1972.

Robert C. Wood, *Suburbia: Its People and Politics,* Boston, Houghton Mifflin, 1958.

Index

About the Editors

Louis H. Masotti is Professor of Political Science and Director of the Center for Urban Affairs at Northwestern University. He is the author of *Education and Politics in Suburbia, A Time to Burn? A Critical Evaluation of the Present Crisis in Race Relations* (with Jeffrey Hadden and others) and *Shoot-out in Cleveland: Black Militants and the Police* (with Jerome Corsi), and editor of *Riots and Rebellion* (with Don Bowen) and *The Urbanization of the Suburbs* (with Hadden).

Jeffrey K. Hadden is Professor of Sociology at the University of Virginia. He is author of *Gathering Storm in the Churches* and editor of *Religion in Transition, Marriage and the Family* (with Marie L. Borgatta) and *Metropolis in Crisis* (with others).